CW00927397

Bulbophyllums and Their Allies

Bulbophyllums
and Their Allies

A GROWER'S GUIDE

Emly S. Siegerist

Foreword by
Gustavo A. Romero-Gonzalez

TIMBER PRESS
Portland, Oregon

Illustration Credits

By permission of the American Orchid Society, West Palm Beach, Florida: Plates 1, 2, 20, 25, 26, 39, 40, 46, 49, 56, 59, 62, and 66.
By permission of Wilbur A. Chang, Kaneoke, Hawaii: Plates 52, 55, and 69.
By permission of Leslie A. Garay, Blacksburg, Virginia: Plates 29, 31, and 32.
By permission of Fritz Hamer, Sarasota, Florida: Plates 10 and 44.
By permission of James Harper, Galena, Ohio: Plates 23 and 38.
By permission of Marilyn M. LeDoux, Labadie, Missouri: Plates 3, 4, 48, 51, 53, 58, 63, and 68.
By permission of Mrs. Ralph Levy, Memphis, Tennessee: Plates 5, 6, 9, 11, 12, 13, 16, 17, 18, 19, 21, 22, 24, 27, 30, 34, 35, 43, 45, 47, 67, 70, 73, 75, 76, and 77.
By permission of Charles Nishihira, Honolulu, Hawaii: Plates 36 and 57.
By permission of Clair Ossian, Carrolton, Texas: Plates 7, 28, and 54.
By permission of Karlheinz Senghas, Heidelberg, Germany: Plates 41 and 61.
By permission of Walter L. Siegerist, St. Louis, Missouri: Plates 15, 37, and 42.
By permission of Tamlong and Heike Suphachadiwong, Chonburi, Thailand: Plates 8, 14, 33, 50, 60, 64, 65, 71, 72, and 74.

ISBN 0-88192-506-3

Printed in Hong Kong

Published in 2001 by
Timber Press, Inc.
The Haseltine Building
133 S.W. Second Avenue, Suite 450
Portland, Oregon 97204, U.S.A.

Library of Congress Cataloging-in-Publication Data

Siegerist, Emly S.
    Bulbophyllums and their allies : a grower's guide / Emly S. Siegerist; foreword by Gustavo A. Romero-Gonzalez.
       p.   cm.
    Includes bibliographical references (p.   ).
    ISBN 0-88192-506-3
    1. Bulbophyllum. 2. Bulbophyllum—Identification. I. Title.

SB409.8.B84 S54 2001
635.9′344—dc21

00-066669

Contents

Color photos follow page 160.

Foreword

The orchids were traditionally regarded as the largest group of flowering plants. Recent accounts in the botanical literature, however, place the sunflower family, Asteraceae or Compositae, ahead of the orchids, at least as far as number of recorded species is concerned. But few botanists would doubt supremacy of orchids in the realm of contrasts. Again, referring to the sunflower family, plants may occupy waste lands to pristine habitats, and may range from small, annual herbs to rather large trees, and the inflorescences, flowers to the casual observer, vary from minute to the large size of the familiar sunflower. However, the orchids remain unsurpassed in other features such as the diversity and intricacy in flower form, the range of color, including unusual blues and even tones approaching black, and fragrances that range from exquisite scents to disagreeable smells that attract carrion flies. It is with pleasure that I write this foreword to the present contribution to the classification and cultivation of *Bulbophyllum* and closely allied genera, a unique group which is itself a microcosm of the tremendous variability observed in the orchid family.

Bulbophyllum is by far the largest genus in the subtribe Bulbophyllinae, encompassing thousands of species distributed worldwide, but with the bulk of the species found in Asia. Within Orchidaceae, this subtribe closely resembles subtribe Pleurothallidinae, perhaps the largest group in the family. *Pleurothallis* and allies, however, are restricted to the New World. These two subtribes, Bulbophyllinae and Pleurothallidinae, are similar in many respects: both are extremely diverse in number of species and in ecological adaptations, the great majority of the species are pollinated by flies, they have the widest range in plant size among orchids but excel in the number of miniatures, and both, despite their diversity, are poorly represented in most greenhouses. Granted, not many species of *Bulbophyllum* and allied genera would win beauty contests, and some produce such foul fragrance you would not want to keep them indoors when in flower, while others are so small you need a magnifying glass to see the flowers. Few other orchids, however, present such diversity in inflorescence and floral morphology, or such intricate details in the ornamentation of the labellum. Other reasons why this group is not more commonly cultivated are the limited availability of species, perhaps a function of a limited demand, because most growers only know a few species, and their seemingly particular growing requirements. I am confident that *Bulbophyllums and Their Allies: A Grower's Guide* will not only give orchid growers a better appreciation for the diversity of species in this group, but also help them find suitable growing conditions in their greenhouses.

Emly Siegerist has compiled a comprehensive volume that includes an introduction to the orchids, a brief history of the group, and a description of *Bulbophyllum* and its numerous sections, covering also some fascinating topics such as pollination biology. Orchid growers will undoubtedly find the detailed glossary and index extremely useful. Emly amassed a great deal of information on roughly 375 species of *Bulbophyllum*, 40 species of *Cirrhopetalum*, 80 species of closely related genera, as well as about 50 hybrids. For each species and hybrid, the reader is presented with a brief but informative historical introduction, a complete, concise description, the habitat where the species is found in nature, and suggestions on how to best grow it in cultivation.

I am certain this book will contribute tremendously to the popularity of *Bulbophyllum* and, most importantly, will guide the beginner as well as the advanced orchid grower in meeting the growing requirements of the species and hybrids treated in this book.

Gustavo A. Romero-Gonzalez, Ph.D.
Keeper, Oakes Ames Orchid Herbarium

Acknowledgments

Many people around the world have been helpful in furthering my obsession with this genus of orchids, but foremost among them is, of course, my mentor and very good friend, Leslie A. Garay. Without his most generous sharing of knowledge and material my interest in this fascinating field would not have grown to the extent it has.

Others have been unselfish in sharing plants as well as photographs, in particular Mrs. Ralph Levy of Tennessee and Wolfgang Bandisch of Papua New Guinea. Also unstinting in their support have been Tamlong and Heike Suphachadiwong of Thailand who have not only made many beautiful hybrids but have generously shared their excellent photographs. Thanks also to one of the best orchid growers in the St. Louis area, Marilyn M. LeDoux, and to the superb illustrator, Fritz Hamer of Florida.

Photographs have kindly been shared by the American Orchid Society, Wilbur A. Chang, James Harper, Charles Nishihira, Clair Ossian, Karlheinz Senghas, and Walter L. Siegerist.

But most important of all, my heartfelt thanks to my most avid supporter who, many years ago, gave me a rather shopworn cattleya that he had carried home on his lap from California and thus started my undying interest in orchids.

CHAPTER 1

The *Bulbophyllum* Alliance

Orchids constitute one of the largest plant families on Earth. Unless you live in an igloo on an ice floe, native orchids could be growing in your neighborhood.

What makes an orchid different from other plants? First, orchids are trimerous, that is, they have three sepals and three petals, and one of the latter is transformed into a labellum, or lip, upon which the pollinator lands. Second, orchids have bilateral symmetry, that is, there is only one plane on which an orchid flower can be dissected to have each half produce a mirror image of the other. (The scientific term for this type of flower is *zygomorphic*.) Third, orchids have a structure called a column in which all the reproductive parts are located. Orchids can be monopodial or sympodial, that is, they can have one central stem from which all leaves and flowers arise as in *Vanda*, or they can have a rhizome (an internode between the pseudobulbs) that creeps along the surface of the growing medium and from which the pseudobulbs emerge as in *Cattleya*.

Orchids can be epiphytic, lithophytic, or terrestrial. A few are even subterrestrial, spending their entire life cycle beneath the ground with only a small opening at the surface through which they can be pollinated. The epiphytes are by far the largest group of orchids with the majority of them growing on tree trunks or tree limbs in jungles. A common bit of misinformation embraced by many people is that an epiphyte is the same as a parasite, which is, of course, not true. An epiphyte uses the host plant merely as a support, not as a source of nourishment. Its nourishment comes from the accumulation of organic matter that is washed down with the rains. The lithophytes grow on rocks, often along roaring streams or on mountain sides, and the terrestrials exist as "normal" plants growing in the ground.

Most orchids are warm-growing epiphytes and live in close proximity to the equator, but even Alaska has some native terrestrial orchids, so there are some that can exist in almost all habitats. At least 2700 species have been published as belonging to the genus *Bulbophyllum*, giving orchid growers many plants to choose from for their collection.

Classification of Orchids

John Lindley, in the mid-1700s, proposed one of the earliest systems of classifying the orchid family by dividing the known orchids into what seemed to him to be natural groups based on sets of characteristics common to each group. He decided there were six tribes, Cypripedieae, Epidendreae, Malaxideae, Neottieae, Ophrydeae, and Vandeae, which he further divided into subtribes. His tribe Malaxideae had four subtribes, Dendrobiinae, Genyorchidinae, Malaxidinae, and Thecostelinae. Subtribe Dendrobiinae had but two genera, *Dendrobium* and *Bulbophyllum*. In 1881 George Bentham published in the *Journal of the Linnean Society* his system of classification which combined Lindley's tribes Malaxideae and Epidendreae. In any case, the genus *Bulbophyllum* is related to several other genera, namely, *Acrochaene*, *Chaseella*, *Cirrhopetalum*, *Codonosiphon*, *Drymoda*, *Epicrianthes*, *Ferruminaria*, *Hapalochilus*, *Ione*, *Mastigion*, *Monomeria*, *Monosepalum*, *Osyricera*, *Pedilochilus*, *Rhytionanthos*, *Saccoglossum*, *Sunipia*, *Synarmosepalum*, *Tapeinoglossum*, *Trias*, and *Vesicisepalum*. Some interesting intergeneric hybrids have been made and will be discussed in chapter 9.

History of the Genus *Bulbophyllum*

In 1758 Louis-Marie Aubert Du Petit-Thouars was born in France. He became one of the foremost plant scientists of his time, exploring such places as the French island possessions off the east coast of Africa then known as Île de France, Île de Bourbon, and Madagascar but now called Mauritius, Réunion, and Madagascar. Some flora from these islands had reached France, and they were so different from former collections that they excited botanists everywhere. Madagascar is almost 777,000 square kilometers (300,000 square miles) in area, separated from Africa by the Mozambique channel. The other two smaller islands are farther east and together are less than 5180 square kilometers (2000 square miles) in size. These Indian Ocean islands with their unusual flora fascinated Thouars because many species found there were unknown on the African mainland. For more than a million years the plant (and animal) life on these islands evolved independently into a unique flora with more than 1100 species of orchids alone.

Thouars planned to sail to Madagascar with his brother Aristide and explore the fauna, but the French Revolution delayed the trip until 1792. He spent the next nine years on the smaller islands with perhaps only six months of this time on Madagascar. As was customary, he sent some of his collected plants to European botanists, and a number of these plants were named after him as a result. In 1802 he returned to France and published several descriptions of various plants and treatises on the geography of the islands. He was especially interested in the orchids of the area, and the main work he published was *Histoire Particulière des Plantes Orchidées Recueillies sur les Trois Îles Australes d'Afrique* in 1822. This became a most important work, detailing all aspects of orchids and containing more than 100 exceedingly well-done plates illustrating some of the Madagascan and Mascarene orchids. His description of his new genus *Bulbophyllum* is contained in this book. Although he had earlier called some of the plants of this genus by his generic name *Phyllorkis* in 1809, the newer name is used today because it was more widely accepted. The name *Phyllorkis* is derived from the Greek *phyllon* meaning "leaf" and *orchis* which refers to the genus.

Thouars used a most unconventional method of describing his new species, using pages that fold out from the book and contain a tabular form instead of the usual narrative. But perhaps the most unusual nomenclature is found in the compound names he used in most of his illustrations: he took the first syllable of the specific name and the last portion of the generic name and combined them. *Bulbophyllum densum* became *Densophylis* and *B. nutans* was called *Nuphylis*. To add to the confusion, he did not always use these terms but sometimes substituted their synonyms. Another idiosyncrasy of his was the combination of portions of a plant's generic and family names. In this manner the name *Phyllorchis* which he had formerly used, although spelled slightly differently, was used for the genus *Bulbophyllum* as its alternate name.

Thouars' book on the Madagascan and Mascarene orchids is still very valuable to scientists today, mainly because of its botanical plates. There is an amusing anecdote about the illustration of *Angraecum sesquipedale*, which shows its remarkably long spur that contains nectar. Years later when Charles Darwin, after his long voyage on the *Beagle*, found this species growing in a collection in England, he predicted that there must be a moth with a proboscis between 25 and 27.5 centimeters (10–11 inches) long so that it could reach the nectar. (It had to be a moth because the flower is white and most fragrant at night and only a moth flies at night and can see and smell the white flower.) When this idea reached England, the scientific community was more than a little unhappy with it; in fact, they laughed out loud at the very thought of a moth with a tongue that long. It was too bad that Darwin did not live long enough to laugh back, because he was vindicated when such a moth was indeed found years later.

Another noted botanist who contributed greatly to the understanding of the genus *Bulbophyllum* and allied genera in the 1800s was John Lindley, secretary of the Royal Horticultural Society in England and the first editor of the famous *Gardener's Chronicle*, a fascinating journal which is much sought after today by collectors of botanical literature for the insights it gives into the personalities of the botanists and horticulturists of the day, as well as the information it gives on the various plants being grown at that time. Lindley not only was an authority of the time on the cultivation of orchids but also was a close associate of all the well-known orchid horticulturists. In this capacity he received many new orchids which he dutifully described and named in his *Genera and Species of Orchidaceous Plants* (1830–1840). Listed in this volume besides *Bulbophyllum* were *Cirrhopetalum* Lindley, *Cochlia* Blume, *Epicrianthes* Blume, *Lyraea* Lindley, and *Megaclinium* Lindley, which are included in the *Bulbophyllum* complex.

In 1926 Rudolf Schlechter described the subtribe Bulbophyllinae and included the genera *Bulbophyllum*, *Chaseella*, *Drymoda*, *Monomeria*, *Pedilochilus*, *Saccoglossum*, and *Trias* but listed the subtribe Sunipiinae separately. There is still much discussion about the classification of these plants as you will see from the list of synonyms for each species, and perhaps the final decisions are still to come as more knowledge is gained.

Definition of *Bulbophyllum*

In addition to the characteristics common to all orchids, that is, they are trimerous, zygomorphic, and have one petal formed into a labellum, *Bulbophyllum* species have a column which extends into a distinct foot forming a mentum. The labellum is attached to the column foot and moves very easily, with even the slightest breath of air setting it into motion. The genus and its allies are epiphytes, with only a very few exceptions, and they are sympodial, that is, they grow on creeping rhizomes, and have pseudobulbs that produce one leaf (sometimes two or three). They have an inflorescence that arises from the base of the pseudobulb, never from its sides or top. Some dendrobiums resemble bulbophyllums but have an inflorescence that arises from the sides or the top of the pseudobulbs, which is never the case with *Bulbophyllum*. The genus name comes from the Greek words *bolbos* which means "bulb" and *phyllon* or "leaf."

The *Bulbophyllum* alliance is pantropic, and botanists believe that the genus originated in or around Malaysia and engaged in peripheral speciation with one center of evolution migrating eastward through Indonesia and New Guinea, Australia, and adjacent areas. The other area of distribution went westward through India to Madagascar and Africa with a few species going as far as South America and some to Central America. Very few found their way to North America. This migration explains the evolutional changes in the species that are endemic to certain areas. For instance, the group called *Megaclinium* is very distinctive with two leaves per pseudobulb and a rachis (the major axis of an inflorescence) that is flattened and has small flowers arranged along either side of it. This particular set of characteristics is not found in the members of the genus that grow in Malaysia or the areas to the east, and there are only a very few that are similar to it in South America. Such a distribution strongly suggests that these characteristics evolved in Africa and Madagascar and that a few plants migrated to South America where they adapted to local conditions. The largest diversity is found, naturally, in Malaysia and its immediate surroundings with many, many new species being discovered even today, especially on the island of New Guinea. And, as mentioned before, Madagascar is another area rich in genetic diversity.

Pollination Mechanisms of *Bulbophyllum*

Bulbophyllums have pollen (the male part of the flower) enclosed in a structure which has a sticky appendage. This structure is called the pollinia. To effect fertilization, the pollinia must be deposited onto the stigmatic surface (the female section of the flower), either its own or that of another orchid. Both the pollinia and stigma occur on the same structure which is called the column. Since this genus is not as a rule wind pollinated, another factor is required, usually a carrion fly or a small, nectar-seeking fly. Of course, in laboratories the factor is frequently a toothpick or scalpel.

We know that nothing in nature is without a reason. The colors and odors of flowers are lovely to look at and smell, but their real purpose is to attract pollinators to the flower. The movement of the labellum, the fluttering of the palae on sepal and petal tips, catches the attention of the flies, bees, birds, and so forth that are necessary to transport the pollen from one flower to another. For instance, the lovely fragrance of white flowers that is so evident in the evening attracts the night-flying moths that Darwin correctly theorized were the pollinators of some angraecums. The pollinators land on the labellum, inadvertently have the pollinia adhere to their bodies, then move on to the next flower where the pollinia becomes attached to the stigmatic surface and the process repeats itself.

The dark red color of *Bulbophyllum phalaenopsis* flowers and the narrow yellowish protuberances on the back of the petals appear to the flies to be the maggot-riddled flesh of dead animals, and of course, the accompanying odor accentuates this fallacy. In fact, it has been compared to the stench of dead elephants that have been in the sun for many days. This species is one of the bulbophyllums best suited to growing outdoors in a warm climate for obvious reasons, but there are many species of *Bulbophyllum*, *Cirrhopetalum*, and allied genera and their hybrids that adapt quite easily to conditions that hobbyists can create. Many of these orchids are exceptionally attractive.

Allied Genera

With a genus as large as *Bulbophyllum*, it is natural that botanists have tried to divide it, forming new genera or subgenera with varying degrees of success. The closely allied genera were enumerated earlier and a few of them have been successfully crossed with bulbophyllums to form intergeneric hybrids. *Cirrhopetalum*, of course, hybridizes easily with *Bulbophyllum*, and so have some members of the genera *Rhytionanthos* and *Trias*. Theoretically, all the allied genera mentioned should be able to produce hybrids with one another.

Synonymy

In the plant descriptions, synonyms are listed for each species. To avoid unnecessary duplication when purchasing plants, it can be very helpful to know the several different names by which that one plant is sometimes called. Other related genera, some of which were at one time or another called *Bulbophyllum*, will also be discussed, as well as many of the beautiful and easily grown hybrids. The dimensions of plants, leaves, and flower parts are approximate, naturally, because of the difference in individual plants and growing conditions, but they will serve as a general guide.

CHAPTER 2

Sections of *Bulbophyllum*

*B*ulbophyllum has been divided into sections for ease of studying the various similar plants. These sections are listed and described here and mentioned in the descriptions of the species to facilitate understanding of the genera. The species upon which the description of the section is based is called the type. In some instances a type is not designated because the original author of the section did not name one. Some of the species described in later chapters have not been assigned to a section because the revision of the grouping of these plants is still under study and any assignation to various sections would be misleading. An enumeration of the various sections described in this book follows.

Section *Adelopetalum* (Fitzgerald) J. J. Vermeulen (1993)
    The pseudobulbs of these orchids are usually close together with single leaves that are small, only occasionally growing as long as 11 cm. There are only a few flowers per inflorescence, and they are held well above the leaves. These small flowers are generally cupped, and the labellum rarely is lobed. All members of this section can be found in Australia and New Zealand. Type: *Adelopetalum bracteatum* Fitzgerald (1891).

Section *Aeschynanthoides* Carr (1930)
    This section consists of small plants that have a single leaf and grow on frequently vining rhizomes. The pseudobulbs are minute or nonexistent except as small swellings on the rhizomes under the leaves. The very short inflorescence has only one or two flowers. Type: *Bulbophyllum dryas* Ridley (1915).

Section *Alcistachys* Schlechter (1924)
    These are large plants with flat two-leaved pseudobulbs that are yellow or red and not fully developed at flowering time. Leaves are oblanceolate and

present during flowering. Bracts are as large as or larger than the flowers, and lateral sepals are free.

Section *Altisceptrum* J. J. Smith (1914)

These are large plants with a single leaf per pseudobulb and long inflorescences that are either pendent or have their tops reflexed and bear many flowers. Lectotype: *Bulbophyllum elongatum* (Blume) Hasskarl (1844).

Section *Aphanobulbon* Schlechter (1911)

These single-leaved species are without pseudobulbs or with very much reduced pseudobulbs. The long inflorescence has rather flaccid, usually yellow or cream-colored flowers. Type: *Bulbophyllum odoratum* (Blume) Lindley (1830).

Section *Bifalcula* Schlechter (1924)

These are large two-leaved plants with an inflorescence that is much longer than the pseudobulb. The flowers surround the terete or angular rachis, and the bracts are not longer than the flowers. The stelidia are usually longer than the anther, and there are basal teeth on the labellum. Type: *Bulbophyllum implexum* Jumelle & Perrier (1912).

Section *Biflorae* Garay, Hamer & Siegerist (1994)

The single-leaved pseudobulbs of plants in this section are not close together, there are only a few flowers per inflorescence, and the lateral sepals separate from one another soon after the flowers fully open. Type: *Bulbophyllum biflorum* Teijsmann & Binnendijk (1853).

Section *Brachyostele* Schlechter (1912)

This section is of interest although it does not consist of plants that are good inhabitants of civilized areas. The specific name of the type specimen indicates the reason for this statement. There is one leaf per pseudobulb, and the flowers are yellow green with red markings and are pollinated by blow flies. *Bulbophyllum pachyglossum* Schlechter (1919) and *B. santosii* Ames (1915) belong to this section. They grow in New Guinea and the Philippines. Type: *Bulbophyllum foetidum* Schlechter (1913).

Section *Brachypus* Schlechter (1913)

The single-leaved pseudobulbs are close together, and there are many short, single-flowered inflorescences in this section.

Section *Bulbophyllaria* (Reichenbach fil.) Grisebach (1864)

The pseudobulbs of this section have two leaves each, and the long, cylindrical rachis has very small flowers. Type: *Bulbophyllum bracteolatum* Lindley (1838).

Section *Bulbophyllum* Thouars (1877)
These are large plants with an inflorescence longer than the two-leaved pseudobulbs. The flowers surround the terete or angular rachis, and the bracts are as long as or shorter than the flowers. The stelidia are almost always shorter than the anther, and the labellum is without basal lobules. Type: *Bulbophyllum nutans* Thouars (1822).

Section *Careyana* Pfitzer (1888)
There is one leaf per pseudobulb, and the inflorescence consists of small flowers tightly packed around the scape thus forming a cylinder of flowers. Type: *Bulbophyllum careyanum* (Hooker fil.) Sprengel (1826).

Section *Cirrhopetaloides* Garay, Hamer & Siegerist (1994)
The plants have one leaf per pseudobulb, and the outer margins of the lateral sepals are curved in and seemingly joined along their central portion. The tips of the sepals are always free, are not fleshy, and are setaceous. Type: *Cirrhopetalum longissimum* Ridley (1896).

Section *Cochlia* (Blume) J.J. Smith (1914)
The basionym for this section is the genus *Cochlia* Blume (1825). The pseudobulbs have one leaf each and are appressed to the pendent rhizomes, the inflorescence is capitate with ringent flowers, and the labellum is reflexed at the apex. Type: *Cochlia violacea* Blume (1825).

Section *Cocoina* Pfitzer (1888)
The pseudobulbs are close together and have one leaf each. The inflorescence is much longer than the leaves. There are many pale flowers in the racemes. Type: *Bulbophyllum cocoinum* Lindley (1837).

Section *Corymbosia* (Blume) Pfeiffer (1870)
The basionym for this section is *Diphyes* section *Corymbosia* Blume (1825). There are small flowers on long pedicels with long sepals that are narrow and have somewhat incurved margins. There is one leaf per pseudobulb. Type: *Diphyes laxiflora* Blume (1825).

Section *Cylindracea* Pfitzer (1888)
The pseudobulbs of this section are very small, and sometimes it seems that they are nonexistent. There is only one leaf per pseudobulb, and the

flowers are held on tall, pendent scapes forming dense, cylindrical clusters. Type: *Bulbophyllum cylindraceum* Lindley (1830).

Section *Densiflora* Ridley (1907)

The members of this section have rhizomes that are densely sheathed and bear widely spaced pseudobulbs. The scape is short with tiny flowers clustered close to the rhizomes.

Section *Desmosanthes* (Blume 1825) J. J. Smith (1933)

Small species with one leaf per pseudobulb, umbellate inflorescences, and lateral sepals that do not twist much and are not connate but are often spreading are typical of this section. The flowers are usually greenish or yellow and have a stronger colored labellum. The basionym for this section is *Diphyes* Blume (1825). Type: *Diphyes crassifolia* Blume (1825).

Section *Diceras* Schlechter (1913)

Plants of this section are pendent epiphytes with one leaf per pseudobulb. They have a pair of hornlike growths on the basal portion of the labellum. Type: *Bulbophyllum diceras* Schlechter (1913).

Section *Didactyle* (Lindley) Cogniaux (1902)

This section represents some of the few species found in South America. It is distinguished by the two extra staminodes below the normal pair on the column and by the large heavy rib on the labellum.

Section *Elatae* Garay, Hamer & Siegerist (1994)

There is one leaf per pseudobulb and graceful, erect inflorescences with flowers carried in a pseudoumbellate rachis. The lateral sepals are free with the inner surfaces parallel but never joined. Type: *Cirrhopetalum elatum* Hooker fil. (1890).

Section *Emarginatae* Garay, Hamer & Siegerist (1994)

The pseudobulbs of this section are remote and well developed and have only one leaf each. The inflorescence has few flowers, and the lateral sepals are fused along their inner margins with the apices more or less free and the outer margins incurved, partially connivent but not fused. Type: *Cirrhopetalum emarginatum* Finet (1897).

Section *Ephippium* Schlechter (1913)

These plants have pseudobulbs that are spaced slightly apart and have only one leaf each. There is one flower per inflorescence, and the petals are much shorter than the sepals, while the labellum is rather long. Type: *Cirrho-petalum blumei* Lindley (1830).

Section *Epibulbon* Schlechter (1912)

In this section the rhizomes are rooted only at the base, there is but one leaf per pseudobulb, the flowers have sepals that are long and pointed, and the glabrous surface of the labellum is red.

Section *Fruticicola* Schlechter (1912)

The rhizomes of this section are usually hanging and are covered by sheaths. The pseudobulbs lie against the rhizomes and have one leaf each. The single flowers are hirsute on the underside of the labellum. Type: *Bulbophyllum fruticicola* Schlechter (1905).

Section *Globiceps* Schlechter (1913)

The pseudobulbs are very small and have one leaf each. The flowers face in all directions on a compact rachis, and the floral segments are short and broad. Lectotype: *Bulbophyllum globiceps* Schlechter (1905).

Section *Habrostachys* Schlechter (1913)

These small plants have pseudobulbs that are somewhat flattened hori-zontally and that retain their two leaves when flowering. The slender pedun-cle is often setaceous, and the flowers surround the terete or angular rachis. The bracts are not longer than the flowers, the stelidia are longer than the anther, and the labellum is basally lobed. Type: *Bulbophyllum jumelleanum* Schlechter (1913).

Section *Hedyothyrsus* Schlechter (1912)

Plants of this section have creeping rhizomes and pendent flower spikes. Type: *Bulbophyllum hedyothyrsus* Schlechter (1912).

Section *Hirtula* Ridley (1907)

These plants have abbreviated rhizomes with pseudobulbs that are small and clustered and have a single leaf. The inflorescence is slender and sub-umbellate with only a few somewhat pubescent flowers. Type: *Bulbophyllum hirtulum* Ridley (1907).

Section *Humblotiorchis* Schlechter (1925)

The plants of this section are small with a heavy, many-flowered inflo-rescence that is not longer than the leaf. The dorsal sepal is free and larger than the lateral sepals, the labellum is glabrous, and the stelidia are longer than the anther. Type: *Bulbophyllum humblotii* Rolfe (1890).

Section *Hyalosema* Schlechter (1911)
This section has large pseudobulbs with one leaf and long peduncles and there is a single large flower with very long dorsal and lateral sepals. The dorsal sepal is broader than the lateral sepals and forms a cap or hood over the flower. Type: *Bulbophyllum grandiflorum* Blume (1848).

Section *Hybochilus* Schlechter (1911)
The pseudobulbs of this section each have one leaf and are very small and widely spaced on the rhizomes. A single flower is carried on a very thin pedicel, and the central lobe of the labellum is hirsute or glandular to some degree.

Section *Intervallatae* Ridley (1897)
The plants in this section are medium sized, the pseudobulbs are fairly close together and have a single leaf, and the floral scape can be as long as 30 cm. The flowers are a nice size and are borne in succession as the scape elongates over a prolonged period of time. Type: *Bulbophyllum tardeflorens* Ridley (1896).

Section *Ischnopus* Schlechter (1912)
The pseudobulbs are not close together on the rhizomes and have a single leaf. The inflorescence is erect with a pendent rachis that has many small flowers. Lectotype: *Bulbophyllum habropus* Schlechter (1913).

Section *Lemniscata*
The pseudobulbs of these plants have two or more leaves which are deciduous. The long, pendulous rachis carries numerous small flowers. Each sepal has a long, hanging apical appendage.

Section *Leopardinae* Bentham (1883)
These single-leaved orchids have a short peduncle, usually bearing only two or three large flowers, rarely one flower, and the lateral sepals are spreading. Type: *Bulbophyllum leopardinum* (Wallich) Lindley (1830).

Section *Lepidorhiza* Schlechter (1911)
This section is from Indonesia, the Philippines, and New Guinea. There is one leaf per pseudobulb, and the flowers are large and colorful, bloom successively, and have lateral sepals that tend to fold over once but never join one another as is done in the genus *Cirrhopetalum*. Type: *Bulbophyllum amplebracteatum* Teijsmann & Binnendijk (1862).

Section *Leptopus* Schlechter (1905)

This section consists of hanging plants with roots emerging all along the rhizomes and creeping under the sheaths. There is a single leaf per pseudobulb, and the column has long stelidia. Lectotype: *Bulbophyllum leptopus* Schlechter (1905).

Section *Lichenophylax* Schlechter (1924)

These orchids are small with the two-leaved pseudobulbs somewhat flattened. The rachis is terete or angular, the bracts are not longer than the flowers, the column is without ornaments below the stelidia, the leaves are present during flowering, and there is but one flower per inflorescence. Type: *Bulbophyllum lichenophylax* Schlechter (1924).

Section *Loxosepalum* Schlechter (1924)

The inflorescence is longer than the leaf, and there is one leaf per pseudobulb. The rachis is often slightly swollen and has numerous small flowers on short pedicels. The labellum is recurved and slightly flattened horizontally.

Section *Lupulina* Pfitzer (1888)

The two-leaved pseudobulbs are fully developed when flowering and the flowers occur in a two- to four-ranked spike. The lateral sepals are not reflexed, the petals are linear and somewhat falcate, the column foot is at a right angle to the column, and the bracts are longer than the flowers. Type: *Bulbophyllum occultum* Thouars (1822).

Section *Lyraea* (Lindley) Moore (1877)

The two leaves per pseudobulb are present when flowering. The rachis is swollen. The lateral sepals are navicular, connate, with margins inrolled, and are prominently keeled. Type: *Bulbophyllum prismaticum* Thouars (1822).

Section *Macrobulbon* Schlechter (1912)

As indicated by the sectional name, this group of bulbophyllums is distinguished by its large pseudobulbs. There is one leaf per pseudobulb, and the inflorescence is short with two or more flowers on a compressed rachis. All members of this section are endemic to New Guinea. Type: *Bulbophyllum macrobulbon* J. J. Smith (1910).

Section *Macrostylidia* Garay, Hamer & Siegerist (1994)

The pseudobulbs in this section are distant on the rhizomes and have one leaf. The floral scapes are graceful, and each inflorescence has only a few flowers. These flowers have long lateral sepals that are free from a divergent base and are twisted once so they appear temporarily connivent, at least in part. The petals always have a sharply pointed tip. Most distinctive are the conspicuous and twisted stelidia. Type: *Cirrhopetalum macraei* Lindley (1830).

Section *Medusa* Pfitzer (1888)

There is one leaf per pseudobulb, the flowers are displayed in all directions, the lateral sepals are separate from one another at the base, and the flowers are frequently elongated. Type: *Cirrhopetalum medusae* Lindley (1842).

Section *Megaclinium* Summerhayes (1935)

In this section the pseudobulbs each have two leaves, only rarely one or three leaves, and a peduncle bearing a flattened rachis. There is a single row of small flowers on either side of this rachis and they open successively. In 1824 John Lindley established the genus *Megaclinium* to describe this very unusual group of African orchids. Heinrich Gustav Reichenbach, whose father is also well known in botanical circles, considered *Megaclinium* a section of the genus *Bulbophyllum* in 1861, but some taxonomists of the time, including Ernst Pfitzer and Friedrich W. L. Kraenzlin, agreed with Lindley that it should have its generic status maintained. Today most taxonomists agree with Reichenbach. The distribution of this section is limited to lowland forests that are rarely as high as 1400 m above sea level in Africa and the adjacent islands. There have been more than 40 species described with these characteristics. Unfortunately, many of them are seldom seen in cultivation although they are all well worth growing if they can be obtained. Type: *Bulbophyllum falcatum* (Lindley) Reichenbach fil. (1861).

Section *Megaloglossum* Carr (1933)

These plants are similar to those in section *Micromonanthe* with small creeping rhizomes that branch and grow as a compact mass, but the pseudobulbs are large and rather square. There is one flower per inflorescence, and it is approximately 1 cm in size. The column has long, slender stelidia.

Section *Micrantha* Cogniaux (1902)

The pedicels of plants in this section are long and graceful with many very small flowers. The pseudobulbs have only one leaf each. Type: *Bulbophyllum micranthum* Barbosa Rodrigues (1822).

Section *Microbulbon* Garay, Hamer & Siegerist (1994)

A single leaf per pseudobulb, very small disclike pseudobulbs that are several centimeters apart, flowers that seem to originate from a central point and spread out horizontally, and sharply pointed stelidia are the identifying characteristics of this section. Type: *Cirrhopetalum sarcophyllum* King & Pantling (1895).

Section *Micromonanthe* Schlechter (1913)

These plants are small with creeping rhizomes that branch and have single-leaved pseudobulbs that are varying distances apart but grow as a compact mass. There is only one flower per inflorescence and as a rule it is less than 1 cm in size. All sepals are roughly the same length. Lectotype: *Bulbophyllum neoguineense* J. J. Smith (1908).

Section *Minutissima* Pfitzer (1888)

These are very small plants with pseudobulbs crowded together on the rhizomes, single rudimentary leaves, and single flowers. Type: *Bulbophyllum minutissimum* F. von Mueller (1878).

Section *Monilibulbon* J. J. Smith (1914)

These are small plants with pseudobulbs close together, either lying on the rhizome or enclosing it, and there is but one leaf. The inflorescence has a single flower. The word *monili* means "necklace" and refers to the appearance of the pseudobulbs, which resemble a beaded necklace. Type: *Bulbophyllum tenellum* Lindley (1830).

Section *Nematorhizis* Schlechter (1912)

The plants of this section are very small and widely creeping with thin rhizomes. They have one leaf per pseudobulb and short, blunt stelidia on the column. Type: *Bulbophyllum nematorhizis* Schlechter (1912).

Section *Oxysepala* (Wight) Reichenbach fil. (1861)

The rhizomes hang from trees or rocks, and the pseudobulbs are quite small with single, fleshy leaves. Inflorescences arise all along the rhizomes, are sessile, and bear a single small yellow or white flower. The sepals have elongated apices, and the petals and labellum are small. This section covers a large area from India throughout Thailand, the Malay peninsula, east to Java, New Guinea, and Australia. There are even some species reported from Brazil. Type: *Oxysepala ovalifolia* Wight (1852).

Section *Pachyanthe* Schlechter (1912)

This section has one leaf per pseudobulb and large flowers that are vertically rather flat while in bud, have a flat labellum with keels or tubercles, and the column has a distinct foot but shows no mentum in the open flower. The section is endemic to New Guinea. Type: *Bulbophyllum pachyanthum* Schlechter (1912).

Section *Pachychlamys* Schlechter (1924)

This section from Madagascar has two leaves per pseudobulb. The inflorescence is erect, has several sheaths and numerous relatively small flowers that are alternately held on the apical portion. The lateral sepals are partially connate.

Section *Pahudia* Schlechter (1911)

These plants are vigorous with large, elongate, single-leaved pseudobulbs and several large, spreading flowers on each inflorescence. The lateral sepals fold upon themselves or are twisted but are never parallel to each other. Type: *Cirrhopetalum pahudii* De Vriese (1854).

Section *Pahudiella* Garay, Hamer & Siegerist (1993)

The cylindrical pseudobulbs of this section are not close together and have one leaf each. There are only a few flowers per inflorescence, and these are rather large with broad sepals but never with margins inrolled. Type: *Bulbophyllum subumbellatum* Ridley (1896).

Section *Papulipetalum* Schlechter (1912)

This section has one leaf per pseudobulb, and the pseudobulbs are seldom well developed. The single flower is on a long inflorescence, the lateral sepals are longer than the dorsal sepal, and the tiny petals have long papillae at their apices. Type: *Bulbophyllum papulipetalum* Schlechter (1912).

Section *Pelma* (Finet) Schlechter (1913)

This sectional name was chosen by Rudolf Schlechter in reference to the genus *Pelma* which was defined by Achille Finet in 1909. The rhizomes are pendulous and not rooting except at the base of the entire plant. The pseudobulbs are at an angle to the rhizomes, have a single leaf, and are enclosed in sheaths as are the inflorescences. The flowers are very small. Type: *Dactylorhynchus flavescens* Schlechter (1913).

Section *Peltopus* Schlechter (1913)

These plants have creeping rhizomes, one leaf per pseudobulb, single flowers with tiny petals, and a labellum with a basal depression. They grow at elevations of 2000 m above sea level or higher. Type: *Bulbophyllum peltopus* Schlechter (1928).

Section *Pendula* Pfitzer (1888)

This section has globose pseudobulbs that are close together on the rhizomes, and the many-flowered racemose inflorescence is recurved or pendent. The sepals are all similar in size and smooth. Ernst Pfitzer likened the inflorescence to a slender bunch of grapes.

Section *Pleiophyllus* J. J. Smith (1914)

The pseudobulbs of plants in this section have two or three leaves which are deciduous at flowering time. The small flowers are held on a racemose inflorescence.

Section *Polyblepharon* Schlechter (1911)

A main feature of this very large section is that the height of a pseudobulb with its single leaf is usually less than 7 cm. The rhizome is pendent, the inflorescence is single flowered, the lateral sepals are connate by their outer margins, and the labellum is ciliate. Species in this section have been found from India throughout New Guinea and as far as Australia. Type: *Bulbophyllum polyblepharon* Schlechter (1911).

Section *Ptiloglossum* Lindley (1862)

There is one leaf per pseudobulb, the labellum is exceptionally mobile and feathery, and the plants grow on tree trunks or in moss. Type: *Bulbophyllum calamarium* Lindley (1861).

Section *Pygmaea* Reichenbach fil. (1861)

Minute pseudobulbs on creeping rhizomes, single leaves less than 5 cm tall, and only a very few small flowers per inflorescence are typical of this section. Type: *Bulbophyllum pygmaeum* (J. E. Smith) Lindley (1861).

Section *Racemosae* Bentham & Hooker fil. (1883)

This section has large pseudobulbs that are some distance apart on the rhizome and have a single leaf. The reddish-brown flowers are borne on long racemes. Type: *Bulbophyllum racemosum* Rolfe (1893).

Section *Saurocephalum* Schlechter (1911)

This section has but one leaf per pseudobulb and a thickened or swollen rachis with small flowers arranged all around it and pressed down upon it. The name refers to the presumed resemblance of the flowers to the head of a snake. Lectotype: *Bulbophyllum saurocephalum* Reichenbach fil. (1886).

Section *Sestochilos* (Breda) Bentham & Hooker fil. (1883)

Sestochilos is one of the most interesting and perhaps most often discussed sections of the genus *Bulbophyllum*. These orchids have good-sized pseudobulbs on creeping rhizomes, one leaf per pseudobulb, and almost always one flower, rarely two or three, per inflorescence. The rhizomes and pseudobulbs are encased in long, stiff bristles. The flowers are large with large sepals and petals. Type: *Sestochilos uniflorum* Breda (1828).

Section *Sphaeracron* Schlechter (1912)
    The small pseudobulbs have a single leaf and are closely appressed to the
rhizomes. The flowers appear either singly or in pairs from many points
along the short stem. Lectotype: *Bulbophyllum sphaeracron* Schlechter (1912).

Section *Stenochilus* J. J. Smith (1914)
    The pseudobulbs have one leaf, and the flowers are nonresupinate, that is,
they do not rotate 180 degrees as they do in most orchids, and the labellum
remains upright with the dorsal sepal in the inferior position. When photographs of flowers from this section are published, they are frequently shown
upside down, and even editors of magazines that are devoted solely to horticulture "correct" the illustrations of these orchids by printing them with the
labellum in the inferior position. The rhizomes are creeping, and there are
many roots which often are branching. Type: *Bulbophyllum macranthum* Lindley (1844).

Section *Stictosepalum* Schlechter (1913)
    This section is monotypic with cylindric pseudobulbs, a long single leaf,
and a scape shorter than the leaf with several flowers. Type: *Bulbophyllum stictosepalum* Schlechter (1913).

Section *Trichopus* Schlechter (1924)
    These orchids are not more than 10 cm tall, have one leaf per pseudo-
bulb, and have no more than six flowers per inflorescence. Each inflorescence is more than 10 cm tall, and the flowers are widely spaced on the rachis,
the sepals are not connate, and the labellum is ciliate. Type: *Bulbophyllum
intertextum* Lindley (1862).

Section *Tripudianthes* Seidenfaden (1979)
    There are many flowers on the decurved rachis of plants in this section
which have two leaves per pseudobulb that are usually deciduous during
flowering. The lateral sepals are conjoined and larger than the dorsal sepal.

Section *Umbellatae* Bentham (1883)
    There is one leaf per pseudobulb, and the flowers have lateral sepals that
fold inward once or more. The margins of these folded parts are parallel to
some degree. Lectotype: *Bulbophyllum umbellatum* Bentham (1883).

Section *Uncifera* Schlechter (1912)
    The rhizomes of orchids in this section are usually pendulous, there is at
least one flower per inflorescence, and the labellum is not lobed. There has
been a bit of dissention about this section because in 1910 Rudolf Schlechter

loaned his specimens to J. J. Smith so he could copy them. Smith received material from New Guinea that was similar, and Schlechter felt that Smith was trying to upstage him and be the first to publish these new species. Schlechter claimed that Smith's descriptions were insufficient for him to use and did not do so. Lectotype: *Bulbophyllum ochroleucum* Schlechter (1905).

Section *Xiphizusa* (Reichenbach fil.) Cogniaux (1902)

This New World section has tiny round pseudobulbs that are very close together on the rhizomes. The tall inflorescence has several lax flowers that have hirsute petals, and the labellum is very noticeable with a linear ciliate projection at the apex.

CHAPTER 3

Growing Conditions

There are so many diverse orchid habitats with so many factors to consider—altitude, rainfall, temperature extremes, air circulation, and so forth—it is a wonder that we can grow so many different species well. This book is written to give you enough information to have a good chance of success with most bulbophyllums and, after a bit of experience, enough knowledge to know which species to avoid. A single windowsill, or even a home greenhouse, cannot possibly successfully nurture all *Bulbophyllum* species. So the first step is to be familiar with your own limitations and then choose plants accordingly.

In 1830 John Lindley published the conditions he considered necessary to successfully cultivate orchid plants—very high temperatures, great humidity, and extreme shade. The successful growers of the time, especially Sir Joseph Paxton, who cultivated the plants for the Duke of Devonshire at Chiswick House, in England, recognized the fallacy of these conditions and grew his orchids quite well at more reasonable temperatures and with adequate light and humidity, taking into consideration the altitude at which the various plants grew in nature.

Most bulbophyllums presented here will adapt to most home growing conditions with the required temperature extremes being the most limiting factor. If you are planning to grow orchids on a windowsill in your warm family room, it certainly is a waste of money and time to invest in a group of cool-growing plants, but many of the most desirable species will adjust to those conditions with ease.

Temperature

The temperature ranges that are indicated for the various species are approximate and are meant only as loose guidelines. Intermediate conditions should be between 13 and 18°C (55 and 65°F) at night in the winter and a bit higher during the day, perhaps as much as 5 to 7°C (10–15°F) more. In other words, it should be a temperature that is comfortable for people as well as plants. When a plant is said to be an inhabitant of a warm environment, it is a tropical species that likes to be at least 18°C (65°F) during the night and prefers to be a good deal warmer in the daytime with the temperature possibly as high as 32°C (90°F) or a bit more—just what you would expect in the tropics. And when cool temperatures are specified, night temperatures during the winter should range from 7 to 13°C (45–55°F) and rise 6 to 11°C (10–20°F) during the day.

Light Intensity

Most orchids do not tolerate direct, bright sunlight. The majority of those discussed in the following pages need medium light conditions, which means slightly shaded situations or between 22,000 and 38,000 lux (2000 and 3500 foot-candles). Plants that grow in the tops of forest trees can usually benefit from slightly more bright light but not direct sunlight. Those species that are found in the understory of forests require less than 22,000 lux (2000 foot-candles) which translates to shade from direct sunlight but not the gloom of a cave. Common sense is the best guide. If the leaves turn light green or yellow or, heaven forbid, develop burned brown spots, move the plants immediately to a more shady location. On the other hand, if the plants have new, fully developed growths and show no signs of flowering, move them to a slightly brighter area. Flowering may also sometimes be induced by a slight drop in temperature, especially at night.

Air Circulation

Good air circulation is always an asset when growing healthy plants. When the air moves over the leaves many plant diseases are discouraged from gaining a foothold. Although the plants want high humidity, they do not relish having drops of water standing on the leaves or in the crowns of plants. A few well-placed fans assure good air movement in a greenhouse and a ceiling fan accomplishes the same goal in a house. When plants are grown in a lath house in warm areas, Mother Nature usually takes care of things very well, but if the air is especially stagnant, just add a well-insulated ceiling fan.

Humidity

Humidity is possibly the most difficult factor to supply. Most orchids prosper in 40 to 60 percent humidity which is not too difficult to provide in a greenhouse but can be a problem in the home environment. A tray with pebbles in it and water just up to the bottom of the pots but not touching them will help. Spritzing the plants with water in a spray bottle is another ploy that adds humidity. Some growers have found that developing a garden area with a small pool or fountain in one room of the house provides a delightful growing area that is enjoyed by the plants as well as the owners.

Potting Media

The *Bulbophyllum* complex is generally adaptable to many types of growing media, including osmunda, tree fern shreds or pieces, Canadian peat, cypress mulch, redwood (*Sequoia sempervirens*) fiber, charcoal of various sizes, styrofoam pellets, fir bark in many sizes, corks from wine bottles, coconut husks or chunks, vermiculite, perlite, certain types of rocks, or any mixture thereof used either in pots or baskets. The addition of moisture-retentive material, such as varying amounts of spaghnum or peat moss, and the size of the chunks or pellets determine the amount of moisture held in the mix. There are many different mixes on the market and most growers have a favorite one, either a commercial mixture or one of their own making, but they all seem to give good results under the conditions for which they were formulated. Perhaps it would be best for the beginner to either use a standard commercial mix that is airy and light or to use a mix devised by a friend who is growing under similar conditions. One type of mixture that retains moisture very well (sometimes too well) is medium fir bark, vermiculite, peat, perlite, and lime in various proportions.

As a rule, osmunda and spaghnum moss hold too much moisture to use alone as a potting medium for bulbophyllums, but spaghnum is very useful as a top dressing on the pot or basket. Be certain that the spaghnum is sterile, and if there is any doubt, bake it in the oven at 230°C (450°F) for four hours. If the pot is deep, it is helpful to put a layer of rock, broken pot shards, or large charcoal pieces in the bottom, then top it with the normal potting medium where the roots will grow. This prevents the potting mix from decaying too rapidly due to excess accumulation of moisture. The addition of cypress mulch to a mix is helpful in counteracting mold. It goes without saying that all potting media must be sterile, that is, free of all pathogens. The popularity of true New Zealand spaghnum moss is due to the fact that it has a pH of 4 and supposedly no pathogens can grow in it.

When using pots in a rather dry environment, such as in the home, it is often useful to top dress the medium with a thin layer of fluffed spaghnum moss or chopped coconut fiber to keep the roots moist a bit longer, but be warned that orchids rarely can exist in a continually wet habitat. Plastic pots are obviously going to keep the growing medium more moist than clay pots and are often preferred for growing in the comparatively dry home environment. The few species that require constant moisture or a moisture-retentive potting mix will be identified in the plant descriptions. Such a plant does not require that its roots be kept constantly wet, only that they should be moist most of the time with a few dry hours each day and that the atmosphere should be humid. Remember, orchids are not aquatic plants.

Some growers have success top dressing the pots or baskets with corks from wine bottles. Their non-orchid-growing friends are usually delighted to save corks for the orchids, so that it is easy to amass quite a stash of free top dressings. The residue of the wine tannins on the corks seems to subtly supply the plants with extra nutrients. Since the corks decay more rapidly than most media, it is best to use them as top dressing only, not as a complete potting medium; as a top dressing they can be easily removed and replaced with fresh ones when necessary. If using corks as top dressing on plants that are grown outdoors, it is helpful to cover them with a piece or two of fine netting to discourage thieving birds and squirrels. Pliable aluminum mesh works well, as does nylon mesh, just be certain to fasten it securely.

Slab Culture

If you can supply adequate humidity, mounting the plants on pieces of cork bark, tree fern, coconut husks, wood, or twigs is very effective. If available, sassafras twigs and limbs are very good mounts. Any of these can easily be hung in the growing area and allowed to move a bit in the breezes. *Opuntia cholla*, usually called just "cholla," comes from the deserts of the American Southwest. The dried skeleton of this cactus is especially attractive for mounting small plants as it gives a rather airy, exotic appearance. Good results have been obtained by lightly filling the center of cholla pieces with spaghnum or chopped coconut fiber to retain a bit more moisture, then tying the plants around it.

Another novel mounting device is the Florida cypress "knee" so often seen for sale along the highways in that state. (These "knees" are root formations of the bald cypress, *Taxodium* species.) Depending on their natural growing conditions, moisture-loving plants can be bedded down on wisps of spaghnum or coconut fiber before mounting, or the whole knee can be allowed to stand in a tray containing a small amount of water. Be certain that only the cypress knee is in the water, not the plants. Tying the plants on the mount is the usual method of attaching them but some growers use glue guns successfully. If tying, use something that will withstand the humidity, such as florist wire, phone wire, nylon fishing line, or strips of old nylon stockings.

Many growers find it impossible to properly maintain plants on mounts because they cannot keep the plants moist enough for good development. At the risk of being redundant, let me emphasize that by this it is not meant that they must be constantly wet but that they need to be given a drink each day and then allowed to dry, all the while maintaining air humidity at a comfortable level. This humidity requirement as well as the nuisance of daily watering almost always precludes growing plants on mounts in the home environment. But if there is a small water garden or an area where other plants give a tropical atmosphere, it is worth experimenting with a few bulbophyllums on slabs. If they appear to be in distress, just remove them from the slab and pot them.

In greenhouse culture or when growing orchids in a lath house or other outdoor area, slab mounting is often preferred. Some very successful growers in Thailand mount their bulbophyllums on pieces of coconut husk with wire hooks projecting from the top and bottom of the husk. They suspend them one from another in a long column from the top of the shade house to within 30 to 60 cm (1–2 ft.) of the ground. The top plants are watered copiously, and the water cascades down the column. Of course, they have wonderful air circulation and constantly high humidity in Thailand.

A clever way of handling rampant growers is to settle the plant into a wire basket lined with sheets of spaghnum moss, then fill with a loose medium such as tree fern or bark chunks. This arrangement gives the plants the opportunity to grow on the outside of the basket as well as within it while retaining more moisture than is possible with a piece of cork or other slab.

Very Small Plants

There are many lesser known, smaller bulbophyllums that should be interesting to the amateur grower. In the home environment they often can be grouped in a tray filled with pebbles, water added to the tray to supply humidity, and placed in a bright window. Even those species that are best grown on slabs can be handled in this manner, but be certain that the plants do not rest in the water. The pendent species are a bit more difficult without a greenhouse, but daily misting might provide enough humidity to keep them happy. Direct sunlight is a no-no because the leaves will certainly burn. However they are housed, these plants add interest and variety to any collection.

Sanitation

Although bulbophyllums seem to be less prone to fungal and viral infections than some other genera of orchids, it is still very important to keep things as clean as possible. If there is any doubt about the sterility of a potting mix, by all means bake it in an oven at 230°C (450°F) for a few hours and allow it to cool before using. Clay pots that are to be reused should be washed thoroughly in hot, soapy water, rinsed very well, then baked in an oven or soaked in an antifungal solution and allowed to dry before using. Plastic pots need to be scrubbed and rinsed. It is rarely advisable to reuse slabs of any sort and, of course, potting mix should be discarded or added to the compost pile after use.

Fertilizer

Fertilizer is, naturally, of prime importance in growing prize orchids. Some of the most successful growers dip their plants in a mixture of dehydrated chicken manure and water as frequently as every week in the spring and summer. This mixture is not without odor and certainly not recommended for family room culture, but in a greenhouse or lath house it works wonders for the plants. The proportion of manure to water is not critical and suspending a porous bag full of manure into a vat or barrel and allowing it to remain there is not overkill.

For in-home growing a more fragrant method of fertilization is recommended. Granules which release a small amount of fertilizer with each watering can be distributed on top of the growing medium in pots and baskets. Powders and liquids can be diluted and applied when watering, and these are quite successful in supplying the necessary nutrients. The main thing to remember when using these commercial products is to follow the directions of the manufacturers very carefully as it is easy to overdose. A safe method would be to use less than the recommended amount until you are familiar with the product.

Many growers vary the fertilizer with the seasons. In spring and summer they use a 30–10–10 mix (30 parts nitrogen, 10 parts phosphorous, and 10 parts potassium) diluted as the label indicates, 0.6 milliliter per liter of water (1/2 teaspoon per gallon) applied every other week. In the rainy summer season they switch to a 20–20–20 mix and in the fall and winter use 10–30–20. In the spring most growers find that fertilizer can be applied more often as this is the season of rapid growth. And some growers dilute the fertilizer even more and apply a weak solution with every watering, usually using a proportioner of some sort to simplify the task. Hobbyists using this latter method apply the principle that God doesn't say, "It's the third Thursday of the month, I must send fertilizer."

Repotting

Repotting is usually most successful in spring or early summer, but if a plant is in obvious distress, don't wait—do it now! Decayed potting medium is the cause of many a plant's decline and ultimate demise. Most mixtures do not last more than two years, and it is often helpful when there are a number of plants in the collection to keep potting records on the plant tag so repotting can be done before the plant is in distress. Plants grown on slabs rarely need repotting, but if the growth is too rampant and there are many hanging rhizomes, those with several pseudobulbs could be severed and remounted on another slab, either to increase the collection or to share with a friend.

Records

Plant records are often successfully kept on the name tag of the plant. If there are more than a few plants, a number should be assigned to each as it is acquired. This can be a simple sequential numbering of plants or it can be more complex with the year of acquisition followed by the group number and then the individual number within the group. For instance, say that the first group of plants purchased in 2000 contained five plants. They would be numbered 00-1-1, 00-1-2, and so forth. The second group that year would be 00-2-1, and so on. On the back of the tag the date of blooming could be added, perhaps including the number of flowers, and also the dates of repotting. Of course, if the collection is small, just keep the name of the plant on the tag and enjoy it when it flowers.

American Orchid Society Awards

In the 1940s the American Orchid Society (AOS) established formal rules for the judging of orchid plants. Judging centers were formed and plants could be sent to them for evaluation once each month. In St. Louis, Missouri, at the First World Orchid Conference in 1954, the system of point judging was refined, standardizing the system used in all judging centers and at all AOS–sponsored orchid shows. By the 1960s there were judging centers throughout the United States and more have been added since then so that there is one within reach of most orchid growers including those in Hawaii and Canada.

To become an American Orchid Society judge requires a long training period starting with a three-year minimum as a student judge. The prospective student judges must have grown orchids for some years and be familiar with botanical terms and the basic orchid genera. They are interviewed by a group of judges and if deemed knowledgeable they then become, in effect, apprentice judges, and work with a mentor as well as all the other judges at regional judgings and orchid shows. In addition, they prepare and present many papers on orchids and their evaluation and also attend workshops on judging. At the end of the three-year period, but not longer than a six-year period, they are either elevated to the rank of probationary judge or dropped from the program. Again, there is a minimum three-year period of service in this capacity before elevation to accredited judge, during which time the training programs continue and attendance is required at a minimum number of judging and training events each year. This rigorous training for becoming an AOS judge is necessary to effectively evaluate all genera and species of this huge family. The learning process does not end with accreditation but continues with required attendance at a certain number of judging events and seminars each year.

A standardized group of AOS awards is in use, including some for recognition of new species either as a botanical species or as one desirable for horticulture, awards given to the grower for excellence in growing a particular plant, and quality awards for excellent flower form.

The Certificate of Botanical Recognition (abbreviated CBR/AOS) is awarded to a plant new to horticulture and is given to an orchid species or natural hybrid that is considered rare, novel, and of educational value. The species may not have received a prior AOS award and must have at least two-thirds approval of the judging team. The name must also be verified by a botanical taxonomist approved by the American Orchid Society.

The Certificate of Horticultural Merit (CHM/AOS) may be granted to a species or natural hybrid that is well grown, well flowered, and is considered attractive enough to contribute to the horticultural aspects of orchid growing. The award is voted upon by the judging team who score the plant using a point scale. If the average points awarded are 80 or above, the CHM/AOS is awarded. Again, this is a provisional award that requires a taxonomist's verification.

The Certificate of Cultural Merit (CCM/AOS) is perhaps the most coveted AOS award because it is given to the grower, not the plant. The grower must have had the plant in his possession for at least six months and the plant must be extremely healthy with a large number of flowers. Again, the plant is scored by the judges on a specific point scale and if the average of the team is 80 or more, the CCM/AOS is granted. This award, unlike the two previously mentioned, may be given to other plants of the same species or the same hybrid.

The merit awards, Highly Commended Certificate (HCC/AOS), Award of Merit (AM/AOS), and First Class Certificate (FCC/AOS), are given to orchid flowers that are exhibited either on the plant or as cut flowers. They recognize orchids that are unusually fine specimens. The flowers are evaluated by a team of judges and scored on specific point scales for each genus. If the average points of the team range from 75 to 79, the HCC/AOS is awarded; if the points range from 80 to 89, the award is an AM/AOS, and if they are 90 or above the FCC/AOS is given. Upon completion of scoring, the awarded plant is described, measured, and photographed for publication in the *Awards Quarterly* (AQ) which is a quarterly publication of all awards granted in the preceding period.

CHAPTER 4

Bulbophyllums with Two Leaves
per Pseudobulb

Perhaps some of the least-known but most intriguing plants of the genus *Bulbophyllum* are those with two leaves. The largest number are indigenous to Madagascar and central and southern Africa with smaller numbers in Asia and even a few in South and Central America. Almost all those from Africa have small, but occasionally very striking, flowers. Many are true miniatures, while others are very large, but the majority fall into the medium size range so there are some that will fit easily into any growing facility.

The multileaved plants from Asia are almost all delightful. Many of them are deciduous at certain stages of their growth cycles which can be caused by various environmental influences such as temperature, day length, and light intensity. Most often the leaves are present during the wet season and the flowers appear during the dry season which greatly increases their visibility. Some Asian species have very interesting large flowers, and almost all of them are worth space in an orchid collection.

The few members of the genus that have reached the Americas are, unfortunately, not as attractive as the others. The plants are a bit stiff and uninteresting, and the flowers are sometimes rather drab and certainly very small. They range throughout Mexico, Central and South America, the West Indies, and even occasionally are found in Florida. They grow as epiphytes on trees in humid forests less than 300 m above sea level and are not often found in orchid collections. The swollen rachis with the small flowers spaced around it would lend interest to a large collection. All the New World species listed here belong to the section *Bulbophyllaria*. The pseudobulbs of these plants are deeply ridged and sheathed. The rachis is long and cylindrical with very small flowers.

Where there have been well-defined botanical sections published, they will be mentioned in the descriptions of the species. Since there are, naturally, many similarities in the plants within these sections, it is often interesting to grow several of the same section and compare them to one another. They frequently require the same type of environment, thus simplifying care.

Bulbophyllum acutebracteatum De Wildeman (1921)

SYNONYM

Bulbophyllum platyrachis De Wildeman (1906)

This attractive, small species has pseudobulbs that are slightly flattened and angled. The leaves are sometimes as long as 7 cm and are always present when the flowers are open. The scape is about 16 cm tall and has almost 50 flowers on the somewhat flattened, reddish rachis. The flowers are distichously alternate, and the floral bracts are as long as the yellow-orange flowers. This species grows as an epiphyte at low altitudes in the West African countries near the Gulf of Guinea but also has been found in Republic of the Congo and as far south as Zimbabwe. Small pieces of cork bark, tree fern, or tree branches are appropriate for mounting this species. The growing area should be slightly shaded, warm, and humid.

Bulbophyllum afzelii Schlechter (1918)

The pseudobulbs of this species belonging to the section *Lichenophylax* are close together, perhaps 1 cm apart, on the readily branching rhizomes. The leaves are 2 cm long and are present during flowering. There is only one small flower per 6-cm long scape. The oval sepals are 1 cm long, the petals are minute, the column is without ornaments below the stelidia, and the labellum is fleshy, keeled, and about the length of the petals. This species grows as an epiphyte in the forests of Madagascar and can be cultivated by hanging the plants on moisture-retentive mounts in warm temperatures with good air circulation and moderate shade. Perhaps very small tree fern slabs or pieces of cholla with a layer of moss would be best, although wooden mounts or pieces of tree branches would work well also. This tiny plant is attractive because the flowers are held well above the leaves and, because the plant forms dense mats, there will be a nice display of flowers at one time despite the fact that there is only one flower per inflorescence. The variety *microdoron* (Schlechter) Bosser (1965) is quite similar but the apices of the sepals are a bit shorter and the base of the labellum is narrower. The variety can, of course, be grown under the same conditions as the species.

Bulbophyllum ambreae Perrier (1938)

This species was named after the mountain in Madagascar on which it was first found in 1932 and is part of the section *Lyraea*. It is a nice medium size, between 8 and 12 cm tall, and the rounded, knobby pseudobulbs are only 2 cm apart on the rhizomes. The elliptical leaves are about 4 cm long and are present when flowering, and the inflorescence is held well above them. The scape is perhaps 15 cm long and has a rachis that carries 10 to 15 flowers, each of which is less than 1 cm in size. The lateral sepals are connate with their margins inrolled and are prominently keeled, while the labellum is bilobed. This plant is endemic to the forests of Madagascar at more than 1200 m altitude and prefers a mossy medium on which to grow. Warm to intermediate conditions are appropriate with, of course, adequate moisture, good air circulation, and moderate shade. Although the individual flowers are small, they are numerous and presented well above the plant, making them very desirable additions to the collection.

Bulbophyllum ankaizinense (Jumelle & Perrier) Schlechter (1924)
SYNONYM
Bulbophyllum ophiuchus var. *ankaizinensis* Jumelle & Perrier (1912)

Named for the area in Madagascar in which it grows on trees in mossy forests at about 1000 to 2000 m elevation, this orchid which belongs to the section *Lyraea* has deeply ridged, narrow pseudobulbs that are 2 to 4.5 cm tall and only 1 to 3 cm wide. The leaves are present when flowering and can be as long as 16 cm, and the peduncle 13 cm long. The swollen rachis is densely covered with tiny, brown, papillose flowers. The lateral sepals are connate with their margins inrolled and are prominently keeled. The plant can best be grown in a pot with a medium that retains moisture. It requires semishade and intermediate temperatures.

Bulbophyllum aristatum (Reichenbach fil.) Hemsley (1883)
SYNONYMS
Bolbophyllaria aristata Reichenbach fil. (1866), *Phyllorchis aristata* (Reichenbach fil.) Kuntze (1891)

This Central American species of the section *Bulbophyllaria* has deeply ridged, sheathed pseudobulbs and the rachis is long and has very small flowers. It is differentiated from the other species in the section by the shape of its petals which form a long wedge or sometimes look almost spoonlike and have a long, narrow bristlelike projection. The peduncle is about 9 cm tall and is taller than the leaves. Successful cultivation requires warm temperatures and high humidity with shelter from direct sunlight.

Bulbophyllum auricomum Lindley (1830)
SYNONYMS
Bulbophyllum foenisecii Parish & Reichenbach fil. (1865)
Bulbophyllum tripetaloides (Roxburgh) Schlechter (1914), *Dendrobium tripetaloides* Roxburgh (1814)
Phyllorchis auricoma (Lindley) Kuntze (1891)

The pseudobulbs of this species of the section *Pleiophyllus* are about 3.5 cm tall and only 1 or 2 cm apart on the rhizome. The leaves, which are deciduous when flowering takes place, are 12 cm long and only 1.5 cm wide. The racemose inflorescence rises from the base of the pseudobulbs, then arches gracefully with as many as 25 flowers arranged along it. These flowers are less than 1 cm in size, yellowish to white, and darker at the base. The lateral sepals are hirsute, the petals are ciliate, and the finely hirsute labellum is green at the base, then yellowish with brown markings. The plants grow in India, Thailand, Myanmar, Sumatra, and Java and require a warm, moist growing environment with light shade and good air movement. They can be grown in pots or baskets, or on slabs with equal success.

Bulbophyllum averyanovii Seidenfaden (1992)

This interesting member of the section *Pleiophyllus* has smooth pseudobulbs that are about 2 cm tall and equally as wide, so close to one another on the rhizome that they touch. The leaves are 5 cm long and 1 cm wide, and are deciduous when the flowers appear. The thick flower scape is 1.7 cm long and sharply curved apically, and the rachis is about 1 cm long with as many as 10 flowers crowded together. The flowers are less than 0.5 cm in size, white, with outer portions of the sepals densely hirsute, and have a dark purple, rugose labellum. The species grows only in Vietnam. It requires intermediate temperatures and moderate amounts of moisture, and must be kept in the shade. Pots, baskets, or mounts are satisfactory.

Bulbophyllum bathieanum Schlechter (1916)

This orchid is a member of the section *Alcistachys* and has clustered pseudobulbs that are large, oval, flattened, and not fully developed at flowering time. The leaves are as long as 20 cm and are present at flowering. The scape is considerably longer than the leaves, up to 35 cm, holding many clustered flowers on a slightly recurved inflorescence. The flowers are about 2 cm long, pale green with a rich dark red labellum that has two raised, granular, longitudinal lines. The lateral sepals are free, and the flowers are held in large bracts. This species grows as an epiphyte in forests in Madagascar at about 600 m altitude. Although large in size, it has very attractive flowers and can easily be grown in good-sized pots in any standard mix that holds a reasonable amount of moisture. Warm conditions, partial shade, and good air circulation are necessary.

Bulbophyllum bequaertii De Wildeman (1921)

SYNONYMS
Bulbophyllum bequaertii var. *brachyanthum* Summerhayes (1953)
Bulbophyllum cochleatum var. *bequaertii* (De Wildeman) J. J. Vermeulen (1987), *B. cochleatum* var. *brachyanthum* (Summerhayes) J. J. Vermeulen (1986)

The pseudobulbs of this species are 10 cm tall, enveloped in sheaths, and several centimeters apart on the rhizomes. The flowers appear on a scape that sometimes is 50 cm or more long but is usually much shorter. The rachis is frequently a bit rounded, and the many small dark reddish flowers are closely spaced around it. The flowers are turned away from the rachis and the bracts are prominent. The species is native to Congo (Zaire), Uganda, Tanzania, and Kenya in rain forests from sea level to 2000 m altitude. It grows well in large pots with an open, well-draining potting mix and requires light shade, warm temperatures, and daily misting to keep the humidity at a proper level.

Bulbophyllum bifarium Hooker fil. (1864)
SYNONYM
Bulbophyllum pallescens Kraenzlin (1914)

The pseudobulbs of this species are about 4 cm tall and 1 cm wide, four angled, and a bit more than 3 cm apart on the rhizomes. The leaves are some-times as long as 10 cm and 1 cm wide and are present when flowering. The scape is almost 20 cm long and has many small flowers with reflexed lateral sepals. These flowers are subtended by yellow floral bracts that are 1 cm long, which is longer than the flowers. The plants grow as epiphytes, only rarely as lithophytes, in forests of Kenya, Cameroon, and the Ivory Coast at altitudes of about 2000 m above sea level. The floral bracts are dominant and make an unusual picture displayed at right angles to the rachis with the smaller pale flowers nestled in them. Cultivation is easiest in pots or baskets at intermediate temperatures in lightly shaded areas.

Bulbophyllum blepharistes Reichenbach fil. (1872)
SYNONYMS
Bulbophyllum malayanum J. J. Smith (1912)
Cirrhopetalum blepharistes (Reichenbach fil.) Hooker fil. (1890)
Cirrhopetalum distans Reichenbach fil., name published without designation
    of type
Cirrhopetalum longiscapum Teijsmann & Binnendijk (1862), *Phyllorchis
    longiscapa* (Teijsmann & Binnendijk) Kuntze (1891)
Cirrhopetalum spicatum Gagnepain (1950)

The pseudobulbs of the monotypic section *Blepharistes* are somewhat glo-bose and a good distance apart on the rhizomes, and the two leaves are often as long as 8 cm and a bit fleshy. The flowers form an umbel on a scape 20 to 30 cm long and open successively. They are yellow with purple lines and dots, the lateral sepals are connate, and the petals are oblong and fimbriate. The labellum is exceedingly mobile, moving upwards at the faintest touch and staying in that closed position several seconds, presumably to trap a vis-iting insect and thus effect pollination. *Bulbophyllum blepharistes* grows in rain forests in Myanmar, Thailand, Laos, Malaya, and Vietnam at moderate to low elevations. These plants are easily grown in pots or baskets or on slabs and are attractive and interesting to grow assuming they are given warm, moist conditions and no direct sun.

Bulbophyllum bracteolatum Lindley (1838)

SYNONYMS
Bolbophyllaria bracteolata (Lindley) Reichenbach fil. (1852), *Phyllorchis bracteolata* (Lindley) Kuntze (1891)

This species, the type of the section *Bulbophyllaria* as described by August H. R. Grisebach in 1864, grows in Guyana, Surinam, and Bolivia and has deeply ridged, sheathed pseudobulbs. It can be identified by the lateral sepals that are connate to their middle and by the dentate upper margin of the projection on either side of the column. The swollen rachis is pendent with many widely spaced flowers. Pots or baskets with a potting mix that holds some moisture, and warm, humid conditions with light shade are the keys to successful cultivation.

Bulbophyllum brevipetalum Perrier (1937)

This Madagascan species is a member of the section *Alcistachys* and can be up to 40 cm tall, with thick rhizomes and pseudobulbs that are shaped somewhat like a slightly flattened turnip. The leaves are oblanceolate and can be as long as 18 cm and 3 cm wide, and they are present during flowering. The scape is 40 cm tall with long sheaths. The yellow flowers have red markings, are often 2 cm long, and are covered by rigid bracts. This plant grows on trees in forests more than 1500 m above sea level and requires light shade, pots or baskets with a mix that holds some moisture, intermediate temperatures, high humidity, and good air circulation to prosper.

Bulbophyllum bufo (Lindley) Reichenbach fil. (1861)

SYNONYMS
Bulbophyllum bakkosorum Schlechter (1901)
Bulbophyllum deistelianum (Kraenzlin) Schlechter (1905), *Megaclinium deistelianum* Kraenzlin (1902)
Bulbophyllum falcatum var. *bufo* J. J. Vermeulen (1987)
Megaclinium gentilii De Wildeman (1902)
Bulbophyllum longibulbum Schlechter (1901)
Bulbophyllum lubiense De Wildeman (1921)
Bulbophyllum seretii De Wildeman (1916)
Megaclinium bufo Lindley (1841), *Phyllorchis bufo* (Lindley) Kuntze (1891)

Bulbophyllum bufo has conical pseudobulbs 4 to 5 cm long and 1.3 cm wide, each bearing two leaves that may be as large as 15 × 3 cm. The raceme is about 20 cm long with flowers arranged in single file on each side of the com-

pressed rachis. These flowers open successively, thus assuring a long blooming period. The dorsal sepal has a shortly acuminate tip, and all floral parts
are less than 1 cm long. Flowers are hirsute, pale beige with pink overlay, and
the labellum is dark red. Perhaps the most innovative description of this
plant is found in Heinrich Gustav Reichenbach's words in *Walper's Annuals of
Botany* (1861, p. 258) as follows:

> Let the reader imagine a green snake to be pressed flat like a dried
> flower, and then to have a row of toads, or some such spreckled reptiles,
> drawn up along the middle in single files their backs up, their fore legs
> sprawling right and left and their mouths wide open, with a large pur-
> ple tongue wagging about convulsively; and a pretty considerable
> approach will be gained to an idea of this strange plant, which if Py-
> thagoras had but known of it, would have rendered all arguments about
> the transmigration of souls superfluous.

Bulbophyllum bufo is endemic to central Africa and can be successfully grown
in a pot with a loose medium. Intermediate to warm temperatures, some
shade from noon sun, and moderate watering will encourage flowering.

Bulbophyllum burttii Summerhayes (1953)

This African species has angled pseudobulbs that are less than 6 cm tall
and 2 cm wide, and are covered with sheaths. The leaves can be as long as 17
cm, are relatively narrow, and are present when flowering. The inflorescence
is sometimes 30 cm long with as many as 50 flowers. These flowers are distichous and, although many open at one time, they do not open completely.
All floral parts are yellow or pale green and are less than 1 cm in size, the
most striking aspect of which is the sharply recurving lateral sepals. The
plants grow on trees at approximately 2000 m altitude in Congo (Zaire) and
Rwanda and require an intermediate temperature range and shade to thrive.
Using pots with a mix that drains well is the easiest way to grow this species.

Bulbophyllum calyptratum Kraenzlin (1895)

This member of the section *Megaclinium* has pseudobulbs about 6 cm tall,
angled, somewhat flattened and as much as 5 cm apart on the rhizome. The
narrow leaves can be as long as 26 cm, and the scape 60 cm tall with as many
as 50 small flowers. The rachis is usually erect but can be somewhat spreading, wide, and flat, with edges that may be sharp; it is sometimes as large as 31
cm long and 2 cm wide, and has a glabrous surface. The flowers are distichous, often 3 cm apart, held well out from the rachis, less than 1 cm overall, and white with tan or dark red markings. The dorsal sepal is the dominant
portion of the flower, spathulate, and recurved with a fleshy portion on either
side of the apex. The species grows as an epiphyte throughout central Africa

from the lower elevations to 1000 m above sea level. It can be grown in pots or on large and substantial mounts but requires semishade, warm temperatures, and considerable moisture to grow well. Gentle air circulation is very helpful.

Bulbophyllum cariniflorum Reichenbach fil. (1861)
SYNONYMS
Bulbophyllum birmense Schlechter (1910)
Bulbophyllum densiflorum Rolfe (1892), not *B. densiflorum* Ridley (1896)
    which is *B. singaporeanum* Schlechter (1911)

This rather small species from the eastern Himalayas has pseudobulbs 2 cm tall with two, or very rarely three or four leaves, each about 17 cm long and 3 cm wide. The inflorescence is about 12 cm tall with a deflexed spike that has many 0.6 cm, yellow-green flowers with dark yellow labellums. These attractive little flowers are densely held and all open at the same time. This species can easily be grown in pots with a good mix of tree fern, bark, and charcoal or any mix that doesn't hold too much water. Intermediate temperatures and filtered, never direct, sunlight give the best results.

Bulbophyllum carnosilabium Summerhayes (1954)

This member of the section *Megaclinium* grows in Gabon and Congo (Zaire) at low altitudes. The pseudobulbs are about 3 cm apart on the rhizomes, flattened, and about 7 cm tall. The leaves are narrow and can be 22 cm tall. The scape is sometimes 40 cm long with more than 30 flowers on the rachis. The rachis is wide and flat, to 30 cm long and 0.8 cm wide, glabrous, and with sharp edges. The small flowers are distichous, almost 2 cm apart, red, and only a few are open at any time. The plants can be grown in pots or on slabs in a warm, shaded environment and need considerable moisture.

Bulbophyllum cirrhosum L. O. Williams (1940)

This species is endemic to Mexico and is a member of the section *Bulbophyllaria*. The peduncle is taller than the leaves, and the flowers are verrucose with long, narrow petals. Plants can be grown in pots with a mixture that retains some moisture, in warm, humid, lightly shaded areas.

Bulbophyllum coccinatum Perrier (1938)

The pseudobulbs of this species of the section *Lyraea* are sharply angled, 3 cm tall and 0.8 cm wide, and about 4 cm apart on the rhizomes. The leaves are often as long as 11 cm and 1 to 2 cm wide and are present when flowering. The inflorescence is taller than the leaves, and the swollen rachis is red with as many as 30 very small, red flowers fairly close together. The lateral sepals are connate, their margins are inrolled, and they are prominently keeled. The species is endemic to Madagascar and can be grown in pots or on mounts of wood, tree fern, or cork with a bit of mossy padding under the roots. The temperature should be warm to intermediate, the atmosphere moist, and the area shaded.

Bulbophyllum cochleatum Lindley (1862)
SYNONYMS
Bulbophyllum jungwirthianum Schlechter (1922)
Bulbophyllum pholidotoides Kraenzlin (1914)
Bulbophyllum talbotii Rendle (1913)
Phyllorchis cochleata (Lindley) Kuntze (1891)

The slender, sheathed pseudobulbs of this species are about 6 cm tall and are 3 cm apart on branching rhizomes. The leaves can be as long as 12 cm and less than 1 cm wide and are present when flowering takes place. The inflorescence is held well above the leaves and consists of many yellowish flowers that are less than 1 cm in size and are presented in bracts about the same length. The species is found in forests throughout central Africa between 900 and 2000 m above sea level. It can be grown on slabs of any sort or in pots or baskets with a well-draining mix. Intermediate temperatures, good air circulation, protection from direct sunlight, and regular watering are necessary for optimum growth.

Bulbophyllum colubrinum (Reichenbach fil.) Reichenbach fil. (1861)
SYNONYMS
Bulbophyllum decipiens Schlechter (1901)
Bulbophyllum gabunense Schlechter (1901)
Bulbophyllum imschootianum (Rolfe) De Wildeman (1895), *Megaclinium*
    imschootianum Rolfe (1895)
Bulbophyllum inaequale Reichenbach fil. (1886), not *B. inaequale* (Blume)
    Lindley (1830) of the section *Monilibulbon*, *Phyllorchis inaequalis*
    (Reichenbach fil.) Kuntze (1891)
Bulbophyllum makakense Hansen (1959)
Megaclinium colubrinum Reichenbach fil. (1855), *Phyllorchis colubrina*
    (Reichenbach fil.) Kuntze (1891)

Bulbophyllum colubrinum has the distinction of being one of the very few members of the genus once known as *Megaclinium* that have only a single leaf per pseudobulb. The pseudobulbs are about 5 cm tall and a few centimeters apart on the rhizome. The leaves are 20 cm long, and the inflorescence may be twice that long with many, many small flowers. The rachis bends slightly and is wide and flat with sharp edges. The purple flowers are less than 1 cm long and spaced along the side of the rachis, where they open sequentially. These orchids are found in forests from sea level up to about

900 m altitude along the western coast of Africa. They can be grown in warm areas, in pots or baskets, or they can be mounted. They require good air circulation, frequent watering, and light shade.

Bulbophyllum comorianum Perrier (1938)

As the name implies, this member of the section *Lyraea* is endemic to the Comoro Islands. The pseudobulbs are about 2 cm tall and 1 cm wide, and at least 4 cm apart on the rhizomes. The leaves are small, too, only 2 to 5 cm long and not more than 1 cm wide and are present when flowering. The swollen rachis is held above the leaves and is about 9 cm tall with 15 small flowers that are less than 0.5 cm long. The connate lateral sepals have inrolled margins and prominent keels. This tiny plant can be grown in light shade on small pieces of tree fern, cork, or bark with a bit of padding under the roots, warm temperatures, and considerable amounts of moisture.

Bulbophyllum comosum Collett & Hemsley (1890)

SYNONYMS

not *Bulbophyllum comosum* Perrier (1934) which is *B. pogonochilum*
    Summerhayes, name published without designation of type, *Phyllorchis comosa* (Collett & Hemsley) Kuntze (1891)

This member of the section *Pleiophyllus* is deciduous at flowering and has terete pseudobulbs that are about 2 cm tall with two leaves which can be 20 cm long. The scape is considerably taller than the leaves, usually about 25 cm, and the pendent rachis bears many small, dangling, pale ivory, hirsute flowers. *Bulbophyllum comosum* grows in Myanmar, Thailand, and India as high as 2000 m above sea level. The densely crowded racemes were described by J. D. Hooker in *Flora of British India* as "like a bottle brush" with flowers in a horizontal plane and having long hairs. This species does well in wooden baskets with a loose, airy medium such as medium-sized chunks of tree fern, charcoal, and bark mixed together, frequent watering, and warm temperatures. A top dressing of used wine corks is always welcomed by the plants. Be sure to remember that these plants are deciduous, and resist the impulse to over water. Also be sure not to discard them when they drop their leaves.

Bulbophyllum complanatum Perrier (1937)

SYNONYM

Bulbophyllum sigilliforme Perrier (1937)

This very small species has pseudobulbs that are less than 1 cm in diameter, closely set, and flattened. The thick leaves are obtuse and approximately 1 cm long and are present during flowering. The inflorescence is shorter than the leaves and has one to seven yellowish flowers that are minute and surround the rachis. This species grows as an epiphyte in dry forests or on limestone in Madagascar at low elevations and requires warm temperatures. It can best be mounted on very small pieces of bark or cork without any moss padding and requires only moderate amounts of water and protection from direct sunlight.

Bulbophyllum coriophorum Ridley (1886)

SYNONYMS
Bulbophyllum compactum Kraenzlin (1893)
Bulbophyllum crenulatum Rolfe (1905)
Bulbophyllum cyclanthum Schlechter (1916)
Bulbophyllum mandrakanum Schlechter (1925)
Bulbophyllum robustum Rolfe (1918)

This medium-sized plant, part of the section *Lyraea*, is more than 30 cm tall with 8-cm tall pseudobulbs and persistent leaves that are 22 cm long. The scape is 25 cm tall, usually arching slightly, and the swollen rachis is often as large as 8 cm tall and 2 cm wide with many flatly compressed small flowers. These flowers are between 0.5 and 1 cm in size and are crowded together on the rachis. The lateral sepals are connate, have inrolled margins, and are keeled. The labellum is green, two-lobed, almost perfectly round, and uppermost. This species is common in the forests of Madagascar and the Comoro Islands at altitudes that range from 1000 to 1600 m and can be grown in large pots with a light potting mix that allows good drainage. As with all forest plants that do not grow in the crowns of trees, it needs shade from the hottest sun. Intermediate to warm temperatures and good air movement are also needed. Again, there are a lot of colorful flowers that show to good advantage above the plant which makes it quite desirable.

Bulbophyllum elliotii Rolfe (1890)

SYNONYM
Bulbophyllum malawiense Morris (1968)

Robert A. Rolfe published the description of this interesting small species in the *Journal of the Linnean Society* from the type specimen which was collected by Scott Elliot in 1890 in Madagascar. The oval, very slightly compressed pseudobulbs are not more than 2 cm apart on the rhizomes and have two rather small, 4-cm long, somewhat rounded, thick, persistent leaves. The inflorescence may be 10 cm long with many flowers on the swollen, sometimes drooping rachis. The flowers are shaded green or yellow with dark red markings, and the labellum is dark red with white hirsute edges. Besides Madagascar and Malawi, the species has been found in what was the Transvaal region of South Africa and Congo (Zaire), in Tanzania, Burundi, Zambia, and Zimbabwe. It grows as high as 1700 m above sea level as an epiphyte on the upper parts of trees and is often found growing with lichens. It would be wise to mount these plants on tree fern or cedar slabs or perhaps on pieces of cypress knees with a small pad of moss under the roots. Careful attention to watering and ample fertilizer in warm conditions and bright light should assure excellent growth and flowering. These flowers are very colorful and quite attractive above the plant.

Bulbophyllum falcatum (Lindley) Reichenbach fil. (1861)

SYNONYMS

Bulbophyllum dahlemense Schlechter (1919)

Bulbophyllum hemirhachis (Pfitzer) De Wildeman (1921), *Megaclinium hemirhachis* Pfitzer (1908)

Bulbophyllum leptorrachis Schlechter (1905)

Bulbophyllum oxyodon Reichenbach fil. (1888), *Megaclinium oxyodon* Reichenbach fil. (1888)

Bulbophyllum ugandae (Rolfe) De Wildeman (1921), *Megaclinium ugandae* Rolfe (1913)

Megaclinium falcatum Lindley (1826), *Phyllorchis falcata* (Lindley) Kuntze (1891)

This species is perhaps the most popular of those once considered members of the genus *Megaclinium*. It is the type species of the section *Megaclinium* as described by Victor S. Summerhayes in 1935, and its specific name means "sickle shaped." The pseudobulbs are somewhat angled, approximately 6.5 cm tall and 2 cm wide, 5 cm apart, and bear the usual two leaves which can be as long as 20 cm but are usually much shorter. The rachis is flattened and is sometimes, but rarely, 16 cm long. It is dark red and has 12 to 20 flowers that are placed alternately on either side. The lateral sepals and lip are dark red, while the dorsal sepal is yellow. This species grows in western Africa just north of the equator and is seldom found above 1200 m elevation. It is most commonly an epiphyte in trees in lowland forest areas, but it does also occasionally grow as a lithophyte. It can be found in Uganda, Sierra Leone, Guinea, and Congo (Zaire). *Bulbophyllum falcatum* is a very interesting species to grow because of the unusual flattened rachis and relatively small size of the plant. A fascinating description of it was given by John Lindley (1830):

> The lip of this plant is elastically articulated with the column, and exhibits a beautiful instance of vegetable irritability, analogous to that of some species of *Pterostylis*. The lip moves up and down with great rapidity, much in the same way as the head of the Chinese images of Mandarins.

Bulbophyllum falcatum grows extremely well in pots with a good potting mix that does not decay rapidly. It thrives with good air circulation, frequent fertilization, and watering, and prefers slightly shaded conditions. By all means, try to add this delightful species to your orchid collection.

Bulbophyllum filiforme Kraenzlin (1895)
SYNONYMS
Bulbophyllum daloaense Cribb & Perez-Vera (1975)
Bulbophyllum longispicatum Kraenzlin & Schlechter (1908)
Bulbophyllum macrostachyum Kraenzlin (1908)
Bulbophyllum resupinatum var. *filiforme* J. J. Vermeulen (1987)

This small African plant is a member of the section *Megaclinium* and has a lovely, slightly fractiflex, arching inflorescence that can vary from 3.5 to 4 cm long. The flowers are about 1 cm apart, less than 1 cm in size, and are yellow with dark purple markings. The plant grows as an epiphyte at low elevations, often in mangrove forests. It does well in pots or on slabs with moss to hold the necessary moisture, and it requires light shade, high humidity, and warm temperatures.

Bulbophyllum fimbriatum (Lindley) Reichenbach fil. (1861)
SYNONYM
Cirrhopetalum fimbriatum Lindley (1839), not *Bulbophyllum fimbriatum* Perrier
(1941, 1951) which is *B. peyrotii* Bosser, name published without
designation of type

This species, a member of the section *Tripudianthes*, has pseudobulbs that are 1.5 to 2 cm tall and very close together, and has two leaves about 5 cm long which are shed before the flowering period. The scape is roughly 10 cm tall with 6 to 12 pale ivory or green flowers that form a declined, umbellate inflorescence. The lateral sepals are 1.5 cm long and coherent. The dorsal sepal is less than 1 cm long with a sharp apical point and is fringed with long red-purple cilia. The petals are 0.2 cm long and also have numerous red or purple cilia. These flowers are very pretty with the lateral sepals projecting away from the stem to form a whorl and the cilia appearing as a fuzzy circle of dark red hairs at the center of the umbel. The flowers are very easily enjoyed because the leaves have dropped when they appear. This species is indigenous to southern India at low elevations and can be grown in small pots or baskets with any good mix. It needs warmth, some shade, and moisture to grow well.

Bulbophyllum hildebrandtii Reichenbach fil. (1881)
SYNONYMS
Bulbophyllum maculatum Jumelle & Perrier (1912)
Bulbophyllum madagascariense Schlechter (1915)
Bulbophyllum melanopogon Schlechter (1918)

Another plant indigenous to Madagascar is this member of the section *Bifalcula* that is only very rarely unifoliate. The pseudobulbs are about 3 cm tall and 4 cm apart on the rhizome, while the leaves are approximately 7 cm long and 2 cm wide. The inflorescence is 17 cm tall and the fractiflex rachis is sometimes 15 cm long. There are many flowers, each less than 1 cm long, greenish yellow with a red, densely ciliate labellum. The stelidia are longer than the anther and the basal teeth on the labellum. The plants grow epiphytically along edges of streams from sea level to 600 m altitude. They need a warm environment and can be cultivated in heavy pots with a mix that retains some moisture. They must be protected from direct sunlight.

Bulbophyllum hirtum (J. E. Smith) Lindley (1830)

SYNONYMS

Bulbophyllum suave Griffith (1851)

Phyllorchis hirta (J. E. Smith) Kuntze (1891), *Stelis hirta* J. E. Smith (1816),
    Tribrachia hirta (J. E. Smith) Lindley (1826)

This small species is a member of the section *Pleiophyllus* and is very similar to *Bulbophyllum comosum*. It, too, is deciduous when flowering and has small pseudobulbs with relatively tall, arching, many-flowered, racemose inflorescences. The terete pseudobulbs are about 2 cm tall and have two leaves, only rarely one leaf, which can be 20 cm long. The scape is considerably taller than the leaves, and the drooping floral spike bears many small, white, very hirsute flowers. *Bulbophyllum hirtum* can be found from 800 to 1800 m above sea level and is native to the subtropical Himalayas, Nepal, Thailand, Vietnam, and Myanmar. These are well-behaved little plants, not rapidly outgrowing their containers, and are small enough to grace a coffee table when in flower. This species, too, likes wooden baskets or clay pots with an airy potting mix and a nice top dressing of corks or spaghnum. Warm conditions, light shade, and frequent watering with a slight dry season will produce many appealing small flowers. PLATE 1

Bulbophyllum imbricatum Lindley (1841)

SYNONYMS

Bulbophyllum laurentianum Kraenzlin (1899)

Bulbophyllum stenorachis Kraenzlin (1895)

Bulbophyllum strobiliferum Kraenzlin (1889)

Bulbophyllum triste (Rolfe) Schlechter (1905), not *B. triste* Reichenbach fil.
    (1861) which is *B. tristellidium* Kittredge nom. nov. of the section
    Lepidorhiza, *Megaclinium triste* Rolfe (1894)

Megaclinium imbricatum (Lindley) Rolfe (1897), *Phyllorchis imbricata*
    (Lindley) Kuntze (1891)

The specific name *imbricatum* refers to overlapping margins. The pseudobulbs of this orchid that is part of the section *Megaclinium* are 4 to 8 cm tall and may have only one leaf, but they can have as many as three which are 13 cm long and 2.5 cm wide or larger. The rachis is 13 cm long and 8 cm wide, flattened, and almost black. The dorsal sepal is 1 cm long, the petals incurved, the labellum recurved, and the base of the labellum has small teethlike projections. The flowers are a velvety, light green so heavily spotted with black that they appear almost solid black. The native habitat of *Bulbophyllum imbricatum* is the area from Sierra Leone to Congo (Zaire) at elevations below 1000 m. It can be grown in pots with a well-draining potting mix or on slabs of any sort in warm areas with light shade and regular watering. This plant adds great interest to a mixed orchid collection.

Bulbophyllum jumelleanum Schlechter (1913)

The type species of the section *Habrostachys* which Rudolf Schlechter described in 1913, this orchid has pseudobulbs that are compressed, less than 1 cm in size, and 1 cm apart on the rhizome. The two thick leaves are only about 1 cm long. The inflorescence is 7 cm tall with about eight tiny flowers loosely displayed on the setaceous rachis. The bracts are not longer than the flowers and the labellum is basally lobed. The species is endemic to Madagascar and grows on trees in forests more than 1200 m above sea level. It can be cultivated on small supports of any nature or in small pots at intermediate temperatures. It is a nice addition to a miniature collection because of its very small size and the inflorescence that is held well above the plant, making it quite visible.

Bulbophyllum kanburiense Seidenfaden (1970)

Another very interesting two-leaved species is *Bulbophyllum kanburiense*, a member of the section *Tripudianthes*. At first glance the many flowers on the decurved rachis resemble the samaras of maple trees and present an unusual picture. The conjoined lateral sepals are 3.5 to 5 cm long, and the dorsal sepal is less than 0.8 cm long with entire edges and is slightly hirsute on the apical surface with the edges nearest the stem recurved. The petals are tiny, with a long apical protrusion and hirsute edges and surface. Even the very small labellum has hirsute edges. The species has been found in Myanmar, Thailand, and Vietnam and requires a dry period during which the leaves drop and flowering takes place. This orchid can be successfully cultivated in small baskets or pots with a loose medium or on tree fern or cork mounts in shaded areas with careful attention to watering, remembering that "dry season" does not mean a complete absence of water, only a reduction in frequency and quantity. PLATE 2

Bulbophyllum lemniscatoides Rolfe (1890)

SYNONYM

Bulbophyllum lemniscatoides var. *exappendiculatum* J. J. Smith (1920)

This species was described by Robert A. Rolfe in the *Gardener's Chronicle* and is a member of the section *Lemniscata*. It has smooth pseudobulbs 2 cm tall that are crowded together on the rhizomes. The two leaves are about 10 cm long and are deciduous when flowering takes place. The inflorescence is erect for 25 cm, then the cylindric raceme of 20 to 30 flowers bends sharply downwards. The sepals are almost black with bristly white hairs on the outside and have 0.5- or 0.6-cm long, very slender, round, purple appendages that are quite mobile and no doubt very attractive to pollinators. The flowers form a dense pendulous cluster which is most striking. The species is native to Java, Sumatra, Thailand, and Vietnam and is found on mountain sides at about 1500 m above sea level. It should be grown slightly dry and requires good air circulation and shade. Since it naturally grows on tree trunks, it adapts well to mounting on cork or tree bark slabs without any moss padding under the roots.

Bulbophyllum lemniscatum Parish (1872) ex Hooker fil.

SYNONYMS

Bulbophyllum lemniscatum var. *tumidum* Parish & Reichenbach fil. (1874),
    Phyllorchis lemniscata (Parish ex Hooker fil.) Kuntze (1891)

This plant, belonging to the section *Lemniscata*, has pseudobulbs that are 2 cm in diameter, crowded together, and covered with warty protuberances. There are three leaves per pseudobulb and they are deciduous at flowering time. The species is notable for the very slender, 1-cm long, many-angled red and white mobile palae on the petals. The green and purple flowers are hirsute, only 2 cm long with the palae, and form a dense pendulous cluster atop a 16-cm cylindric scape. The species is native to Thailand, India, and Myanmar, and it, too, benefits from a relatively dry season each year. It grows well in small pots or on pieces of bark or tree fern and prefers no direct sunlight and good air circulation in intermediate temperatures.

Bulbophyllum lemuraeiodes Perrier (1937)

This very small plant of the section *Lyraea* has ovoid pseudobulbs about 1 cm tall and 3 to 4 cm apart on the rhizome. Although it sometimes is as tall as 9 cm, it is usually shorter. The two leaves can each be 3 cm long and are present while flowering. The scape is about 12 cm tall with a bent rachis that is only slightly thickened and has as many as 10 flowers, each less than 1 cm long. The lateral sepals are connate and keeled, and the labellum has two lobes. These flowers are dark red and are displayed nicely above the horizontally extended leaves. The plant grows epiphytically in the forests of

Madagascar between 1500 and 2000 m above sea level. It can be cultivated on slabs of any sort that are large enough to accommodate the plant's slightly rambling habit. Temperatures should be intermediate, water must be abundant, and shade from the noon sun is necessary.

Bulbophyllum lichenophylax Schlechter (1924)

SYNONYM
Bulbophyllum quinquecornutum Perrier (1937)

This is the type species of Rudolf Schlechter's section *Lichenophylax* which he described in 1924. The plants are miniature, at most 5 cm tall overall. The pseudobulbs are less than 0.5 cm tall, somewhat flattened, and the leaves are only 4 cm long and 0.1 cm wide, which gives them a grassy appearance. The pedicel is 4 cm long and bears a thin, greenish flower which is less than 1 cm long. The bracts are not longer than the flowers, and the column is without ornaments below the stelidia. This species is epiphytic on lichen-covered trees higher than 2000 m above sea level and would grow well on small mounts with a base of moss in intermediate conditions with some shade and a reliable supply of moisture.

Bulbophyllum masoalanum Schlechter (1916)

The pseudobulbs of this member of the section *Lyraea* are about 3 cm tall and about the same distance apart on the rhizomes. The leaves can be 11 cm long and almost 2 cm wide with the reflexed inflorescence displayed above them. The flowers are pale yellow with red veins and are shown to best advantage if the plants are mounted on a piece of bark, or some similar mount, with a good bit of moss padding under and over the roots to keep them moist. The plant grows in forests of Madagascar at 300 m above sea level or higher and appreciates warm temperatures and shade.

Bulbophyllum maximum (Lindley) Reichenbach fil. (1861)

SYNONYMS
Bulbophyllum ciliatum Schlechter (1906)
Bulbophyllum cyrtopetalum Schlechter (1911)
Bulbophyllum djumaense (De Wildeman) De Wildeman (1921), *B. djumaense*
    var. *grandifolium* De Wildeman (1921), *Megaclinium djumaense*
    De Wildeman (1903)
Bulbophyllum moirianum A. Hawkes (1956)
Bulbophyllum nyassanum Schlechter (1915)
Bulbophyllum oxypterum (Lindley) Reichenbach fil. (1861), *Megaclinium*
    oxypterum Lindley (1839), *Phyllorchis oxyptera* (Lindley) Kuntze (1891),
    Bulbophyllum oxypterum var. *mozambicense* (Finet) De Wildeman (1921),
    Megaclinium oxypterum var. *mozambicense* Finet (1910)

Bulbophyllum purpuratum (Lindley) Lindley (1862), *B. purpuratum* Schlechter
(1906), *Megaclinium purpuratum* Lindley (1862)
Bulbophyllum subcoriaceum De Wildeman (1921)
Megaclinium maximum Lindley (1830), *Phyllorchis maxima* (Lindley) Kuntze
(1891)

The pseudobulbs of this member of section *Megaclinium* are ovoid with
four sharp angles, sometimes as tall as 10 cm, and are 3 to 10 cm apart on the
rhizome. The leaves are 10 to 20 cm long, and the peduncle is wiry and quite
variable in length, occasionally reaching 40 cm long. The rachis curves and
is 30 cm tall, wide and flat, with undulate purple edges. The flowers are quite
small, only about 0.5 cm long, but there are often as many as 40 to 50 of them
opening successively. The sepals are recurved, the labellum oblong, grooved
at the base and only 0.2 cm long. The flowers are yellow, heavily speckled
with purple. The species can be found from sea level to 1900 m altitude,
growing as an epiphyte or lithophyte in moist areas, often around waterfalls.
It grows throughout most of Africa and is well deserving of its specific name
maximum. It should be planted in a pot or basket with a medium that retains
a bit of moisture such as a shredded bark, charcoal, and tree fern mixture
with a little moss added, given intermediate conditions, partial shade with
good air circulation, and high humidity. It can also be successfully grown
hanging on a sturdy tree fern or wood mount. PLATE 3

Bulbophyllum muscarirubrum Seidenfaden (1979)

This small species is a member of the section *Tripudianthes* and has dorsal
and conjoined lateral sepals that are approximately the same size, about 0.3
cm long. The flowers are light red purple with darker spots and are densely
held on 3-cm long inflorescences. The species is deciduous when flowering
and occurs in Thailand as high as 1100 m above sea level. It may be grown in
small pots with a loose, airy potting mix or on mounts with careful attention
to watering. Protection from direct sunlight is a must. This is a most attractive miniature and easy to grow.

Bulbophyllum nigericum Summerhayes (1962)

The pseudobulbs of this species are about 2 cm apart on the rhizome and
have thick oblong-elliptic leaves that are as long as 7 cm and present when
flowering. The inflorescence may be more than 20 cm long, sometimes with
as many as 30 flowers. The rachis is unusual in that it is swollen and four
angled with two of the sides concave, and it is from these that the flowers
emerge. The flowers open widely and face upward with lateral sepals that are
reflexed and broad petals. Although the flower is made up of parts less than
1 cm in size, it is yellow with purple markings and quite attractive. As the
specific name indicates, this species is found in east central Africa, primarily

in Nigeria. The plants grow as lithophytes between 1000 and 2000 m above sea level and can be grown on moderately large pieces of rock or on wooden slabs in intermediate temperatures with shade and a regular supply of water.

Bulbophyllum nitens Jumelle & Perrier (1912)

This is another Madagascan species that is quite interesting to grow. It is part of the section *Lyraea* and has pseudobulbs that are four angled, 2 cm apart on the rhizomes, and about 3 cm tall. The leaves are present during flowering, are 6 cm long, and the peduncle is as tall as 30 cm with a reflexed cylindrical rachis that is 6 cm long. There are many yellow-green flowers densely arranged around the rachis, and although they are considerably less than 1 cm in size, they are easily seen because they are held so attractively above the leaves. The lateral sepals are connate, their margins are inrolled, and they have a prominent keel. These are epiphytes that grow with lichens from 1500 to 2000 m altitude and there are several varieties named by H. Perrier that are self-explanatory: *intermedium, majus, minus, pulverulentum,* and *typicum*. They can all be grown in the same manner, in pots with the usual mix that holds moisture to some degree but still has good air circulation, intermediate temperatures, light shade, and high humidity.

Bulbophyllum nutans Thouars (1822)

SYNONYMS

Bulbophyllum andringitranum Schlechter (1925)
Bulbophyllum chrysobulbum Perrier (1951)
Bulbophyllum nutans var. *flavem* Cordemoy (1894), *B. nutans* var. *genuinum*
    Cordemoy (1894), *B. nutans* var. *nanum* Cordemoy (1894), *B. nutans* var.
    pictum Cordemoy (1894), *B. nutans* var. *rubellum* Cordemoy (1894),
    Nuphyllis nutans Thouars (1822), *Phyllorchis nutans* (Thouars) Kuntze
    (1891)
Bulbophyllum serpens Lindley (1830)
Bulbophyllum tsinjoarivense Perrier (1937)

This attractive species has far more than its share of synonyms and confusion. Add a brief transfer to the genus *Phyllorchis* and you have a lot of superfluous names for a very nice species that is the type of the section *Bulbophyllum* as described by Louis-Marie Aubert Du Petit-Thouars in 1877. The unusual name, *Nuphyllis nutans*, is one of the compound names that Thouars gave to some of the illustrations of his orchids by combining the first syllable of the specific name and the last portion of the generic name. The plants are a manageable size, not more than 10 cm tall, with angled pseudobulbs less than 1 cm tall and about 3 cm apart on the rhizome. The leaves are 2 cm long and 1 cm wide, and the inflorescence is much longer than the leaves, sometimes up to 27 cm tall, with as many as 30 flowers which are about 1 cm in size and which surround the rachis. The floral bracts are not longer than the flowers, and the labellum lacks basal lobes. The flowers are yellowish with a bright red labellum which makes them very conspicuous and quite attractive. The species grows either as an epiphyte or a lithophyte at altitudes from sea level to 2200 m in boggy, humid areas of Madagascar and Mauritius. It may be best to mount these plants on tree fern or other appropriate material, always with a sizeable layer of moss under the roots, and with careful attention to supplying ample humidity and warmth and to avoiding direct sunlight.

Bulbophyllum occlusum Ridley (1885)

A large plant that is worth the space is this member of the section *Alcistachys*. The widely oval, 6-cm tall compressed pseudobulbs are clustered on the very thick rhizomes and have oblanceolate leaves that are 30 to 40 cm long and are present when flowering. The inflorescence is usually as tall as the leaves, with many sheaths and about 20 large flowers that are encased in the good-sized, light-colored bracts. The 2.5-cm long flowers are greenish yellow with red markings. This species, too, grows only on trees in the forests of Madagascar below 1500 m altitude and can be grown in light shade either on large, hanging cork slabs with moss padding or in large pots with a mix that retains some moisture. Temperatures should be warm to intermediate, and high humidity is necessary for the plants to grow well. The plants take a considerable time to adapt to a change of venue, but once they are comfortable they reward the grower with flowers that are a nice size, colorful, and attractive.

Bulbophyllum occultum Thouars (1822)

SYNONYM
Diphyes occulta (Thouars) Kuntze (1891)

This interesting species frequently has the specific name misspelled with an *a* inserted to make it *occulatum*. It is the type species of the section *Lupulina* which was described by Ernst Pfitzer in 1888. The pseudobulbs are 3 cm tall and 2 cm wide, are fully developed when flowering, and are spaced 3 cm apart on the rhizome. The very thick, flat leaves can be as large as 12 cm long and 3 cm wide. The inflorescence is about 25 cm tall, and the wide triangular rachis is sometimes as long as 14 cm. This rachis is recurved and covered with tan bracts which enclose the tiny red flowers. The lateral sepals are not reflexed and the column foot is at a right angle to the column. The species grows as an epiphyte in Madagascar and Mauritius from sea level to 1500 m altitude and can be cultivated either in pots with a mix that drains well or on large slabs of bark or cork with a thin layer of moss or some other padding under the roots. It requires warm to intermediate temperatures, light shade, and a sizeable amount of moisture. Despite the fact that the flowers are hidden within the bracts, this is an interesting plant because of the attractive arrangement of the bracts.

Bulbophyllum oerstedii (Reichenbach fil.) Hemsley (1883)
SYNONYMS
Bolbophyllaria oerstedii Reichenbach fil. (1855), *Phyllorchis oerstedii*
   (Reichenbach fil.) Kuntze (1891)

This species grows throughout Central America and into Venezuela and Ecuador and is a member of the section *Bulbophyllaria*. The peduncle is erect but shorter than the leaves, the column has wings that are enlarged apically, and the stelidia have apices that are triangular. Pots or baskets in warm and humid conditions with light shade are required for successful cultivation.

Bulbophyllum ophiuchus Ridley (1885)
SYNONYM
Bulbophyllum moramanganum Ridley 1935

The pseudobulbs of this species belonging to the section *Lyraea* are four sided and carry leaves that are as large as 13 cm long and 2 cm wide. The inflorescence is often as tall as 50 cm, and the many-flowered rachis is thickened and dark red. The flowers are only 0.5 cm in size, but they are extremely well displayed. The lateral sepals are navicular, keeled, connate, and have inrolled margins. These epiphytes grow in the forests of Madagascar at 900 to 1200 m altitude and can be cultivated in pots with the usual bark, tree fern, or other mix, intermediate temperatures, some shade, and frequent watering.

Bulbophyllum oreonastes Reichenbach fil. (1881)
SYNONYMS
Bulbophyllum hookerianum Kraenzlin (1893)
Bulbophyllum infundibuliflorum J. B. Petersen (1952)
Bulbophyllum planiaxe J. B. Petersen (1952)
Bulbophyllum rhopalochilum Kraenzlin (1914)
Bulbophyllum zenkerianum Kraenzlin (1912)
Phyllorchis oreonastes (Reichenbach fil.) Kuntze (1891)

The pseudobulbs of this popular plant are only a few centimeters apart on the rhizome and carry two persistent leaves that are each about 8 cm long. The inflorescence can be as long as 18 cm. The rachis is flattened and holds the tiny flowers about 1 cm apart in two rows. The flowers open successively and all floral parts are less than 1 cm long. These handsome little flowers are yellow or reddish yellow. This species can be found throughout central

Africa growing on trees, bushes, or rocks in rain forests from low elevations up to about 1600 m above sea level. It can be mounted or grown in pots with a well-draining medium at warm to intermediate temperatures, in mottled shade, and with careful attention to watering. Another good addition to an orchid collection, this species is small but the flowers are very pretty and easily seen above the plant.

Bulbophyllum pachyrrachis (A. Richard) Grisebach (1864)

SYNONYMS

Bolbophyllaria pachyrrachis (A. Richard) Reichenbach fil. (1861), *Phyllorchis pachyrrachis* (A. Richard) Kuntze (1891), *Pleurothallis pachyrrachis* A. Richard (1850)

This species has been found as far north as Florida as well as in Jamaica, Cuba, El Salvador, Belize, and Venezuela and belongs to the section *Bulbophyllaria*. The peduncle is erect but shorter than the leaves. The column does not have enlarged wings, and the stelidia are narrow, pointed, and somewhat flat. Like the other American species, this one can be grown in warm, lightly shaded, humid conditions in either pots or baskets.

Bulbophyllum platyrhachis (Rolfe) Schlechter (1905)

SYNONYM

Megaclinium platyrhachis Rolfe (1897)

This very close ally of *Bulbophyllum maximum* in the section *Megaclinium* is considered by some taxonomists to be conspecific. It differs mainly in being much larger overall but having narrower leaves. It is native to Congo (Zaire), Uganda, Kenya, Tanzania, Malawi, and Mozambique from low elevations to 1400 m above sea level and prefers to grow in rather moist conditions. Plants grow best in large pots with a moisture-retentive media, warm to intermediate temperatures, and light shade.

Bulbophyllum porphyrostachys Summerhayes (1951)

The pseudobulbs of this species which is part of the section *Lupulina* can be as tall as 6 cm, are as far apart on the rhizomes as 7 cm, and are fully developed when flowering. The leaves are often 20 cm long. The inflorescence can be longer than 20 cm, and the swollen rachis is four angled with as many as 50 tiny yellow and red flowers that do not open widely. The lateral sepals are not reflexed, the petals are linear, and the column foot is at a right angle to the column. These flowers are enclosed in bracts that emerge from the two concave sides of the rachis. The plants grow in the rain forests of Nigeria and Cameroon and can be cultivated in warm to intermediate conditions on large slabs or pots with a medium that does not dry out too rapidly. Slight shade and high humidity are necessary for good growth and flowering.

Bulbophyllum proudlockii (King & Pantling) J. J. Smith (1912)

SYNONYM
Cirrhopetalum proudlockii King & Pantling (1897)

This species in the section *Pleiophyllus* is named after R. L. Proudlock, curator of the Botanic Garden in Calcutta, who collected the first specimen. The pseudobulbs are 1.5 cm long, crowded on the rhizome, and leafless at flowering time. The inflorescence is 4.5 cm tall and erect, and the decurved raceme is about 1.5 cm long with from 6 to 10 straw-colored flowers that are each 1.5 cm long. The species grows in India at about 1200 m above sea level and can be grown in intermediate temperatures with some protection from direct sunlight and with frequent watering and fertilizing. Small mounts or pots are appropriate as well as a slight reduction in moisture when the leaves drop.

Bulbophyllum purpureorachis (De Wildeman) Schlechter (1914)

SYNONYM
Megaclinium purpureorachis De Wildeman (1903)

This spectacular species belongs to the section *Megaclinium*. The pseudobulbs are somewhat rectangular, 11 cm tall and 6 cm wide, and the leaves are 30 cm long and 8 cm wide. The inflorescence can be about 100 cm tall, and all floral parts are less than 1 cm long. The flowers are cream with rosy markings and the lip is red purple. The habitat is the Ivory Coast, Cameroon, Gabon, Republic of the Congo, and Congo (Zaire) at low elevations. This is obviously a large plant and can be grown successfully in any warm indoor environment, or outdoors in tropical climates. A very large, relatively shallow pot with regular fertilization and good air circulation is necessary for optimum growth, and direct sun is never conducive to good culture. A well-grown specimen of this species was the center of attraction at the 41st International Orchid Show in Miami, Florida, in 1986. It had six inflorescences with 40 open flowers and almost 200 buds and was grown by Marshall Orchids. It was the focal point of a display and certainly brought attention to a genus with which all too many people were not familiar at that time.
PLATE 4

Bulbophyllum refractum (Zollinger) Reichenbach fil. (1861)

SYNONYM
Cirrhopetalum refractum Zollinger (1847)

This species is quite similar to *Bulbophyllum kanburiense* and is also a member of Seidenfaden's section *Tripudianthes*. It has small pseudobulbs and a pair of 7-cm leaves which are deciduous during the dry season when flowering occurs. The inflorescence is about 22 cm or more tall, hanging down as do the others of this section, with the pendent rachis bearing a dozen or more flowers. The dorsal sepal is about 1 cm long and slightly hirsute. The connate lateral sepals are 5 cm or more long and the petals are about 0.4 cm long, narrowing to form a point, and are apically hirsute on the surface and edges. The labellum has very dark cilia about 0.1 cm long. The flowers are yellow orange and have reddish spots. Unfortunately, these flowers have a rather unpleasant odor, but their appearance is very attractive. The natural habitat is India, Thailand, Sumatra, and Java, and plants thrive in small containers with a loose medium or on mounts of any sort. They should never be allowed to dry out completely, and they do not tolerate direct sunlight.

Bulbophyllum reichenbachii (Kuntze) Schlechter (1915)

SYNONYMS
Bulbophyllum gracile Parish & Reichenbach fil. (1874), not *B. gracile* Thouars
    (1822) of the section *Pachychlamys*, and not *B. gracile* (Blume) Lindley
    (1830) which is *B. scheffleri* (Kuntze) Schlechter (1915)
Phyllorchis reichenbachii Kuntze (1891)

The pseudobulbs of this member of the section *Pleiophyllus* are slightly less than 2 cm in diameter and are close together on the rhizomes. The leaves are thin and deciduous at flowering time. The inflorescences are 15 cm tall, reflexed, and have a raceme of many minute flowers that are green with brown markings. The species grows in India at about 1000 m above sea level and can be cultivated in small pots at intermediate temperatures with light shade and regular attention to watering.

Bulbophyllum rubiginosum Schlechter (1925)

This small but attractive plant of the section *Lyraea* has densely sheathed pseudobulbs only 1 cm tall and about 1 or 2 cm apart on the rhizome. The leaves are persistent, oval, and only about 2 cm long. The inflorescence is short, not as long as the leaves, and the rachis is slightly swollen and compressed. There may be as many as eight very small (less than 0.5 cm) green flowers. The lateral sepals are connate with inrolled margins and the labellum is bilobed. This species grows in the forests of Madagascar below 1000 m altitude, and it would be very happy on small mounts of some sort with warm temperatures, a bit of shade, and lots of humidity and air movement. If you are attracted to small and interesting plants, by all means grow this one, but be sure to supply some sort of magnification for your visitors so they, too, can enjoy the tiny flowers.

Bulbophyllum rubrolabium Schlechter (1916)

This species, sometimes spelled *rubrilabium*, is of the section *Lyraea* and grows as an epiphyte in forests up to 1500 m above sea level. The pseudobulbs are 4 cm apart on the rhizomes, sharply four angled, and about 3 cm tall. The leaves are narrow, oblong, to 9 cm long. The inflorescence is slightly shorter than the leaves, sheathed, and a bit thickened. There are about 15 flowers that are less than 1 cm long. The lateral sepals are connate and, as implied by the specific epithet, the red, two-lobed labellum is the drawing card here. The plants can be grown on slabs of any sort, but they do require adequate water, shade, and air movement. The labellum, which really attracts attention, makes this plant a fine addition to the species collection.

Bulbophyllum rubrum Jumelle & Perrier (1912)

SYNONYM
Bulbophyllum ambongense Schlechter (1925)

Another species that is endemic to Madagascar, this one belongs to the section *Bifalcula*. Its pseudobulbs are close together but not touching, and its leaves are about 7 cm long, with a pedicel to 14 cm long and a rachis almost 10 cm long. There are usually many flowers which are less than 1 cm long and are held in bracts which are not longer than the flowers. The flowers are yellow with a dark red labellum, and the stelidia are longer than the anther. This plant grows on trees that are near the sea or at very low altitudes and requires a warm temperature, good air circulation, light shade, and a moist environment. Clay or plastic pots with a bit of moss added to the usual potting mix should give excellent results.

Bulbophyllum ruginosum Perrier (1937)

A member of the section *Habrostachys*, this Madagascan species has pseudobulbs that are about 2 cm tall and 0.5 cm wide, compressed, and close together on the rhizomes. The leaves are small, about 4 cm long and 2 cm wide. The inflorescence is sometimes as tall as 24 cm with as many as 30 small flowers that are less than 1 cm long and surround the rachis. The sepals are about 0.7 cm long, and the minute petals have papillose margins. The bracts are not longer than the flowers, and the labellum is basally lobed. This species grows in forests at 1000 m above sea level and is best cultivated in small pots or baskets with a standard potting mix and intermediate temperatures and light shade.

Bulbophyllum rugosibulbum Summerhayes (1960)

This very small plant is lithophytic and has heavily sheathed pseudobulbs that are barely 1 cm tall and are held closely together on very thin rhizomes. The leaves are present when the plant flowers and can be as long as 5 cm and are only 1 cm across. The inflorescence is often slightly curved and is held well above the leaves. The flowers are less than 1 cm in size, pale yellow with a brownish ciliate labellum. This species is found in Tanzania, Malawi, and Zambia on exposed rocks at slightly below 2000 m above sea level. It can be grown on small pieces of rock or wood in rather bright sunlight with frequent watering and good air circulation. Warm to intermediate temperatures are suitable.

Bulbophyllum rutenbergianum Schlechter (1925)
SYNONYMS
Bulbophyllum coursianum Perrier (1955)
Bulbophyllum peniculus Schlechter (1925)
Bulbophyllum spathulifolium Perrier (1951)

A member of the section *Bulbophyllum*, this species is a handsome little plant that is only about 10 cm tall with the 2-cm tall pseudobulbs close to each other on the rhizomes. The leaves are about 5 cm tall and the inflorescence is as much as 9 cm long. There are a number of small yellow to white flowers that are well spaced on the rachis. This species, too, is endemic to Madagascar and can be easily grown in small pots or on mounts in a warm, lightly shaded environment with a good water supply.

Bulbophyllum sandersonii (Hooker fil.) Reichenbach fil. (1878)
SYNONYMS
Bulbophyllum bibundiense Schlechter (1906)
Bulbophyllum melleri Reichenbach fil. (1878)
Bulbophyllum mooreanum Robyns & Tourney (1955)
Bulbophyllum pusillum (Rolfe) De Wildeman (1921), *Megaclinium pusillum* Rolfe (1894)
Bulbophyllum tentaculigerum Reichenbach fil. (1878)
Megaclinium sandersonii Hooker fil. (1871)

Most of these synonyms were once assigned to the genus *Megaclinium* and this species is now a part of the genus *Bulbophyllum*, section *Megaclinium*. The pseudobulbs are 5 cm tall, 2 cm wide, and four angled. The leaves are 16 cm long and 1.8 cm wide, and the inflorescence can be 24 cm tall. The flowers are placed slightly off-center along a thickened, compressed rachis. The floral parts, like those of other plants in this section, are less than 1 cm long, are fleshy and pale with dark purple markings. The species is found growing as an epiphyte in the rain forests and woodlands of Uganda, Kenya, Tanzania, Zambia, Zimbabwe, Angola, South Africa, and Mozambique from very low elevations to 1800 m above sea level. It can best be cultivated on cork or tree fern slabs with a padding of some absorbent material such as spaghnum or osmunda and grown in partial shade in warm to intermediate conditions. Abundant water is, of course, essential to good culture.

Bulbophyllum sanitii Seidenfaden (1970)
This small plant of the section *Tripudianthes* was named by Seidenfaden after the helicopter pilot, Captain Sanit of the Royal Thai Airforce, who took

him to many otherwise inaccessible places in northern Thailand. The pseudobulbs are less than 3 cm tall and are close together on the rhizomes. The
two or rarely three leaves are 8 cm long and 1.6 cm wide, and the scape is 17
cm tall. The sharply deflexed rachis is 6 cm long and carries many flowers.
The hirsute dorsal sepal is slightly more than 1 cm long and 0.2 cm wide.
The lateral sepals are about 2 cm long, connate only in the distal half, and
marginally ciliate. The petals are less than 0.5 cm long, aristate, and fimbriate, and the finely ciliate labellum is half that size and has a globular apex.
The flowers are light cream colored and have purple markings. Cultivation
is best accomplished in small pots or baskets in intermediate conditions with
some shade and frequent watering.

Bulbophyllum sarcorhachis Schlechter (1918)

This species of the section *Lyraea* has oblong, four-angled pseudobulbs
about 2 cm tall and 1 cm wide, and 2 cm apart on the rhizomes. The two
leaves are approximately 6 cm long and 1.5 cm wide, and the inflorescence
can be 12 cm long. The peduncle is heavily sheathed, and the rachis is
swollen and has 15 to 20 or more flowers that are less than 1 cm long and
papillose. Several varieties have been named by Perrier: *berforonense, flavomarginatum*, and *typicum. Bulbophyllum sarcorhachis* var. *berforonense* (Schlechter)
Perrier (1937) had been the victim of a typographical error in 1925 and the
name was misspelled *Bulbophyllum befaonense* which has led to some confusion. Variety *berforonense* differs from the species in that it has narrower and
longer pseudobulbs and leaves, and the inflorescence is often almost 20 cm
tall. Variety *flavomarginatum* has a more robust inflorescence with pseudobulbs as large as 5 cm tall and 2 cm wide, leaves wider than the species, and
the dorsal sepal has a clear yellow margin, hence the varietal name. All of
these are endemic to Madagascar and can be grown in warm and shaded
environments and need almost daily watering to thrive.

Bulbophyllum scaberulum (Rolfe) Bolus (1889)
SYNONYMS
Bulbophyllum bambiliense De Wildeman (1916)
Bulbophyllum chevalierii De Wildeman (1921)
Bulbophyllum clarkei (Rolfe) Schlechter (1905), *Megaclinium clarkei* Rolfe
    (1891)
Bulbophyllum congolanum Schlechter (1901)
Bulbophyllum ealaense De Wildeman (1916)
Bulbophyllum eberneum (Pfitzer ex Kraenzlin) De Wildeman (1921),
    Megaclinium eberneum Pfitzer ex Kraenzlin (1908)
Bulbophyllum jespersenii De Wildeman (1916)

Bulbophyllum pobequinii (Finet) De Wildeman (1921), *Megaclinium pobequinii* Finet (1910)
Bulbophyllum summerhayesii Hawkes (1956)
Bulbophyllum zobiaense De Wildeman (1916)
Megaclinium scaberulum Rolfe (1888)

This plant is part of the section *Megaclinium* and, without flowers, it is so similar to *Bulbophyllum sandersonii* that it can easily be mistaken for it. The most distinguishing floral difference is that this species has a flower with a slightly shorter dorsal sepal and narrower lateral sepals than the other. It can be found throughout tropical and southern Africa, especially Kenya, Uganda, and Tanzania. It grows in riverine forests from 100 to 1800 m above sea level and should be cultivated on slabs with a padding of moss or in pots or baskets in warm to intermediate moist conditions and partial shade. Both this species and *B. sandersonii* are of manageable size and nice additions to the collection.

Bulbophyllum suavissimum Rolfe (1889)
SYNONYM
Bulbophyllum suavissima (Rolfe) Kuntze (1891)

This species is quite similar to *Bulbophyllum proudlockii* and *B. reichenbachii*, other members of the section *Pleiophyllus*, with the small, crowded, deciduous thin-leaved pseudobulbs, decurved raceme, and many small flowers. The flowers are yellow with a bright yellow labellum and have a very nice sweet scent. The species grows in India, Myanmar, and Thailand and can be housed in warm temperatures with moderate protection from direct sun and with high humidity. It is best not to overpot these small plants and to give them a top dressing of some sort to hold the humidity.

Bulbophyllum sulfureum Schlechter (1924)

A member of the section *Alcistachys*, this species is very similar in appearance and habitat to both *Bulbophyllum bathieanum* and *B. occlusum*, but the sheaths and bracts are sulfur yellow, hence the specific name. It can be grown in weighted pots to support the large plants, with a good potting mix that retains a bit of moisture but does not stay constantly wet. It needs warm temperatures, light shade, and good air circulation. This orchid is an interesting addition to a mixed collection with the bright yellow bracts and sheaths attracting much attention.

Bulbophyllum tetragonum Lindley (1830)
SYNONYMS
Bulbophyllum quadrifarium Rolfe (1903)
Bulbophyllum wrightii Summerhayes (1962)

The slightly flattened, four-angled pseudobulbs of this member of the section *Lupulina* can be as far apart on the rhizome as 9 cm. The thick leaf can be 25 cm long and is fully developed when flowering. The inflorescence is about 28 cm long, often with as many as 50 small flowers. The four-angled rachis is swollen a bit and covered with dark hairs, and the flowers emerge from its two slightly concave sides. The lateral sepals are not reflexed, the petals are linear and somewhat falcate, and the column foot is at a right angle to the column. The floral bracts are white with dark maroon suffusions at the apex, are slightly more than 1 cm long, and are quite prominently displayed at right angles to the rachis. The small flowers open widely, and flowering takes place progressively from the bottom of the rachis to the top. The flowers are pale yellow with red markings. These plants grow as epiphytes from sea level to 900 m altitude in central Africa and do well on slabs with a moisture-retentive layer on the roots, warm temperatures, protection from direct sunlight, and a humid environment. This species is an attractive addition because the widely open, colorful flowers in the conspicuous bracts are unusual.

Bulbophyllum tripaleum Seidenfaden (1979)

This plant, a member of the section *Lemniscata*, has leaves that appear during the rainy season and are shed during the dry season when the flowers appear. The name is derived from the three elongated palae that hang from each of the sepals. These palae are very mobile and act as an attractant for the pollinators. This species comes from a very small area of northwest Thailand which is contained in what is known as the Golden Triangle of opium fame. Unfortunately, *Bulbophyllum tripaleum* is not often seen in collections. It can be grown in intermediate to cool, lightly shaded areas and adapts well to small baskets or mounting on coconut husk.

Bulbophyllum tripudians Parish & Reichenbach fil. (1874)

SYNONYM
Cirrhopetalum tripudians (Parish & Reichenbach fil.) Parish & Reichenbach fil. (1876)

The dorsal sepal of this member of the section *Tripudianthes* is less than 1 cm long with hairy, erose edges and dense cilia on the surface. The lateral sepals are a lovely soft orange yellow with the base marked with small red-purple spots. The labellum is dark and fimbriate. This species occurs in Myanmar, Thailand, Laos, and Vietnam. Culture is best accomplished in small pots or baskets with a loose potting media, shade, good air circulation, and a slightly dry season to induce flowering.

Bulbophyllum triste Reichenbach fil. (1861)

SYNONYMS

Bulbophyllum alopecurum Reichenbach fil. (1880), *Phyllorchis alopecurus*
  (Reichenbach fil.) Kuntze (1891)
Bulbophyllum mackeeanum Guillaumin (1962)
Bulbophyllum micranthum Hooker fil. (1890), not *B. micranthum* Barbosa
  Rodrigues (1822) of the section *Micrantha*, *Phyllorchis micrantha*
  (Hooker fil.) Kuntze (1891)
Phyllorchis tristis (Reichenbach fil.) Kuntze (1891)

This highly desirable, small, deciduous plant has a gracefully arching
inflorescence that carries a large number of small flowers. In many ways it
resembles *Bulbophyllum comosum* and *B. hirtum*, but differs because the flowers
of this species are very colorful with brown-red sepals and petals and a dark
red labellum. The pseudobulbs are flattened, about 2 cm in diameter, and the
same distance apart on the rhizome. The leaves are 12.5 cm long and deciduous when the flowers appear. The scape can be 15 cm tall with a deflexed
raceme that is densely flowered and about 3 cm long. Although the flowers
are less than 1 cm in size, they are vivid. The early descriptions of orchids can
be colorful. For example, it was said that this species had a rhizome as thick
as a duck's quill and a strong, pungently fetid odor. The species comes from
India, Myanmar, and Thailand and can be grown in small pots or baskets or
on mounts of any sort with careful watering, light shade, and intermediate to
warm temperatures.

Bulbophyllum velutinum (Lindley) Reichenbach fil. (1861)

SYNONYMS

Megaclinium velutinum Lindley (1847), *Phyllorchis velutina* (Lindley) Kuntze
  (1891)

This species, a member of the section *Megaclinium*, is quite similar to *Bulbophyllum falcatum*, differing only in the dorsal sepals and petals which are
dark yellow, while the rest of the flower and rachis are dark purple. The
pseudobulbs are slightly angled, 6.5 cm tall and 2 cm wide, and 5 cm apart on
the rhizomes. The leaves are 20 cm long at most, and the flattened rachis is
less than 16 cm long. The flowers are placed alternately on either side of the
rachis. *Bulbophyllum velutinum* grows in Ghana, Sierra Leone, and other African areas just north of the equator in lowland forests and can be cultivated in
pots with a mix that drains quickly, with light shade and warm temperatures.
All African bulbophyllums that were once considered members of the genus
Megaclinium are intriguing additions to the orchid collection because their
very unusual, flattened rachis and commanding appearance are so spectacular that they quickly become the center of interest. Few non-orchid grow-

ers, and even some who grow orchids, recognize these as belonging to the orchid family.

Bulbophyllum viridiflorum (Hooker fil.) Schlechter (1910)

SYNONYMS

Cirrhopetalum viridiflorum Hooker fil. (1890), *Phyllorchis viridiflora* (Hooker fil.) Kuntze (1891), not *Bulbophyllum viridiflorum* Hayata (1912) which is *B. transarisanense* Hayata (1978)

Endemic to the Sikkim Himalayas and Assam (India), this interesting small plant has pseudobulbs that are 2.5 cm tall and are very close together on the rhizomes. It is the only member of the section *Avicula* and can have one or two very soft leaves per pseudobulb. These leaves are present during flowering but are deciduous soon after. The leaves are 7 to 15 cm tall, and the deflexed inflorescence usually rises nicely above them. There are usually about 15 flowers, and they are approximately 2 cm long, imbricate, and as the name indicates, green. This species grows at about 2000 m altitude and can be cultivated in intermediate to cool conditions in pots or baskets with a well-draining mix and light shade.

Bulbophyllum vulcanicum Kraenzlin (1914)

The pseudobulbs of this species are conical-cylindrical, sheathed, to 11 cm tall and 1 cm wide, and sometimes as far apart on the rhizome as 11 cm. The leaves are 15 cm long and 3 cm wide, and present with the flowers. The inflorescence is erect and can be 40 cm tall with many flowers. The rachis is slightly swollen, and the flowers are subtended by distichous bracts slightly less than 1 cm long. The flowers are yellow green to purple and all face in the same direction with many open at the same time. The sepals recurve, thus exposing the very interesting purple labellum which is narrow, finely ciliate at the base, and with apical margins that are fimbriate. The plants grow in mossy forests of Congo (Zaire), Uganda, and Kenya at altitudes of 2000 to 2400 m above sea level. They can be cultivated on large pieces of any suitable mounting material with a padding of moss or fern or anything that will hold some moisture but not keep the roots constantly wet. Intermediate temperatures, high humidity, and slight shade are required for optimum growth.

CHAPTER 5

Bulbophyllums with One Leaf per Pseudobulb

Bulbophyllum absconditum J. J. Smith (1905)

SYNONYMS

Bulbophyllum neocaledonicum Schlechter (1906), *Phyllorchis neocaledonicum* (Schlechter) Finet (1909)

Pelma absconditum Finet (1909)

This species is a member of the section *Pelma*. The pseudobulbs are about 1 cm tall and 0.5 cm wide, and as much as 2 cm apart on the pendent rhizomes which root only at the base of the plant. The leaf is about 3 cm long and 0.5 cm wide and has an acute apex. The inflorescence is only 0.5 cm long and has one wide-opening flower that is less than 0.5 cm in size. The flowers are a very pale translucent shade of yellow or green. The pseudobulbs as well as the inflorescences are sheathed. This species grows in forests from 1000 to 1700 m elevation in Bali, Java, and Sumatra and can be cultivated on pieces of bark, cork, or tree fern in shaded, warm, and humid conditions.

Bulbophyllum acutum J. J. Smith (1905)

SYNONYM

Bulbophyllum hastatum Tang & Wang (1974)

This tiny species is a member of the section *Hybochilus*. The pseudobulbs are less than 1 cm in size and about 2 cm apart on the thin rhizome, and the ovate leaf is less than 3 cm long. The single flowers are about 1 cm long and quite colorful. The sepals are acute, white at the base, shading into purple, and then pale green at the apices. The petals are acute and dark purple, as is the labellum. The flowers do not open widely but present a nice contrast against the dark green plant. This species grows on bare tree branches in slightly shaded situations at medium altitudes in China, Thailand, Malaysia, Borneo, Java, and Sumatra. It would be best to cultivate it on small pieces of cork or branches without a layer of moss or any other type of padding. Temperature should be intermediate to warm and some shade is preferable.

Bulbophyllum adenambon Schlechter (1913)

From the Ymas Lakes, Upper Sepik, West Irian Jaya, comes this colorful plant, a member of the section *Megaloglossum*. The pseudobulbs are about 1.6 cm tall, rather square, and 2 to 2.5 cm apart on the rhizome. The leaves are 7 cm long and 1.8 cm wide, and the flower spike, which is usually about 12 cm tall, rises well above them. The dorsal sepal is 3 cm long, very narrow and drooping forward, the lateral sepals are 3.5 cm long and twisted back, the petals are minute, and the glabrous labellum is less than 1 cm long. Warm temperatures and considerable moisture with light shading are appropriate for growing this interesting plant. PLATE 5

Bulbophyllum affine Lindley (1830)

SYNONYMS
Bulbophyllum kusukusense Hayata (1914)
Phyllorchis affinis (Lindley) Kuntze (1891), *Sarcopodium affine* (Lindley) Lindley (1850)

This species is a member of the section *Sestochilos* and has been found from northern India and Nepal east to China and Taiwan as high as 2000 m above sea level, although it usually grows at much lower altitudes. The cylindrical pseudobulbs are about 5 to 7 cm apart, 2 to 5 cm tall, and encased in long, stiff bristles. The leaves can be as long as 18 cm. The scapes are 7 cm tall and have one pale yellow or white flower with red veins. The sepals and petals are about 2.5 cm long. The plants can be grown in intermediate to warm conditions in pots or baskets in a shredded, loose mix with protection from direct sunlight and with moderate amounts of water.

Bulbophyllum agastor Garay, Hamer & Siegerist (1996)

This species is a member of the section *Macrobulbon* which is noted for having large pseudobulbs and short inflorescences with at least two flowers on a compressed rachis. It is relatively small with pseudobulbs 2.5 cm long and 2 cm wide that are a little more than 1 cm apart on the rhizome. The leaves are only 17 cm long and 4 cm wide, and the small flowers are white with dark red spots and are held very close to the base of the pseudobulbs. Since this species is related to *Bulbophyllum macrobulbon*, it was given the specific name *agastor* which in Greek means "a near kinsman." The type specimen came from Mendi, South Highland Province, Papua New Guinea, at 1560 m elevation. It grows well in pots or baskets with a mix that has some spaghnum or moss of any sort added, and intermediate conditions with high humidity and shade. PLATE 6

Bulbophyllum alagense Ames (1907)

This tiny, creeping orchid belongs to the section *Nematorhizis.* It comes from the Philippines where it grows on mossy branches that extend over rivers at about 400 m elevation. The pseudobulbs are less than 1 cm tall and are widely spaced on the creeping rhizomes. The leaves are about 2.5 cm tall and 1 cm wide, and the tiny flowers are held on peduncles less than 2 cm tall. The single flowers are a very pale yellow. The rambling type of growth would best be handled by mounting, but pots could be used if maintaining enough moisture is a problem. Warm temperatures and high humidity are necessary for optimum growth.

Bulbophyllum alcicorne Parish & Reichenbach fil. (1874)

The pseudobulbs of this species are less than 0.5 cm tall and are about 1 cm apart on the thick rhizomes. The leaf can be 16 cm long and has a blunt apex. The inflorescence is 10 cm tall with a 4-cm long drooping rachis which carries many colorful flowers, each of which is less than 1 cm long. The purple lateral sepals are conjoined and frame the bright yellow labellum. This species grows in India, Myanmar, and Thailand and can be cultivated in warm, moist conditions.

Bulbophyllum ambrosia (Hance) Schlechter (1919)

SYNONYMS
Bulbophyllum ambrosia subsp. *nepalensis* Wood (1986), *Eria ambrosia* Hance (1883)
Bulbophyllum amygdalinum Averyanov (1988)
Bulbophyllum watsonianum Reichenbach fil. (1888)

An orchid that was found on Victoria Peak in Hong Kong is often sold today under the synonym *Bulbophyllum watsonianum.* L. V. Averyanov had called it *B. amygdalinum* in 1988 but, after studying the type of *B. ambrosia*, considered it conspecific. It is a member of the section *Sestochilos* and has been found in Vietnam and China. It has orange-yellow cylindrical pseudobulbs up to 3.5 cm tall that are 5 to 8 cm apart on the creeping rhizomes. The single leaf is about 13 cm long. The inflorescence arises from the base of the pseudobulb on a 7.5-cm stalk and bears one lovely, fragrant flower which has a somewhat oriental appearance. The 2-cm flower opens widely and is white or light ivory with dark red longitudinal stripes on the sepals. This warm-growing plant is easily cultivated in pots or baskets with an open growing medium, intermediate to warm temperatures, good air circulation, regular watering, and frequent repotting, as the plant grows rampantly when happy. PLATE 7

Bulbophyllum anguliferum Ames & Schweinfurth (1920)

This tiny species belongs to the section *Monilibulbon*. It has small flattened pseudobulbs less than 0.5 cm tall which are held closely together on the rhizome, making it resemble a beaded necklace. The elliptic leaves are less than 1 cm long, and the inflorescence has one flower on a 5-cm scape. These attractive flowers open nicely and are relatively large at 1 cm wide. Their overall color is bright yellow orange with darker veins, which makes them quite attractive. This species grows in both wet and dry areas of Borneo at 1500 to 2400 m elevation. It could be cultivated on small, bare pieces of cork or small twigs at intermediate to cool temperatures in light shade and with careful attention to watering.

Bulbophyllum angustifolium (Blume) Lindley (1830)

SYNONYM
Diphyes angustifolia Blume (1825)

John Lindley transferred this tiny species to the section *Desmosanthes* in 1830. The rhizomes and even the pseudobulbs adhere closely to the surface of the twig on which it is growing, often drooping and branching with the short, few-flowered inflorescences rising above them. The flowers open widely, are white with yellow apices, and the whole appearance of the plant gives the impression of a hard struggle against the elements. And, indeed, the species does grow in mountainous areas that are windswept and exposed in Thailand, Malaya, and Java. Plants can be cultivated on slabs with perhaps a slightly cooler temperature than that for intermediate conditions. A bit of padding under the roots and good air circulation with moderate amounts of water give good results. PLATE 8

Bulbophyllum antenniferum (Lindley) Reichenbach fil. (1861)

SYNONYMS
Cirrhopetalum antenniferum Lindley (1843), *Phyllorchis antennifera* (Lindley) Kuntze (1891)

This species is a member of the section *Hyalosema*. It has large pseudobulbs and a long peduncle holding one large flower. The dorsal sepal can be well over 6 cm long, the largest in the section, and it forms a hood over the flower. This species is native to the Philippines, Java, and Papua New Guinea at about 500 m above sea level. It grows well when mounted on wood, cork, or tree fern and requires not only warm temperatures and light shade but moist conditions.

Bulbophyllum apodum Hooker fil. (1890)

SYNONYMS

Bulbophyllum saccatum Kraenzlin (1905)
Bulbophyllum vidallii Tixier (1866)

This species is a member of the section *Aphanobulbon*. The pseudobulbs are minute and from 3 to 8 cm apart on the rhizome, the thick leaf is about 26 cm long, and the scape can be 10 cm or more tall. The pale yellow flowers are less than 1 cm wide, are sometimes slightly fragrant, and appear along almost the entire length of the scape. The plants grow in the lowlands of Thailand, Malaya, Vietnam, Sumatra, Java, Borneo, and the Philippines and can be grown in pots or preferably on slabs in a warm, moist atmosphere with ample air circulation and shade. This is an attractive but wide-scrambling plant that is easy to grow given the right conditions.

Bulbophyllum arfakianum Kraenzlin (1904)

This plant was discovered by Odoardo Beccari at very low elevations of the Arfak Mountains in New Guinea from which the specific name was derived. It is a member of the section *Hyalosema*, and the pseudobulbs are about 2.5 cm apart on the rhizome, 2 to 3 cm tall, and have a leaf that can be 6 cm long. The raceme is approximately 10 cm tall with one lovely, green flower that has brown and red markings on the sepals and petals. The petals are 0.2 cm long and lanceolate, the sepals are about 5 cm long, and the lateral sepals are joined to form a long, shallow receptacle down into which the dorsal sepal curves. This species can be easily grown in pots or baskets with a mix that retains some moisture but does not stay constantly wet. Warm temperatures and light shade are appropriate.

Bulbophyllum argyropus (Endlicher) Reichenbach fil. (1876)

SYNONYMS

Bulbophyllum corythium Hallé (1981)
Thelychiton argyropus Endlicher (1833)

The pseudobulbs of this small species of the section *Adelopetalum* are close together and form dense mats. The leaves are about 2 cm long, and the racemes are 2 cm tall with three tiny flowers. The specific name refers to the "silver foot" of the flowers. The species is endemic to Australia and can be cultivated on small pieces of cork or tree fern in warm, slightly shaded areas.

Bulbophyllum aureobrunneum Schlechter (1913)

This orchid is a member of the section *Leptopus* and can be 30 cm long with the 2-cm tall pseudobulbs lying against the rhizome. The rhizomes hang down, and the roots emerge from the pseudobulbs all along the rhizomes and creep under the sheaths. The single leaf is sometimes 8 cm long.

The flowers are on short bracts and are less than 1 cm in size, brown with yellow stripes. The plants grow on the trunks of large trees in forests of New Guinea at elevations of 800 to 1300 m above sea level. The species can be cultivated on suspended mounts in warm to intermediate conditions and must be kept in a moist and shaded environment.

Bulbophyllum baileyi F. von Mueller (1875)

SYNONYMS
Bulbophyllum caryophyllum J. J. Smith (1914)
Bulbophyllum punctatum Fitzgerald (1883)

Like other members of the section *Stenochilus*, this orchid has a labellum that remains upright with the dorsal sepal in the inferior position. The natural habitat of this species is New Guinea and Australia, where it grows either as an epiphyte or lithophyte at a wide range of elevations in either shade or sun. The pseudobulbs are about 4 cm apart, the leaves can be 14 cm long and 3.5 cm wide, and the flower is pale yellow with red markings. In view of the widely varying natural habitats, it would be prudent to grow these plants in an intermediate temperature unless you know from which area and altitude they came originally. Slight shade is always a safe choice as are pots with a loose potting mix and frequent watering. PLATE 9

Bulbophyllum bandischii Garay, Hamer & Siegerist (1992)

A member of the section *Hyalosema*, *Bulbophyllum bandischii* is especially interesting as it has an unusual petal configuration with antennae ending in a small sphere from which tiny spines protrude. The type plant was collected in Moronse Province, Lae, by a friend, Wolfgang Bandisch of Papua New Guinea, who sent it to St. Louis for identification. It was determined to be a new species and named after the collector. The intriguing flowers are greenish white with dotted red stripes. The plants are very easy to grow with warm conditions, protection from direct sunlight, and a well-draining mix in a pot or basket. PLATE 10

Bulbophyllum barbigerum Lindley (1837)

SYNONYM
Phyllorchis barbigera (Lindley) Kuntze (1891)

A fascinating addition to any collection is *Bulbophyllum barbigerum* which belongs to the section *Ptiloglossum*. It comes from the area of Africa along the coast of the Gulf of Guinea from Sierra Leone to Gabon where it grows in mossy forests at elevations as high as 2300 m above sea level. The pseudobulbs are flattened and about 2 to 3 cm apart, and the many-flowered inflorescence is 18 or 19 cm long. The sepals and petals are pale yellow green, and the sepals are spotted with purple. The column is white with long purple stelidia. The remarkable aspect of the flower is the many fine, long red-brown hairs on the elongated labellum which move with every breath of air, making the flower notoriously difficult to photograph. If adequate moisture can be provided, mounting this plant with a pad of moss under the roots would be very attractive and would be preferable as the plant naturally grows on tree trunks, but pots with spaghnum added to the mix would be appropriate under drier conditions. Warm to intermediate temperatures and light shade are required for maximum growth and good flowering.

Bulbophyllum baronii Ridley (1885)

The pseudobulbs of this small plant that belongs to the section *Loxosepalum* can be as tall as 1.5 cm and are quite close together on the creeping rhizomes. The leaves are shorter than the inflorescence which is 8 to 12 cm long. The rachis is about 8 cm long and carries many small, closely spaced flowers on short pedicels. The sepals are oval, less than 0.4 cm, the petals are about half that size, and the labellum is apically recurved and slightly flattened horizontally. The plants are endemic to the forests of Madagascar, growing as epiphytes or lithophytes at altitudes of 800 to 2000 m above sea level. Cultivation could be on slabs of tree fern or in small pots in a shady, intermediate, moist environment.

Bulbophyllum beccarii Reichenbach fil. (1879)

The section *Beccariana* is monotypic, *Bulbophyllum beccarii* being described by Heinrich Gustav Reichenbach in 1879 in the *Gardener's Chronicle*. It is a plant that, once seen, will never be forgotten. It grows in Borneo by wrapping itself around tree trunks in forests. The leaves are quite large and cupped to hold the decaying matter of the forest which gives needed nutrients to the plant. The flowers are beautiful, white with rose markings, hanging in a pendent cluster below the base of the leaf. There are many stories about the odor of these flowers, all of which open at once, and there can be quite a number of plants in the forest, all flowering at the same time. The smell has been likened to the stink of rotting fish, and one story claims that the artist who drew the flowers fainted from the stench. This is definitely not a plant to cultivate, but it is fun to know that it exists.

Bulbophyllum betchei F. von Mueller (1881)

SYNONYMS
Bulbophyllum atroviolaceum Fleischman & Rechinger (1910)
Bulbophyllum finetianum Schlechter (1906)

This plant is typical of the section *Fruticicola* as it has a rhizome that hangs down with its pseudobulbs appressed to it. The sheaths are persistent, and the plant is fast growing and somewhat branching. The plants can be 20 cm long with the pseudobulbs close together, just slightly ascending, and with leaves as long as 5 cm. The small flowers are yellow orange with dark red stripes, a green labellum that is hirsute on the underside, and they are held on an inflorescence that is only about 1 cm long. The species grows in New Guinea, the Solomon Islands, New Caledonia, Vanuatu, Fiji, and Samoa at elevations of approximately 700 m above sea level. Cultivation should be on a hanging mount in moderately shaded sunlight with frequent watering to keep the humidity high.

Bulbophyllum bigibbum Schlechter (1923)

This very small species is a member of the section *Diceras* and the pseudobulbs are less than 1 cm tall and 2 cm apart on the pendent rhizomes. The leaf is 3 to 4 cm long. There are many very short single-flowered inflorescences in a branching growth pattern. The flowers are less than 1 cm in size, but they open widely. They are an attractive pink color with red veining and have two knobby protuberances at the base of the labellum. This species grows epiphytically in old forests below 2500 m altitude in Indonesia and New Guinea. Successful cultivation should include mounting plants on a hanging piece of wood or cork, intermediate temperatures, moderate shade and humidity, and good air movement.

Bulbophyllum bisetoides Seidenfaden (1970)

In this species the nearly round pseudobulbs are less than 1 cm in size and close together on the rhizomes. The leaves are about 2 cm long and 1 cm wide. The erect inflorescence is less than 2 cm tall, and there are two very small flowers. The sepals and labellum are purple and the petals are light green. The plants are endemic to Thailand at 1300 to 1400 m elevation and can be grown in intermediate conditions in small pots or baskets, with protection from direct sunlight and frequent watering.

Bulbophyllum bisetum Lindley (1842)

SYNONYM
Bulbophyllum cirrhopetaloides Griffith (1851)

In *Annals of Natural History 10* (November 1842), John Lindley said of this species, "A very singular little plant, with flowers as large as a small pea, and deeply keeled sepals. Under each flower is a pair of long filiform bracts." This description hardly does justice to an unusual and interesting small plant. The pseudobulbs are about 2 cm tall, ovoid, spaced about 2.5 cm apart on the rhizomes, and covered with persistent sheaths that turn black when dry. The leaves are 10 cm long, and the pendulous scape is 8 cm long with a raceme of several 1-cm flowers. In all fairness to Lindley, the flowers are light green and round, but they have some purple markings. They also have unusual green terete appendices behind the petals, white cilia on the labellum, and long columnar spurs. This species grows in India and Thailand at elevations above 1800 m and can be grown in pots or baskets in intermediate to cool conditions, but it would be wise to tip the container a bit when flowering so the inflorescences can hang unhindered over the side. Of course, hanging perpendicular slabs would be ideal.

Bulbophyllum bowkettii F. M. Bailey (1884)
SYNONYM
Bulbophyllum waughense Rupp (1950)

This tiny orchid is a member of the section *Micromonanthe*. The pseudobulbs are a bit more than 1 cm long, are 2 to 4 cm apart, and, except for the apical portion, are appressed to the freely branching rhizomes. The leaves are ovate and sometimes as long as 2.5 cm. The inflorescence is 1 cm tall, and the pedicel is decurved. The flowers are less than 1 cm wide and are pink with red stripes, but the overall impression is of a red, drooping flower. The plants grow in Australia from coastal lowlands to cloud forests above 600 m and are usually found as epiphytes, but they also occasionally grow on rocks. It would be best to cultivate these on large mounts of any sort because of the wide spaces between pseudobulbs on the branching rhizomes. Warm, shaded, moist conditions are appropriate.

Bulbophyllum bracteatum F. M. Bailey (1891)
SYNONYM
Adelopetalum bracteatum (F. M. Bailey) Fitzgerald (1891)

This bulbophyllum, the type species of the section *Adelopetalum* which was described by J. J. Vermeulen in 1993, has pseudobulbs that are carunculate, about 1 cm in diameter, close together, and forming dense mats. The single leaves are less than 3 cm long, and the inflorescence can be 10 cm tall with 24 slightly crowded flowers. The flowers open widely and are only about 0.5 cm in diameter, pale yellow with purple spots and pale margins. This species grows on trees in Australian rain forests under good light conditions. The plants can be grown on tree fern or wood mounts in intermediate temperatures with bright light (not direct sunlight) and a reliable supply of moisture.

Bulbophyllum burfordiense Garay, Hamer & Siegerist (1996)
SYNONYM
Bulbophyllum grandiflorum of some authors, not Blume (1901) of the section
   Hyalosema

This orchid caused a mild sensation when it was first exhibited at the Royal Horticultural Society in 1895 by Sir Trevor Lawrence who named it in honor of his collection at Burford Lodge, Dorking, England. It was awarded a Botanical Certificate by the RHS and sent to Kew for identification where Robert A. Rolfe announced that it was *Bulbophyllum grandiflorum* Blume which had not been seen in years. This led to a great deal of vilification of the botanists who had seemingly "misidentified" it, and the name was changed accordingly. Subsequently these species were studied and, though quite similar, they were found to differ in some important characteristics, namely, in *B. grandiflorum* the labellum is glabrous, the petals are ovate and apically acute, the lateral sepals are tapering to an acuminate apex, and the dorsal sepal is at least 14 cm long and 4 cm wide. In *B. burfordiense* the labellum is ciliate, the petals are triangular, the lateral sepals are free, acute to obtuse, and the dorsal sepal is usually smaller. The flowers are a beautiful light greenish brown with white spots throughout. Lateral sepals are 9 cm long and also spotted. The species is a native of Papua New Guinea and can be grown in intermediate to warm situations in pots or on slabs with a steady supply of moisture, light shade, and gentle breezes.

Bulbophyllum calamarium Lindley (1861)

SYNONYMS
Bulbophyllum rupinicola Reichenbach fil. (1865)
Bulbophyllum saltatorium var. *calamarium* (Lindley) J. J. Vermeulen (1986),
    Phyllorchis calamaria (Lindley) Kuntze (1891)

This species, the type of the section *Ptiloglossum* as described by John Lindley in 1862, is a large plant with the flowers opening only a few at a time. It grows on trees in forests at low elevations but sometimes is found in humus deposits. As with the other members of the section, it has a mobile and feathery labellum. Unfortunately, it is rarely seen in cultivation, but if it can be obtained it would be most content in pots with a mix that holds moisture, perhaps including some spaghnum with the other elements. It also needs a very humid atmosphere, shade, good air circulation, and warm temperatures.

Bulbophyllum callichroma Schlechter (1913)

This colorful plant is a member of the section *Hedyothyrsus* and has pseudobulbs that can be 7 cm apart on the rhizomes and leaves that are about 16 cm long. The inflorescence has perhaps 14 bright flowers on its pendulous rachis that is often 13 cm long. The connate lateral sepals are the focal point, often longer than 2 cm, slightly recurved, and a commanding shade of bright purple. The dorsal sepal is white or yellow, also about 2 cm long, and the tiny petals are white. This species grows as an epiphyte in Indonesia and Papua New Guinea at 600 to 2200 m above sea level. It should be grown on rather large mounts of some sort because of the roving growth habit and needs a bit of shade, warm to intermediate temperature, frequent watering, and good air circulation.

Bulbophyllum calyptropus Schlechter (1924)

This very small epiphyte belongs to the section *Micromonanthe* and is only about 3.5 cm tall with 0.4-cm tall pseudobulbs that are not more than 1 cm apart on the rhizomes. The leaf is about 1 cm long, and the inflorescence is 3 cm tall with one tiny but attractive red-purple flower. The sepals are less than 1 cm long, the petals are about 0.4 cm long, and the curved labellum is only 0.5 cm long. This species is endemic to the large island of Madagascar where it grows on lichen-covered trees at 2000 m above sea level. It can be grown on small pieces of tree fern that are padded to retain moisture. The temperature should be intermediate to cool, and light shade is necessary.

Bulbophyllum cameronense Garay, Hamer & Siegerist (1996)

This species grows in the Cameron Highlands (after which it was named) in peninsular Malaysia and is a member of the section *Sestochilos*. The sub-globose pseudobulbs are about 5.5 cm apart on the rhizomes, and both pseudobulbs and rhizomes are encased in long, stiff bristles. The leaf is 31 cm long and 12 cm wide, and the flowers are carried on a short peduncle. The dorsal sepal is 2.5 cm long and 1 cm wide, the lateral sepals about 2 cm long and 1 cm wide, and the petals are 2 cm wide and 0.5 cm wide. In many ways this species resembles *Bulbophyllum siamense* but is larger. It grows well in an intermediate temperature, either potted or slabbed, and needs high humidity and protection from bright sunlight. PLATE 11

Bulbophyllum canlaonense Ames (1912)

This is another tiny member of the section *Nematorhizis* which has the typical very rambling, widely spaced pseudobulb habit of growth with 3-cm tall leaves and small flowers held on 4-cm long inflorescences. Although small, the flowers are a lovely carmine red with yellow stripes. The species grows as an epiphyte in the Philippines at 1300 to 2300 m altitude and can be cultivated on slabs large enough to accommodate a few years of growth in shady, intermediate conditions.

Bulbophyllum capillipes Parish & Reichenbach fil. (1874)

SYNONYMS
Drymoda latisepala Seidenfaden (1981)
Phyllorchis capillipes (Parish & Reichenbach fil.) Kuntze (1891)

This interesting plant grows in Thailand, India, and Myanmar and is a member of the section *Sestochilos*. The Reverend C. Parish noted on the herbarium sheet of this species that is was "a little gem." The pseudobulbs are conical, and the flower stems are sometimes 9 cm tall. Flowers are almost 2 cm wide, and the pale ivory sepals have dark red longitudinal stripes. Growing conditions should be in intermediate temperatures with light shade and ample water and humidity. Since the pseudobulbs are spaced only 4 cm apart at most, the plant will not outgrow its container too rapidly. This entity is not to be confused with *Hapalochilus capillipes* which is discussed in chapter 8.

Bulbophyllum careyanum (Hooker fil.) Sprengel (1826)

SYNONYMS
Anisopetalon careyanum Hooker fil. (1825)
Phyllorchis purpurea (D. Don) Kuntze (1891), *Pleurothallis purpurea* D. Don (1825), *Tribrachia purpurea* (D. Don) Lindley (1826)

One of the more readily available species of the section *Careyana* as described by Ernst Pfitzer in 1888, and the type, is *Bulbophyllum careyanum* despite the Reverend C. Parish's derogatory comment about it as "a worthless plant." The small flowers are tightly packed around the scape, they have prominent declined stelidia on the column, and the labellum is narrow, forming a triangular wedge. The species grows in India, Nepal, Myanmar, and Thailand up to 1200 m above sea level. The plants benefit from warm to intermediate temperatures and a nice piece of tree fern or cork as a support. A regular supply of water, but not constantly wet conditions, with slight shade is appreciated by the plants. They also grow well in pots or baskets with a well-draining potting mix.

Bulbophyllum carunculatum Garay, Hamer & Siegerist (1995)

The internodes between pseudobulbs of this member of the section *Lepidorhiza* are short, and the plant is large, with leaves up to 36 cm long and 7 cm wide. The inflorescence is as long as 45 cm with the large yellow flowers opening successively. The dorsal sepal is 4 cm long and 1.5 cm wide, the lateral sepals 5 cm long and 1.5 cm wide, and the petals 2.5 cm long and 1.2 cm wide. The dark mahogany-red labellum is about 2.5 cm long with a pair of setae at its base, and it is covered with small, lumpy outgrowths (caruncules), hence the specific name. This species grows in the Philippines and thrives in light shade at intermediate temperatures in large pots or baskets but must have a potting mix that drains well. PLATE 12

Bulbophyllum catenarium Ridley (1894)

SYNONYM
Bulbophyllum carunculaelabrum Carr (1932)

Henry N. Ridley named this tiny plant from the Latin word *catenarius* which means "chainlike" in reference to the pseudobulbs. Cedric E. Carr's name is also descriptive of this species and refers to the small, lumpy outgrowths (caruncles) on the labellum. The plant belongs to the section *Monilibulbon*, and the pseudobulbs are very small, less than 0.5 cm long, and rounded. The leaf is also less than 0.5 cm long and almost round. The inflorescence is nearly 2 cm tall, the yellow sepals are 0.5 cm long and have red edges, the petals are minute, and the papillose labellum is dark red. The species grows in Malaya, Vietnam, and Borneo in many different habitats from very wet and moss-covered to more arid and sunny locations, either on moss or on trees. This would indicate that a prudent approach to cultivation would be to mount the plants on very small pieces of bare tree fern or on bark with at most only a very thin layer of moss, and provide moderate water and shade. These plants and flowers may be tiny but they are delightful to see in bloom because the yellow sepals and very dark, warty labellum stand well above the plant and make a striking picture.

Bulbophyllum catenulatum Kraenzlin (1921)

This species is a member of the section *Megaloglossum*. The pseudobulbs are rather square, less than 2 cm tall, and about 2 cm apart on the rhizomes. The leaves are less than 7 cm long, and the inflorescence rises above them. *Bulbophyllum catenulatum* grows in the Philippines and has a yellow flower overlaid with red orange, lightly on the dorsal sepal and petals, heavily on the lateral sepals. The sepals are all similar in shape and less than 1 cm long. The dorsal sepal and the petals have heavily hirsute edges, and the column has long, slender stelidia. It was thought that this species might have been lost but fortunately has been rediscovered. Warm conditions, light shade, and abundant moisture are indicated for good culture.

Bulbophyllum caudatisepalum Ames & Schweinfurth (1920)

Oakes Ames and Charles Schweinfurth described this member of the section *Aphanobulbon* based on a collected specimen from Borneo. It has 3.5-cm tall pseudobulbs that are a bit more than 1 cm apart on the rhizome. The leaves are 13 cm long and only 1.5 cm wide. The inflorescence varies widely in length, from only half as tall as the leaf to considerably longer, and carries many flowers. The dorsal sepal is 0.5 cm long and 0.13 cm wide, the lateral sepals are slightly longer and wider, and the petals are minute. The labellum has three lobes, is sharply decurrent, projecting between the lateral sepals, and the apical half is pubescent. This species also grows in Malaya and can be cultivated in pots or on slabs in warm and shady areas that have high humidity.

Bulbophyllum cauliflorum Hooker fil. (1888)

In horticulture, this attractive miniature has been called a cirrhopetalum. It grows in the Indian Himalayas at altitudes of 1600 to 2000 m which means that it likes intermediate or cool temperatures. The rhizomes are quite long, and the nodes are sheathed. It is from these short sheaths that the flower scapes arise. The tiny flowers are subumbellate, white or cream colored. This species can be grown on small mounts with daily misting, light shade, and good air circulation.

Bulbophyllum cavibulbum J. J. Smith (1929)

This species belongs to the section *Uncifera*, and J. J. Smith named it based on a specimen collected in New Guinea. The small pseudobulbs are about 3 cm apart on the spreading rhizome and have one 3-cm long leaf. The inflorescence is very short, and there are usually two flowers at the base of each pseudobulb. The dorsal and lateral sepals are 2 cm long and acuminate, the petals are less than 0.5 cm long, and the labellum is not lobed and also is less than 0.5 cm long. The flowers are yellow orange with darker permeations. This species grows at about 3000 m above sea level in New Guinea in marshy areas as either a terrestrial or an epiphyte. It can be cultivated on well-padded mounts or in pots with a very moisture-retentive media, shade, and good air circulation at intermediate temperatures. Adding spaghnum or other types of moss that hold moisture to the potting mix is helpful when growing plants in pots. Culture on slabs should be attempted only in a very humid atmosphere when water can be supplied daily.

Bulbophyllum cephalophorum Garay, Hamer & Siegerist (1996)

This interesting species grows in the Philippines and is about 10 cm tall overall. The pseudobulbs are 2.5 cm tall and about 5 cm apart. The leaves are oblong-elliptic and can be as large as 7.5 cm long and 2.2 cm wide. The inflorescence carries many flowers whose sepals are slightly more than 1 cm long with the petals about 0.5 cm long. The labellum is heart shaped with a rounded apex and two raised linear discs. The inflorescence is globose, hence the specific name which is derived from the Greek words *kephale*, meaning "head" and *phoreus*, which means "bearer." These orchids may be grown in warm, shaded conditions and require the normal moisture and air circulation.

Bulbophyllum cerinum Schlechter (1913)

The leaves of this member of the section *Brachypus* can be 40 cm long and are held on small pseudobulbs that are close together on the rhizomes. The inflorescence is only a few centimeters tall with a single 2-cm flower that is cream colored with a few dark spots on the base of the sepals and a dark tan labellum with purple spots. It grows on forest trees at 1000 m altitude in New Guinea and can be cultivated in pots that contain a porous, well-draining medium that retains a bit of moisture. Temperature should be warm to intermediate and some shading is necessary. Other species in this section are quite similar, such as *Bulbophyllum hansmeyeri* J. J. Wood (1981), *B. latibrachiatum* J. J. Smith (1908), and *B. verstegii* J. J. Smith (1908).

Bulbophyllum cheiri Lindley (1844)

SYNONYMS
Bulbophyllum ephippium Ridley (1907)
Bulbophyllum whitfordii Rolfe ex Ames (1905)
Phyllorchis cheiri (Lindley) Kuntze (1891), *Sarcopodium cheiri* (Lindley) Lindley (1850)

This member of the section *Stenochilus* comes from low elevations of Sumatra, Java, Borneo, Malaya, and the Philippines. It is a rampantly wandering plant with the pseudobulbs up to 10 cm apart but less than 1 cm tall. The flowers are pale tan to green, spotted with red, and the dorsal sepal can be more than 6 cm long. The flower segments are arranged in a most graceful manner, making this plant a fine addition to an orchid collection. Because of the wide placement of the pseudobulbs, this species must be accommodated in either a very large basket or pot or can be mounted on a large slab. Warm, shaded conditions and ample moisture are required.

Bulbophyllum chloranthum Schlechter (1905)

This species has the growth habit of the section *Hedyothyrsus*, perhaps even a bit more rampant, with creeping rhizomes and pseudobulbs sometimes as much as 11 cm apart and with leaves to 18 cm long. It has inflorescences that can be almost 45 cm long with the 15-cm raceme drooping attractively and bearing as many as a dozen flowers. The flowers are about 4 cm long and 3 cm wide, and have either pale yellow-green sepals with a colored labellum or purple lateral sepals with a pale purple and cream labellum. It grows in Indonesia, Papua New Guinea, and the Solomon Islands. Obviously, it must be cultivated on large mounts and with light shade, warm to intermediate temperatures, and high humidity. It is well worth the space as the flowers open simultaneously and last about a week, making an admirable display.

Bulbophyllum ciliatum (Blume) Lindley (1830)

SYNONYM
Diphyes ciliata Blume (1825)

This small epiphyte belongs to the section *Micromonanthe* and has pseudobulbs that can frequently be 3.5 cm apart on the rhizomes. The leaf is perhaps 3 or 4 cm long, and the beautiful dark red-pink flowers arise from the rhizomes on tiny inflorescences. The sepals are long and narrow, to 0.6 or 0.7 cm long, the petals are only 0.2 or 0.3 cm long, but the labellum is the center of attraction with its densely hirsute margins and two little "teeth" below the middle. This tiny gem grows in peninsular Malaysia and Java at about 2000 m above sea level. It, too, requires tree fern or similar mounts or pots or baskets with frequent misting, shade, and intermediate temperatures.

Bulbophyllum clandestinum Lindley (1841)

SYNONYMS

Bulbophyllum myrianthum Schlechter (1911)
Bulbophyllum profusum Ames (1912)
Bulbophyllum sessile (Koenig) J. J. Smith (1905), *Epidendrum sessile* Koenig
  (1791), *Phyllorchis sessile* (Koenig) Kuntze (1891)
Bulbophyllum trisetosum Griffith (1851)
Oxysepala ovalifolia Wight (1852)

   This bulbophyllum, the type species of the section *Oxysepala* which was
described by Heinrich Gustav Reichenbach in 1861, is perhaps best known
as *Bulbophyllum sessile*. It is pendulous, branching, and has minute pseudobulbs about 1 to 2 cm apart. The sessile flowers arise all along the rhizomes,
are white with pale yellow elongated apices, and are less than 0.5 cm long.
The species grows throughout Myanmar, Thailand, Laos, Vietnam, Malaya,
Sumatra, Borneo, Java, New Guinea, Guam, and adjacent areas on trees in
open areas and often becomes a large, tangled mass of plants. Despite the
small size of the flowers, this is a congenial small plant to grow because it
adapts so readily to most conditions and produces pretty little flowers in
profusion. The easiest way to care for it is to mount it on tree fern slabs or
some other type of slab with a moss layer under the plants, hang it in an airy
spot in intermediate or warm temperatures, and make sure it is moistened
each day and kept from direct sunlight.

Bulbophyllum cleistogamum Ridley (1896)

   This species belongs to the section *Intervallatae*. It has pseudobulbs that are
3 cm tall and close together, and leaves that can be 24 cm long. The scape is
considerably longer but only rarely reaches 60 cm long as it elongates over
time. The flowers open widely in succession and are very inviting. Both the
dorsal and lateral sepals are as long as 2.5 cm and less than 1 cm wide, pointed
at the apex. The petals are tiny, almost square, with the apical portion
toothed and bearing a long threadlike tip. The sepals and petals are light
yellow with dark maroon stripes. The reflexed labellum is dark maroon,
about 2 cm long, keeled, and has basal auricles. The short column is yellow
and bilobed. Despite the specific name indicating self-pollination, the flowers are rarely cleistogamous. These plants grow on tree trunks in the Philippines, Borneo, Sumatra, and the Malay Peninsula. They can be grown
mounted in shaded, warm to intermediate conditions and, with regular
watering, should produce flowers over a long period of time.

Bulbophyllum cochlia Garay, Hamer & Siegerist (1994)

SYNONYMS

Bulbophyllum violaceum (Blume) Reichenbach fil. (1861), not *B. violaceum* (Blume) Lindley (1830) of the section *Megaloglossum, Cochlia violacea* Blume (1825)

This small pendent species is the type of the section *Cochlia* which was described by J. J. Smith in 1914. The plant has lateral sepals that are basally connate and acute. The labellum has a long, narrow base that is apically reflexed and verrucose. The stelidia are bicuspidate.

Bulbophyllum cocoinum Lindley (1837)

SYNONYMS

Bulbophyllum andongense Reichenbach fil. (1865)
Bulbophyllum brevidenticulatum De Wildeman (1916)
Bulbophyllum vitiense Rolfe (1893)

The flowers of *Bulbophyllum cocoinum*, true to its name, smell like coconut. This species, the type of the section *Cocoina* which was described by Ernst Pfitzer in 1888, is native to Africa, ranging along the northern equatorial region from Sierra Leone to Congo (Zaire) and Uganda. A few specimens are reported from Fiji. It is an inhabitant of rain forests as high as about 1500 m above sea level. This attractive plant is not too spreading, with the pseudo-bulbs only about 2 or 3 cm apart and the gracefully arching inflorescence considerably longer than the leaves, thus making a nice presentation. The individual flowers are loosely arranged on the rachis which is sometimes 40 cm long with 100 flowers. The flowers are pale cream and have pink or rose tips on the long, thin sepals which are held out from the rachis, giving a bristly appearance. A very impressive clone, 'D & B 25' was awarded a CCM/AOS at the Tampa Orchid Club show in October 1997 and was grown and owned by Bill Thoms and Doris Dukes of Florida. The plant was reported to have 3440 flowers and 15 buds on 41 inflorescences. It was grown on a tree fern slab, but plants can also be grown in pots or baskets with a moisture-retentive medium such as the mixtures used for phalaenopsis culture, always keeping in mind that good drainage is paramount. Warm temperatures, light shade, and good air circulation with ample moisture and frequent fertilizing are also necessary.

Bulbophyllum colliferum J. J. Smith (1911)

SYNONYM

Bulbophyllum papulilabium Schlechter (1913)

The pseudobulbs of this interesting member of the section *Pelma* can be 5 cm tall and are about 4 cm apart on the rhizome which can be 100 cm long.

The rhizome roots only at the base of the plant and is pendulous, with the lower portions curving up and outwards. The rhizomes as well as the inflorescences are enclosed in sheaths. The leaf is 7 cm long and 1 cm wide, and the inflorescences that emerge from many points on the rhizome are slightly longer than 2 cm and have only a very few flowers each. The flowers are white with a pale yellow labellum and do not open widely. They only last for four to five days, but since there are hundreds of them blooming at one time on a large plant, they make a dramatic display. The plants grow as epiphytes on trees in forests from 400 to 3000 m above sea level in Papua New Guinea and Indonesia. They can be grown on sturdy pieces of wood or tree fern and need light shade, a good supply of moisture, and warm to intermediate temperatures with ample room to accommodate the spreading nature of the hanging rhizomes.

Bulbophyllum colubrimodum Ames (1923)

In this miniature species of the section *Micromonanthe* the pseudobulbs are close together and less than 1 cm tall. The leaves are about 3.5 cm long, and the flower scape is roughly 5 cm long with but a single flower. This flower is slightly longer than 1 cm, yellow and purple. In describing this species in 1923, Oakes Ames said that the "specific name alludes to the peculiar apical portion of the labellum which—in certain positions—resembles the head of a snake about to strike." This very attractive species opens its flowers widely and grows as an epiphyte at 600 m altitude in the Philippines. It requires warm and moist, shaded conditions for optimum growth and flowering.

Bulbophyllum comatum Lindley (1862)

SYNONYMS
Bulbophyllum hirsutissimum Kraenzlin (1912, 1914)
Phyllorchis comata (Lindley) Kuntze (1891)

The pseudobulbs of this plant are about 3 cm apart on the rhizome, 2 cm tall, and somewhat four angled, and the leaves can be as long as 25 cm. The many-flowered pendulous inflorescence is perhaps 10 cm long, with a swollen apex and a fuzzy surface. The hirsute flowers are held close to the rachis and are a conspicuous shade of red. This plant grows as an epiphyte on forest trees at roughly 1000 m altitude in Nigeria and Guinea. It is best cultivated on a hanging mount of bark in a warm to intermediate temperature, light shade, with generous watering and good air movement.

Bulbophyllum cominsii Rolfe (1895)

Robert A. Rolfe named this member of the section *Hyalosema* from the Solomon Islands after the collector, Comins. The pseudobulbs can be as tall as 2 cm, and the leaves are 12 cm long. The lateral sepals are connate with inrolled sides, almost 6 cm long and 3 cm wide, and the ovate-oblong dorsal sepal is 7 cm long and 3.5 cm wide. The petals are minute and the labellum is less than 1 cm long. The flowers are off-white with red-purple marbling. This species grows in New Guinea and the Solomon Islands and can be grown in pots or baskets in warm, lightly shaded areas with a good supply of moisture. It is a nice plant of manageable size with colorful flowers that are well displayed—a winner on all counts. PLATE 13

Bulbophyllum commocardium Garay, Hamer & Siegerist (1995)

This small orchid was found by Wolfgang Bandisch at Mt. Albert Edward, Murray Pass, New Guinea, at 3000 m elevation and belongs to the section *Peltopus*. The leaves are 4 cm long and 0.6 cm wide, the inflorescence is 5 cm tall, and the pale yellow flowers are about 3 cm in diameter. Like the flowers of *Masdevallia* species, the flowers of *Bulbophyllum commocardium* are single and have tiny petals. The specific name is from the Greek and refers to the decorated, heart-shaped labellum (*commos* means "decoration" and *cardia* means "heart") which is edged with fine cilia. Cooler temperatures, such as would be found in the coolest parts of an intermediate greenhouse, are appropriate for this species. Clay pots and a moisture-retentive media, which can be obtained by adding a bit of moss or osmunda to the usual mix, some shade, and good air circulation are also helpful.

Bulbophyllum compressum Teijsmann & Binnendijk (1862)

This medium-sized species is appropriately named for the distinctively flattened ovoid pseudobulbs which are often as tall as 7 cm and are as much as 13 cm apart on the rhizomes. The leaves are elliptic and can be as large as 14 cm long and 4 cm wide. The inflorescence is slightly taller than the plant and bears many 2-cm long white flowers that are held on 2-cm pedicels. This species is found in Sumatra, Java, Borneo, and Sulawesi at relatively low altitudes of 100 to 600 m above sea level. Despite its wandering growth habit, this plant would be a nice one to cultivate because of the pleasant fragrance of the flowers. It can be grown most easily on large pieces of bark, without any padding, in warm, somewhat shady conditions.

Bulbophyllum conchidioides Ridley (1885)

SYNONYM
Bulbophyllum pleurothalloides Schlechter (1925)

This species is a member of the section *Trichopus*. The plants are quite small, only 2.5 cm high, with a very branching rhizome. The pseudobulbs are minute and have one leaf that is only 1 cm long. The scape is 2.5 cm tall with one to five tiny flowers that have ciliate labellums. The species grows as an epiphyte in mossy forests and on hills from 900 to 1400 m above sea level in Madagascar. It can be cultivated in very small pots or on tiny pieces of cork or coconut husk in warm to intermediate temperatures with high humidity and light shade. These are true miniatures but could be delightful when well grown with the plant densely covering the surface and the flowers held above the leaves.

Bulbophyllum congestum Rolfe (1912)

In this species of the section *Medusa* the pseudobulbs are as much as 5 cm apart on the rhizome, the leaves are about 7 cm long, and the flower scape is slightly shorter than the leaves. The inflorescence is capitate with about a 1.5-cm lateral spread, and the flowers are white to pale yellow. The plants grow in India, China, Myanmar, and Thailand at about 1200 m altitude and can be maintained in pots or on slabs of any type at an intermediate temperature with the usual good air circulation, light shade, and daily misting. They need to be kept cool and dry in December and January to induce flowering. By this it is not meant to dry them out completely, but merely to reduce the amount of water and also reduce the temperature a few degrees. PLATE 14

Bulbophyllum coniferum Ridley (1909)

SYNONYM
Bulbophyllum leibergii Ames & Rolfe (1915)

The pseudobulbs of this species of the section *Globiceps* as defined by Rudolf Schlechter in 1912 are less than 1 cm tall and quite close together on the rhizome with a single 15-cm long leaf. The scape is 20 cm tall with a drooping rachis about 2.5 cm long which holds many very small flowers clustered together. The sepals are papillose, green to yellow with dark purple veins and apices. The lateral sepals are apically connate, and the petals are papillose and fimbriate. The labellum is very small, green, and papillose. This species is endemic to Malaysia, Borneo, Sumatra, Java, and the Philippines and can be cultivated in pots or baskets in warm, moist, lightly shaded areas. A potting mix that retains moisture and careful attention to watering are necessary. Ideally, the plants should be given some water each morning and allowed to become almost completely dry overnight.

Bulbophyllum contortisepalum J. J. Smith (1913)

This species has slightly squared pseudobulbs that are approximately 1 cm tall, are 2 cm apart on the rhizome, and have one leaf that can be 3.5 cm long and 1 cm wide. The inflorescence arises from the rhizome and is 10 cm tall with a 1-cm long ovary. There is one very interesting flower which can be as long as 6 cm but is very narrow. The sepals are very dark purple with some paler markings, the dorsal sepal is about 2 cm long, and the lateral sepals are up to 6 cm long. These lateral sepals are very narrow and twist tightly around one another to form a long tail. The petals are tiny and hirsute with the median lobe threadlike. The labellum is also very small and hirsute. This free-flowering species inhabits the rain forests of Papua New Guinea, Irian Jaya, the Solomon Islands, and Vanuatu at altitudes up to 800 m above sea level. It grows in large clumps on trees that are not covered with moss and thus would grow well on a slab without padding under the roots or in a pot large enough to allow for rapid growth. It requires daily moisture and excellent drainage.

Bulbophyllum copelandi Ames (1905)

This Philippine species is a member of the section *Stenochilus* and has small pseudobulbs about 8 cm apart on the rhizomes, rigid leaves as large as 15 cm, and flowers on peduncles about 5 cm tall. The flowers are yellow with dark red markings and are often 3.5 cm in diameter. This plant grows as an epiphyte in mangrove swamps and therefore appreciates being kept in a warm, shaded, and moist environment. A large slab gives the plant room to wander.

Bulbophyllum corallinum Tixier & Guillaumin (1963)

This very attractive little species is native to Vietnam and Thailand at altitudes as high as 1200 m above sea level. It belongs to the section *Medusa*. The plant is quite small with clustered pseudobulbs, and the inflorescence is held closely near the base of the pseudobulbs. The flowers have only a 0.3-cm spread, and the lateral sepals are dark mahogany, curved, and very glossy. The petals and column are white, and the slightly pointed dorsal sepal is dark reddish brown. Although the flowers are small, they make a striking impression because of the shine on the lateral sepals that look like the cheeks of a chubby little cherub. The plant is quite easy to grow on a tiny piece of cork or tree fern in lightly shaded intermediate to warm conditions with high humidity. The clone 'Emly' was awarded a CBR/AOS in St. Louis, Missouri, in December 1989. PLATE 15

Bulbophyllum cornu-cervi King & Pantling (1895)

The globose pseudobulbs of this species are only 0.3 cm in size and are close together on the rhizomes. The leaf is obovate and can be 3.5 cm long and 2 cm wide. The raceme is as tall as 10 cm and holds many small, green and yellow flowers that have brown markings. The plants grow in India at 800 m above sea level, and they can be cultivated in pots or baskets in warm to intermediate temperatures.

Bulbophyllum cornutum (Blume) Reichenbach fil. (1861)

SYNONYMS

not *Bulbophyllum cornutum* (Lindley) Reichenbach fil. (1861) which is
   Rhytionanthos cornutum (Lindley) Garay, Hamer & Siegerist (1994), not
   Bulbophyllum cornutum Ridley (1886) which is *B. forbesii* Schlechter
   (1913), *Ephippium cornutum* Blume (1825), *Phyllorchis cornuta* (Blume)
   Kuntze (1891)
Bulbophyllum wenzelii Ames (1913)

   This often misnamed member of the section *Sestochilos* has 3-cm tall pseudobulbs encased in long, stiff bristles. The pseudobulbs are 4 cm apart on
creeping rhizomes and have thick leaves 15 cm long. The 3-cm broad flowers occur on inflorescences from 3 to 7 cm tall and are yellow green with
dark red-purple spots. They open widely, making the dark sepals and paler
petals easily visible. This species grows as an epiphyte in forests of Borneo,
Java, and the Philippines at elevations of 1000 m and slightly higher. It can be
cultivated in large baskets or pots that have good drainage, warm temperatures, protection from the sun, and adequate moisture.

Bulbophyllum crassipes Hooker fil. (1888)

SYNONYM

Phyllorchis crassipes (Hooker fil.) Kuntze (1891)

   This species is a member of the section *Careyana* and can be distinguished
from *Bulbophyllum careyanum* by the small stelidia on the column that point
forward and by the labellum which has a broad U shape. It, too, is endemic to
India, Myanmar, Thailand, and Laos and can be cultivated in pots or baskets
or on slabs in intermediate conditions, slight shade, and with a regular supply of moisture.

Bulbophyllum cruentum Garay, Hamer & Siegerist (1992)

   This member of the section *Macrobulbon* can be as tall as 15 cm with pseudobulbs that are 3 cm high and 2 cm wide. The single leaf is elliptic to oblong
elliptic, 12 cm long and 3.5 cm wide. The flowers are dark red, one or two to
an inflorescence, and are presented on short peduncles. The dorsal sepal is
broad elliptic, acute, to 2.8 cm long and 2 cm wide, and the lateral sepals are
connivent, 2.5 cm long and 1.5 cm. The petals are rhombic, acute, heavily
encrusted apically with papillose protuberances, and the fleshy labellum is
slightly curved with two parallel ridges that are covered with short hairs.
This species is closely allied to *Bulbophyllum macrobulbon*, which is also
endemic to Papua New Guinea and Irian Jaya. Pots with a loose mix, intermediate temperatures, light shade, and gentle air movement are needed for
optimum growth. PLATE 16

Bulbophyllum cryptanthum Cogniaux (1899)

SYNONYMS

not *Bulbophyllum cryptanthum* Schlechter (1905) of the section *Polyblepharon*
Bulbophyllum korimense J. J. Smith (1929)
Bulbophyllum ovalifolium (Wight) Parish (1883)
Bulbophyllum volkensii Schlechter (1914), *B. volkensii* var. *aurantiacum*
    Tuyama (1939)

The pseudobulbs of this member of the section *Oxysepala* are about 2 cm apart on the pendent rhizome and 0.5 cm tall, and the single fleshy leaf is 3 cm long. The 0.6-cm flower is carried on an inflorescence that is only 0.3 cm long, but the sepals are extremely thin and graceful, and the labellum is three lobed. The species grows in Northern Mariana Islands, New Guinea, and the Solomon Islands in full sun. It can be cultivated on hanging mounts in sunny, warm areas with a lot of moisture and fertilizer. The flowers are yellow or orange and quite attractive despite their small size.

Bulbophyllum cuneatum Rolfe ex Ames (1905)

The pseudobulbs of this species are very small, and the leaves are about 9 cm tall. The inflorescence is 12 cm tall, sharply recurving, and it carries many small purple flowers that are less than 1 cm in size. The species grows at altitudes of less than 1000 m above sea level in the Philippines and can be cultivated in warm, moist areas.

Bulbophyllum curranii Ames (1925)

This unusual small orchid is an epiphyte of the section *Aeschynanthoides* and grows as a vine with elongated rhizomes and minute pseudobulbs. The leaves are 2 cm long and 3 cm apart. The yellow flowers are less than 1 cm long and occur in pairs on very short inflorescences. The species is endemic to the Philippines at about 3000 m altitude. This plant can be mounted on bark or tree fern and allowed to hang, but it must be kept in semishade at intermediate or cool temperatures and given frequent waterings.

Bulbophyllum cuspidilingue Reichenbach fil. (1861)

SYNONYMS

Bulbophyllum blumei (Lindley) J. J. Smith (1905), *Cirrhopetalum blumei*
    Lindley (1830), *Phyllorchis blumei* (Lindley) Kuntze (1891)
Ephippium ciliatum Blume (1825)

This species is the type of the section *Ephippium* which was described by Rudolf Schlechter in 1913. The pseudobulbs are 3 to 5 cm apart on the rhizome, can be 4 cm tall, and have one leaf which is 10 to 12 cm long. The floral scape is the same length and has a single, delightfully large, colorful flower. The dorsal sepal is more than 2 cm long, apically slender, veined a dark red, and sports white hirsute edges. The lateral sepals are more than 3 cm long, sometimes as long as 8 cm, also veined with dark red but with edges that are more yellow than white. The spreading lateral sepals are broad at the base, and the apices are often joined. The minute petals are pale with dark red markings. The labellum can be as long as 6 cm and has a broad base that quickly narrows to a long, thin point, and it is usually a pale color. This beautiful flower opens widely, and there are often many open flowers at one time on a well-grown plant. Because of the flower's resemblance to a masdevallia, in Papua New Guinea this plant is commonly called *Bulbophyllum masdevalliacium* Kraenzlin (1904) which is a different member of this section. The native habitat is the forests of the Malay Peninsula, Java, Borneo, Papua New Guinea, and Sumatra at low altitudes where it grows on tree trunks and branches with mangrove trees being a favorite host. It can be cultivated in a warm, shaded environment on large slabs as long as there is ample room to expand and a padding of moss or some other material to retain enough moisture for optimum growth. If slabs are not an option, a large wooden or wire basket lined with moss would work well.

Bulbophyllum cylindraceum Lindley (1830)

Sometimes *Dendrobium cylindraceum* is listed as a synonym of this species and that misunderstanding arose because Nathaniel Wallich's original plate gave that name to this plant, although it is an unpublished manuscript name. To add to the confusion there is a *D. cylindraceum* J. J. Smith that is a true member of the genus *Dendrobium*. *Bulbophyllum cylindraceum* gives the appearance of being without pseudobulbs, and the leaf, which can be as large as 26 cm long and 4 cm wide, seems to rise directly from the stout rhizomes. This orchid is the type species of the section *Cylindracea* which was described by Ernst Pfitzer in 1888. The scape can be 45 cm long. and the pendent raceme is densely covered with purple, almost black, 1-cm long flowers. The base of the raceme is often enclosed in a good-sized sheath. The plants grow from India to Thailand at about 2000 to 2300 m elevation and can be cultivated in semishade at intermediate to cool temperatures in large pots with a mix that drains well. This very striking orchid is well worth a place in a mixed collection.

Bulbophyllum dasypetalum Rolfe ex Ames (1905)

SYNONYM

Bulbophyllum vanoverberghii Ames (1912)

This plant is common in the Philippines and has no visible pseudobulbs. The leaves are more than 20 cm tall, and the scape is usually the same size or a bit taller. The species belongs to the section *Aphanobulbon*, and there are many small, fragrant, cream-colored flowers in each raceme. Cultivation requires large pots or slabs with a mixture that holds moisture, shade, and warm temperatures.

Bulbophyllum dayanum Reichenbach fil. (1865)

This species, a member of the section *Leopardinae*, has an unusual flower which prompted the owner of a very nice plant to give it the whimsical but descriptive clonal name 'Hairball'. The name, of course, refers to the extremely hirsute sepals and petals. The rhizomes are creeping, and the flowers, which are clustered together and held very close to the base of each pseudobulb, are yellow and veined or blushed with purple. The species occurs in Myanmar, Thailand, Cambodia, Vietnam, and India at 500 m elevation but occasionally grows as high as 1300 m above sea level. Plants that I imported always met with an early demise, never developing in any manner. When I finally saw specimens growing luxuriously in Tamlong and Heike Suphachadiwong's nursery in Thailand, all with plump leaves and pseudobulbs, happily blooming, the owner told me that this species grows in the understory of dense forests and is very easy to grow and flower if given the proper conditions—damp and very shady at all times, quite the opposite of the conditions I had supplied them. Wooden baskets with a bark mixture topped with spaghnum or other moss suits them well. It is not recommended that they be mounted because of the difficulty in keeping them properly moist, although that is the way they were grown in the nursery—one coconut husk mount hanging beneath another. Of course, the humidity in Thailand is far greater than that found in Missouri, and even there the grower drenched the plants with warm water at least once a day. PLATE 17

Bulbophyllum dearei Reichenbach fil. (1888)

SYNONYM
Phyllorchis dearei (Reichenbach fil.) Kuntze (1891)

This lovely species of the section *Sestochilos* was known in gardening as *Sarcopodium dearei* before it was formally published. The pseudobulbs are less than 2 cm tall, encased in bristles, and are held closely together on the rhizome. The leaf is 13 cm long, and the inflorescence is at least 7 cm long, usually much longer, and bears one slightly fragrant flower. The dorsal sepal is 4 cm long and curves forward over the labellum. The lateral sepals are about the same length but widely spreading, with the lower portion curved. The petals are 3 cm long, spreading, and reflexed. The petals and dorsal sepal are pale yellow to white with darker yellow and purple veins. The lateral sepals are basically the same as the dorsal, but the lower portions are white with dark purple markings in the center. The labellum is pubescent and cordate, and the hypochile is reflexed. The species grows epiphytically at about 1000

m above sea level in Malaya, Borneo, and the Philippines and can be cultivated in pots or baskets in semishaded areas with intermediate to warm temperatures and regular applications of water and fertilizer. PLATE 18

Bulbophyllum dennisii J. J. Wood (1983)

This member of the section *Hyalosema* has angled pseudobulbs that may be
as far apart on the rhizome as 5 cm and as tall as 4 cm. The thick leaves are
often 16 cm long. The raceme is about 13 cm tall, the narrow dorsal sepal is
6 cm long, and the lateral sepals almost 5 cm long. The petals can be from 1
to 5 cm long with a swollen apex, and the labellum is less than 0.5 cm long
and is hirsute. The flowers are maroon with yellow green, shading basally
and apically. This species grows in New Guinea and the Solomon Islands,
and it can be cultivated in warm temperatures with light shade, high humidity, and gentle air circulation.

Bulbophyllum derchianum Ying (1989)

This very small orchid of the section *Aeschynanthoides* grows only in the
forests of Taiwan at about 1200 to 1800 m above sea level. The pseudobulbs
are minute, and the leaves are about 0.5 cm long and have dark purple spots
on the obverse. The tiny flowers are white. This species grows as a mat on a
slab and needs to be kept in the shade in a humid and warm atmosphere.

Bulbophyllum digoelense J. J. Smith (1911)

This delightful member of the section *Intervallatae* grows in the rain forests
of Irian Jaya and Papua New Guinea at low elevations. The pseudobulbs
can be 4 cm apart on the creeping rhizomes and are about 3 cm tall with a leaf
that is approximately 5 cm long. The inflorescence is more than 55 cm long,
arching, with a rachis that is fractiflex and compressed, usually bearing more
than 12 flowers that open successively. The flowers arise from 1-cm bracts,
hang downwards, and are yellow with purple markings. The sepals are about
4 cm long with inrolled margins, the petals are less than 1 cm long with a
threadlike apex, and the labellum is 2 cm long, thick, with verrucose midlobe
margins. Cultivation requires pots, baskets, or slabs with light shade, warm
temperatures, and copious watering. This beautiful species is not difficult to
grow but does require enough space for the extremely long inflorescence to
be enjoyed when in flower.

Bulbophyllum distans Lindley (1862)
Synonyms
Bulbophyllum calamarium var. *albociliatum* Finet (1911)
Bulbophyllum kindtianum De Wildeman (1904)
Bulbophyllum nudiscapum Rolfe (1909)

Bulbophyllum saltatorium var. *albociliatum* (Finet) Vermeulen (1986)
Phyllorchis distans (Lindley) Kuntze (1891)

This species belongs to the section *Ptiloglossum* and has pseudobulbs that can be as large as 5 cm tall and 1 cm wide, and 6 cm apart on the thick rhizome. The elliptic leaf is 11 cm long and 4 cm wide, and the inflorescence is often as long as 60 cm, erect, with many successively opening flowers. The flowers are about 1 cm in diameter, greenish with a hirsute purple labellum which is very articulate. The species has been found in Liberia, Angola, and Congo (Zaire) in rain forests at 1400 m altitude. Culture should be in pots or baskets or on mounts with moss added, intermediate temperatures, and light shade.

Bulbophyllum dryas Ridley (1915)

This true miniature is the type species of the section *Aeschynanthoides* which was described by Cedric E. Carr in 1930. The minute pseudobulbs are at least 2 to 3 cm apart on the rhizomes, and the leaves are about 1.5 cm long. The inflorescence is about 4 cm tall and has a single pale yellow flower which is 1 cm in diameter. This plant grows as an epiphyte on trees in Malaya, Sumatra, and Borneo at heights of about 1500 m above sea level. There the air movement is good and the light is bright. The plant can be grown on a slab hung in filtered sunlight, making certain that it gets adequate circulation of air and a steady supply of moisture. The temperature should be warm to intermediate. This plant is attractive because the flowers are held high enough above the leaves to easily be seen.

Bulbophyllum ebulbe Schlechter (1905)

This species, a member of the section *Aphanobulbon*, is very sprawling and requires much space, but has many 1-cm cream-colored flowers that are nicely fragrant. It grows throughout New Guinea and the Solomon Islands at low elevations in damp, shady areas. Cultivation would require warm temperatures, a large slab, and a thick mat of moss under the roots of the plant.

Bulbophyllum ebulbum King & Pantling (1895)

This species belongs to the section *Aphanobulbon* and has no obvious pseudobulbs. The leaves are about 20 cm long and 3 cm wide, spaced about 7.5 cm apart on the rhizomes. The scape is erect, shorter than the leaf, and the raceme has many pale green flowers that are less than 1 cm long. The species grows in India at 500 m above sea level. Cultivation would require warm temperatures, high humidity, a bit of shade, and good air circulation.

Bulbophyllum echinochilum Kraenzlin (1921)

This species has small, rounded pseudobulbs only slightly separated on the rhizome. The leaf is about 7.5 cm tall, and the raceme is longer than the leaf with the upper third slightly enlarged and bent downward. The flowers are small with fimbriate petals and labellum. The type is said to have originated in the Philippines, but there is some doubt about this and Oakes Ames felt that it had many characteristics that would indicate African origin.

Bulbophyllum echinolabium J. J. Smith

This successively flowering species is most interesting for several reasons. It is one of the largest flowers in the genus with a horizontal length of approximately 40 cm. The very dark labellum is carunculate and the inflorescence is an impressive 70-cm tall. It comes from Borneo and Sulawesi and can be grown in a warm area in pots or baskets with the usual loose potting mix and moist atmosphere.

Bulbophyllum echinulus Seidenfaden (1982)

The flowers of this member of the section *Medusa* are very much like those of *Bulbophyllum corallinum*. The pseudobulbs are close together and less than 1 cm in diameter. The leaves are about 3 cm long and 0.7 cm wide, and the inflorescence is quite short with many flowers in a subumbellate arrangement. The flowers are minute, yellow green with orange shading and an orange labellum. This orchid is endemic to Thailand at elevations of 1300 m above sea level and can be grown in intermediate conditions. As usual, direct sunlight is to be avoided, and regular watering is necessary.

Bulbophyllum ecornutum J. J. Smith (1914)

SYNONYM
Bulbophyllum cornutum var. *ecornutum* J. J. Smith (1905)

This species is quite similar to *Bulbophyllum cornutum*, but the main points of difference are that this species has a bright orange appendage to the pollinia and is without the horns or projections on the column that are found on *B. cornutum*. It is also a member of the section *Sestochilos*, and it grows in open areas as high as 1300 m above sea level in Thailand, Sumatra, and Java. It can be cultivated in intermediate temperatures, light shade, and high humidity.

Bulbophyllum elassoglossum Siegerist (1991)

This species is a member of the section *Megaloglossum* from the Philippines, and its name refers to the very small labellum. The plants can be as large as 11 cm tall and have creeping rhizomes with 3.5-cm pseudobulbs that are 4.5 cm apart. The leaves are 8.5 cm long, and the inflorescence reaches 11 cm and has but a single flower. The floral segments spread widely, the sepals are white with purple spots, and the petals and diminutive labellum are maroon. The plant can be grown in a warm to intermediate setting in a basket or pot with the usual loose mix, protection from direct sunlight, and regular, copious watering.

Bulbophyllum elisae (F. von Mueller) Bentham (1873)
SYNONYM
Cirrhopetalum elisae F. von Mueller (1868)

Sometimes the specific name of this plant is spelled *elizae*. This interesting little orchid of the section *Adelopetalum* has furrowed, gnarled, 3-cm tall pseudobulbs less than 2 cm apart on the rhizomes and one leaf that is about 11 cm long. There are usually a dozen pretty flowers held on each 20-cm long inflorescence. These flowers have drooping lateral sepals more than 2 cm long and only 0.4 cm wide, dorsal sepals that are less than 1 cm long, and minute petals, all of which are yellow green. The glabrous labellum is an interesting shade of dark red brown. This graceful orchid grows on trees or rocks at low elevations in the wet areas of Australia. It can be cultivated on tree fern slabs and needs to be kept moist, very lightly protected from sunlight, and somewhat warm for really good growth.

Bulbophyllum elongatum (Blume) Hasskarl (1844)
SYNONYMS
Bulbophyllum gigas Ridley (1896)
Bulbophyllum sceptrum Reichenbach fil. (1861)
Ephippium elongatum Blume (1825)

Bulbophyllum elongatum is the type species of the section *Altisceptrum* which was described by J. J. Smith in 1914. It is a very large plant with 1-cm tall pseudobulbs spaced 15 cm apart on the rhizome and a leaf that is 60 cm long and 15 cm wide. The inflorescence is also 60 cm long with the apical portion recurved and bearing many small flowers. The flowers are slightly more than 1 cm wide and are white with purple spots, while the labellum is yellow with spots. The species grows in Malaya, Java, Borneo, and the Philippines between 1000 and 1500 m altitude and always near water. It should be cultivated in large pots that have a layer of either broken clay pot shards or rocks in the bottom for balance with a very moisture-retentive mix, warmth, partial shade, good air circulation, and moderate light. Other species in this section that are quite similar are *B. macrophyllum* Kraenzlin (1905), *B. noeanum* Kerr (1927), and *B. penduliscapum* J. J. Smith (1903).

Bulbophyllum emiliorum Ames & Quisumbing (1931)

This member of the section *Stenochilus* was named for Emilio Quisumbing, a civil engineer in the Philippines who also collected orchids. There are about 7 to 10 cm between the small pseudobulbs, one leaf that is 21 cm long, and a single flower on a 6-cm stem. The very waxy flower faces upward, and the lip projects through the opening between the lateral sepals. The flower has a natural spread of 3 cm and is yellow with dark maroon or purple spots and suffusions. It has a strong aroma that surprisingly is not unpleasant. The species was believed to be endemic to the Philippines, growing on trees in dense forests at low elevations but has been found at low elevations in Papua New Guinea also. It requires warm, shaded conditions with adequate moisture and a large slab on which to grow.

Bulbophyllum encephalodes Summerhayes (1951)

This medium-sized plant is a member of the section *Loxosepalum* and has pseudobulbs that are sharply four angled, almost 3 cm tall, and as far apart as 8 cm on the rhizomes. The leaf is narrowly oblong and can be 12 cm long. The inflorescence is perhaps 40 cm tall with many small flowers arising from a square cross section on the bent rachis. The flowers are less than 1 cm in size, are green with dark red margins or sometimes entirely dark red purple and have a labellum that is fleshy, verrucose, recurved, and slightly flattened horizontally. The species grows as an epiphyte on bare tree trunks in montane forests throughout central Africa from 800 to 1500 m above sea level. It can be cultivated on large slabs of cork or cedar in intermediate conditions that are only moderately moist and with shade during the brightest part of the day. Slabs are preferred because the distance between pseudobulbs would make it difficult to restrain this plant in pots.

Bulbophyllum evasum Hunt & Rupp (1949)

This member of the section *Globiceps* has pseudobulbs that are less than 1 cm in size, closely appressed to the brittle rhizomes and covered by bracts, so that they appear to be absent. The pseudobulbs are about 4 cm apart on the rhizomes, and the leaf is roughly 3.5 cm and almost circular. The inflorescence can be 10 cm long, and the rachis is only 0.5 cm long with 15 to 25 flowers in a tight bundle. The flowers are 0.3 to 0.4 cm long and do not spread widely. They are pink with red stripes, and the sepals and petals are tipped with yellow. The plants are endemic to Australia where they grow above 750 m elevation, either on trees or on rocks. The very brittle rhizomes can reach several meters in length This species should be grown on moss-padded slabs in warm conditions with high humidity, light shade, and ample room to spread. Although the flowers are quite small, they are held well away from the leaves and show to good advantage.

Bulbophyllum exaltatum Lindley (1842)

This tiny plant is a member of the section *Didactyle*, which has as one of its distinguishing features two extra staminodes below the normal pair on the column. *Bulbophyllum exaltatum* has small pseudobulbs that are close together on the rhizome, a leaf that is less than 4 cm tall, and an inflorescence that is often more than 42 cm high. The tiny flowers are purple, are partially obscured by large bracts, and are held in an erect raceme. This species grows in Guyana and requires warm temperatures and light shade.

Bulbophyllum exiguum F. Mueller (1860)

SYNONYM
Dendrobium exiguum F. Mueller (1865)

The pseudobulbs of this species of the section *Uncifera* are 1 cm tall and can be as far apart as 4 cm on the rhizome. The leaves are less than 4 cm tall, and the inflorescence is often as tall as 5 cm and carries only a few rather small pale yellow-green flowers which open all at the same time. The specific name means "insignificant." In Australia, where the plant grows on trees or rocks in forests from sea level to 1000 m altitude, it is commonly called "the creeping orchid." It can be cultivated on slabs or in pots in warm and shady conditions.

Bulbophyllum facetum Garay, Hamer & Siegerist (1996)

This is another species in the section *Sestochilos* that is highly recommended to the grower. The specific name was derived from the Latin *facetus* which means "elegant" and refers to the color of the flower which is a pale beige with dark red markings. The species is very similar to *Bulbophyllum ecornutum* but is considerably larger, with the largest dimension of the flower being about 7 cm. It grows in the Philippines and can be nurtured under conditions similar to the others of this section, that is, slightly shaded intermediate to warm temperatures, baskets or pots with shredded tree fern, bark, and charcoal, perhaps topped with old wine corks. Drainage must be good, and daily spraying or misting with tepid water is desirable. PLATE 19

Bulbophyllum flavescens (Blume) Lindley (1830)

SYNONYMS
Bulbophyllum montigenum Ridley (1895)
Diphyes flavescens Blume (1825), *Phyllorchis flavescens* (Blume) Kuntze (1891)

The tiny pseudobulbs of this species are close together on the rhizomes and the leaves can be more than 20 cm long. The raceme is often as long as the leaves, although it is often much shorter, and has many flaccid, pale cream flowers that are punctuated by yellow labellums. Each flower is about

2 cm in diameter and opens widely but, unfortunately, they do not have as pleasant a fragrance as some of the others in this section *Aphanobulbon*. This orchid grows at low altitudes in Malaya, Sumatra, Java, Borneo, and the Philippines. Cultivation would be much the same as for others in the section—warm temperatures, some shade, lots of moisture—except that pots or baskets could be used successfully instead of slabs. It is a nice plant to have as it doesn't outgrow the pot too quickly and has a pleasant display of flowers with only minimum attention from the grower.

Bulbophyllum flectens Cribb & Taylor (1980)
SYNONYM
Bulbophyllum unifoliatum subsp. *flectens* J. J. Vermeulen (1987)

The pseudobulbs of this small plant of the section *Loxosepalum* are almost 3 cm tall and about 4 cm apart on the rhizomes. The leaf is narrowly oblong and can be 8 cm long. The inflorescence is sometimes 16 cm tall and is dark purple, as are the tiny distichous flowers. This species grows in the forests of Tanzania and Malawi between 1700 and 2000 m elevation. Cultivation can be in pots or baskets or on slabs, in shady intermediate conditions.

Bulbophyllum fractiflexum J. J. Smith (1908)
SYNONYMS
Bulbophyllum fractiflexum subsp. *fractiflexum* J. J. Vermeulen (1993)
Bulbophyllum genybrachium Schlechter (1913)

The pseudobulbs of this widely spreading species of the section *Pelma* are 3 cm tall and can be as far apart on the rhizomes as 9 cm. These rhizomes are quite long, root only at the base of the plant, and have the apical portions upturned. The leaves are as large as 12 cm long and 4 cm wide, and the inflorescence is at most 3.5 cm long with as many as eight flowers. It grows in Papua New Guinea and the Solomon Islands at altitudes from 100 to 2000 meters above sea level and can be cultivated on moss-padded slabs of any sort in shady, moist, warm to intermediate areas with adequate room for the drooping plant to hang.

Bulbophyllum fraudulentum Garay, Hamer & Siegerist (1996)
This strange name was given to this member of the section *Hyalosema* because it had for many years been masquerading under the name *Bulbophyllum arfakianum* as described by Kraenzlin despite obvious differences. This species has lateral sepals that are connivent and the petals are oblong, obtuse, and only 0.5 cm long with a recurved apex, while the sepals in *B. arfakianum* are lanceolate with a tapering, elongated apex. This orchid is from Papua New Guinea and grows well in intermediate to warm conditions with light shading, frequent applications of water and fertilizer, and gentle breezes.

Bulbophyllum fritilariiflorum J. J. Smith (1912)

This member of the section *Hyalosema* is quite similar to *Bulbophyllum fraudulentum* but smaller. The inflorescence is 10 to 15 cm tall, the broadly oval dorsal sepal is about 7 cm long, and the connate lateral sepals are about 6 cm long, while the petals are tiny. The labellum is small and ciliate. This species, too, is from Papua New Guinea and needs a warm, somewhat shaded, and moist environment. The Missouri Botanical Garden and Marilyn LeDoux received a CCM/AOS of 82 points for a lovely specimen with the clonal name 'Tower Grove' in St. Louis in 1991. The plant covered a tree fern slab 20 cm long by 32 cm wide and showed off its 11 flowers and five buds to good advantage. PLATE 20

Bulbophyllum fruticicola Schlechter (1905)

SYNONYM
Bulbophyllum fruticula J. J. Smith (1912)

This species is the type of the section *Fruticicola* which was described by Rudolf Schlechter in 1912. It is very similar to other members of the section with its hanging rhizomes, persistent sheaths, and pseudobulbs appressed to the rhizomes. The leaves, however, are narrow, and plants are found growing on shrubs as well as on trees. The labellum is densely papillose, and the flowers are white with red dots near the apices of the sepals. The habitat is about 800 m above sea level in New Guinea. Plants can be cultivated on hanging mounts in slight shade, warm temperatures, and high humidity.

Bulbophyllum gadgarrense Rupp (1949)

This species, a member of the section *Oxysepala*, has pseudobulbs that are about 0.6 cm tall, decumbent, and covered with purple bracts which makes them appear smaller than they really are. The pseudobulbs are about 1 cm apart on the branching, pendent rhizomes which often become tangled, although they are only about 20 cm long. The leaves are very thick, 1.5 to 3 cm long, and channeled. The peduncles are also covered with bracts and are very short with a few pale yellow and white flowers that are 0.5 cm long. The species is endemic to Australia at altitudes above 750 m and can be grown on slabs of any sort in warm conditions, light shade, and with good humidity. The unusual specific epithet is derived from the area in Australia in which plants were found.

Bulbophyllum gibbosum (Blume) Lindley (1830)

SYNONYMS
Bulbophyllum igneocentrum J. J. Smith (1917)
Bulbophyllum korinchense var. *grandiflorum* Ridley (1917)
Bulbophyllum pangerangi Reichenbach fil. (1857)
Diphyes gibbosa Blume (1825), *Phyllorchis gibbosa* (Blume) Kuntze (1891)

The very small pseudobulbs of this member of the section *Aphanobulbon* are close together on the rhizome, while the leaves are often 30 cm long. The raceme is usually the same length as the leaves and carries a number of small but attractive cream-colored flowers that open widely. The species grows in Malaya, Sumatra, Java, and Borneo, usually at low elevations. The plants can be easily grown in pots with a good mix that retains only a small amount of water, and they prefer warm to intermediate conditions with moderate shade.

Bulbophyllum glandulosum Ames (1923)

The pseudobulbs of this miniature orchid that belongs to the section *Hybochilus* are only 0.5 cm tall and 0.3 cm wide, and are 1 cm apart on the rhizomes. The leaf is about 2.5 cm long, and the scapes are about 4.5 cm tall and have only one flower, all parts of which are less than 0.5 cm in size. The petals are only 0.3 cm long and wide at their base, but then they abruptly contract into a glandular tail. The labellum is even smaller and has a central lobe that is distinctly glandulose. The flower is a dark purple and, naturally, the specific name is derived from the glandulose appearance of the petals and labellum. The species grows as an epiphyte in the Philippines at about 1000 m altitude and would do well on small pieces of cork or bark or even tree fern with a bit of padding, in shade, and with intermediate temperatures and high humidity. This is another very interesting addition to a group of miniature orchids.

Bulbophyllum globiceps Schlechter (1905)

This species comes from Papua New Guinea and can be found growing in moss on the high branches of large trees, usually with other orchids and ferns. It is the type species of the section *Globiceps* which was described by Rudolf Schlechter in 1913. These orchids grow near rivers at altitudes of about 750 m above sea level. The pseudobulbs are minute, are close together, and have leaves that are about 6 cm tall. The inflorescence is 15 cm long, arching, and has as many as 25 tiny flowers in a tight umbel. The sepals and petals are diminutive, pink with purple stripes, and the purple-red, papillose labellum is the dominant part of the flower. The plants are best cultivated on slabs of some sort with a heavy layer of spaghnum moss on them, only light shade, warm temperatures, lots of moisture, and strong air movement. Again, these tiny flowers are quite attractive and are easily seen above the leaves.

Bulbophyllum globuliforme Nicholls (1938)

The pseudobulbs of this interesting miniature species of the section *Minutissima* are only 0.1 to 0.2 cm in diameter, almost round, and close together on the creeping rhizome. The leaves are 1 cm long, and the inflorescence is about 1.5 cm tall with a single flower. The flowers are about 0.3 cm in diameter and are white suffused with yellow. This species is endemic to Australia where it grows as an epiphyte from 300 to 750 m above sea level. Small pots or pieces of cork would be appropriate with warm temperatures and a generous supply of moisture in semishaded areas.

Bulbophyllum goebelianum Kraenzlin (1912)

While similar to *Bulbophyllum lobbii*, the flowers of *B. goebelianum* are merely half their size. In these species the pseudobulbs are close together which makes the plants easy to handle in pots or baskets. As usual, an open potting mix of predominantly bark or tree fern, warm temperatures, and frequent watering are all that are required to keep these plants happy. They originate in the Philippines, Borneo, and Malaya.

Bulbophyllum graciliscapum Schlechter (1905)

SYNONYMS

not *Bulbophyllum graciliscapum* Ames & Rolfe (1915) of the section *Megaloglossum*

not *Bulbophyllum graciliscapum* Summerhayes (1954) which is *B. flexiliscapum* Summerhayes nom. nud.

The pseudobulbs of this member of the section *Ischnopus* are less than 1 cm tall and are about 5 cm apart on the rhizomes with recurved leaves that are sometimes 6 cm long. The erect inflorescence can be 15 cm long and have more than 40 flowers on the 10-cm pendent rachis. The flowers are less than 1 cm in size and pale yellow with purple veins, and the labellum is also purple. The plant grows from sea level to above 2000 m elevation in the Solomon Islands, Vanuatu, and Papua New Guinea. Cultivation would be easiest on good-sized slabs with padding, light shade, warm to intermediate temperatures, and considerable moisture.

Bulbophyllum grandiflorum Blume (1848)

SYNONYMS

Ephippium grandiflorum Blume (1848), *Hyalosema grandiflorum* (Blume) Rolfe (1919), *Phyllorchis grandiflora* (Blume) Kuntze (1891)

Living up to its specific name is *Bulbophyllum grandiflorum*, another large-flowered species. It is the type of the section *Hyalosema* which was described by Rudolf Schlechter in 1911. The dorsal sepal is at least 14 cm long and 4 cm wide, the lateral sepals are ligulate and taper to a sharp apex, and the petals are ovate with an acute tip. This orchid is reported from Sumatra to Papua New Guinea and the Solomon Islands where it grows on tree trunks in rain forests at elevations from 300 to 500 m above sea level. The plant needs warmth, a lot of moisture, and good light but not direct sunlight, and can bloom at any time throughout the year.

Bulbophyllum griffithii (Lindley) Reichenbach fil. (1861)

SYNONYM

Sarcopodium griffithii Lindley (1853)

This member of the section *Sestochilos* has pseudobulbs that are less than 2 cm tall, ovoid, and close together on the rhizomes. The leaf is about 5 cm long and 1 cm wide, and deflexed. The inflorescence is very short and carries one pretty flower that is 2 cm in diameter, fleshy, pale yellow white with purple spots. The labellum is white with slightly darker spots. This species comes from India at elevations of 1500 to 3000 m above sea level and can be grown in cool to intermediate temperatures with light shading and high humidity.

Bulbophyllum guamense Ames (1914)

The pseudobulbs of this charming member of the section *Intervallatae* are 2.5 cm tall, 1 to 2 cm apart on the rhizome, and have leaves that are about 15 cm long and almost 4 cm wide. The scape is approximately 25 cm tall and carries the successive flowers well above the leaves. The dorsal sepal is almost 1 cm long, lanceolate, and the lateral sepals are similar in shape and slightly longer. The petals are minute, quadrate, with a long apical projection. The labellum is carunculate and about 1 cm long. This green-flowered species grows on Guam in the Mariana Islands where is it often called "wild onion." It can be cultivated in warm, moist conditions with light shade.

Bulbophyllum hahlianum Schlechter (1905)

SYNONYM

Bulbophyllum macranthum var. *albescens* J. J. Smith (1905)

This species is quite similar to the others in the section *Sestochilos* and grows on tree trunks near the northern coast of Irian Jaya and Papua New Guinea in areas of high rainfall. The lateral sepals are partially joined, and the labellum is quite small. The flowers are cream with darker suffusions. This, too, is an easy flower to grow if given large slabs on which to roam, adequate moisture, warmth, and shade. PLATE 21

Bulbophyllum hirtulum Ridley (1907)

This species is the type of the section *Hirtula* as described by Henry N. Ridley in 1907. The pseudobulbs are less than 0.6 cm tall and crowded together on the rhizome. They have one leaf than can be as long as 15 cm. The inflorescence is 10 cm long, and the small flower is only 0.6 cm long. The lateral sepals are hirsute, the flower is white or beige with brown veins, and the hirsute labellum is dark red. This species grows in Malaya at elevations of 600 m above sea level. It can be grown in small pots or baskets in warm areas with light shade and a regular supply of water.

Bulbophyllum howcroftii Garay, Hamer & Siegerist (1995)

This plant comes from the Sogeri Plateau of Papua New Guinea and is a member of the section *Megaloglossum*. It was named for Neville Howcroft, a noted resident botanist who has contributed substantially to the knowledge of orchids in Papua New Guinea. The pseudobulbs are widely spaced, 3 to 4 cm apart, the leaves are about 11 cm long and 2.5 cm wide, and the single flowers are carried on inflorescences as long as 10 cm. The flowers are close to 2.5 cm long, lemon green with a vivid olive-green band on the lateral sepals, and are somewhat hirsute. Intermediate to warm temperatures, some shade, and good air movement are suitable for growing this plant. PLATE 22

Bulbophyllum humblotii Rolfe (1890)
SYNONYMS
Bulbophyllum album Jumelle & Perrier (1912)
Bulbophyllum laggiarae Schlechter (1918)
Bulbophyllum linguiforme Cribb (1977)
Bulbophyllum luteolabium Perrier (1951)

In this very small species which is the type of the section *Humblotiorchis* as described by Rudolf Schlechter in 1925, the pseudobulbs are about 1 cm tall, 3 cm apart on the rhizomes, and have a single leaf that is 2 to 5 cm long. The inflorescence is slightly shorter than the leaf and often has as many as 10 or 11 tiny white flowers that have a yellow labellum. *Bulbophyllum humblotii* is native to Tanzania, Zimbabwe, Malawi, Seychelles, and Madagascar and grows from 600 to 1200 m above sea level in bright, dry areas. This species is most easily cultivated on tiny slabs of cork or bark without a padding under the roots, with moderate exposure to sun, and if watered only when quite dry. This plant, too, would make a nice addition to a miniature collection.

Bulbophyllum hymenanthum Hooker fil. (1888)

The pseudobulbs are seemingly absent on this very small species, a member of the section *Aeschynanthoides*, and the leaves are ovate-elliptic, fleshy, about 1.5 cm long by 1 cm wide, and 2.5 cm apart on the rhizomes. The scape is 2.5 cm tall and has two flowers which are a bit over 1 cm in diameter and are yellow with purple stripes. Joseph Hooker's description of this species included the following: "Rhizome tortuous, as thick as packthread. . . . A remarkable little species." It grows in India, Thailand, and Vietnam from 1600 to 2600 m above sea level and can be cultivated in intermediate to cool temperatures with light shade. The flowers of this species are colorful and easily seen above the leaves.

Bulbophyllum implexum Jumelle & Perrier (1912)

This tiny plant, the type species of the section *Bifalcula* as defined by Rudolf Schlechter in 1924, has four- or five-sided pseudobulbs about 1 cm in size and 1 to 2 cm apart on the rhizomes. The inflorescence is about 9 cm long, and the rachis is 2 cm long, fractiflex, with two alternate rows of tiny dark red flowers. The species grows in dry forests of Madagascar at low altitudes. It can be cultivated on tiny pieces of wood or cork without a moss padding, and needs warm temperatures and only moderate moisture and slight shade.

Bulbophyllum inflatum Rolfe (1891)

This species is so similar to *Bulbophyllum comatum* in many respects that J. J. Vermeulen has considered it a variety, not a separate species. The rachis is much thicker than that of *B. comatum*, swollen to almost 2 cm in diameter, and the flowers are green with maroon markings. *Bulbophyllum inflatum* grows throughout central Africa and can be cultivated on a hanging slab in intermediate to warm, moist areas that are lightly shaded.

Bulbophyllum insuloides Seidenfaden (1973)

SYNONYM
Bulbophyllum racemosum Hayata (1911)

This species is a member of the section *Racemosae*. The ovoid pseudobulbs are 2.5 cm tall and are close together on the rhizomes with one leaf that is often 12 cm long. There are about a dozen pliable flowers on a 12-cm long inflorescence. The dorsal sepal is about 0.5 cm long, the petals are minute and ciliate, and the lateral sepals are almost 1 cm long and somewhat in-rolled. The flowers are yellow with some light purple spots. This orchid is native to Taiwan in forests at 1500 to 2000 m elevation. It can be grown in pots or baskets at intermediate temperatures with light shade and gentle air movement.

Bulbophyllum intertextum Lindley (1862)

SYNONYMS
Bulbophyllum amauryae Rendle (1913)
Bulbophyllum intertextum var. *parvilabium* Williamson (1980), *Phyllorchis intertexta* (Lindley) Kuntze (1891)
Bulbophyllum pertenue Kraenzlin (1914)
Bulbophyllum quintasii Rolfe (1891)
Bulbophyllum seychellarum Reichenbach fil. (1877)
Bulbophyllum triaristellum Kraenzlin & Schlechter (1908)
Bulbophyllum usambarae Kraenzlin (1904)
Bulbophyllum viride Rolfe (1893)

Another interesting member of Rudolf Schlechter's section *Trichopus* that has a lot of obscure synonyms is the African *Bulbophyllum intertextum*. It also is the type of that section. The pseudobulbs are small, about 1 or 2 cm apart on a creeping rhizome, with one leaf at least 4 cm long per pseudobulb. The scape is fractiflex, and on *B. intertextum* the length can be exceedingly variable, sometimes as long as 30 cm but usually much less. There are generally six or more flowers per inflorescence, pale yellow or green with reddish tips and, although small, they are attractive. The species can be found from the countries bordering the Gulf of Guinea to the eastern coast of mainland Africa and on the Seychelles in riverine forests, where it grows on trees, rocks, or in moss. These plants adapt easily to intermediate to warm temperatures and either mounting or potting as long as there is light shade and adequate moisture.

Bulbophyllum johnsonii Hunt & Rupp (1949)

SYNONYMS
Bulbophyllum kirkwoodae Hunt & Rupp (1949)
Bulbophyllum whitei Hunt & Rupp (1949)

This nice plant is a member of the section *Megaloglossum* with depressed pseudobulbs that are slightly square and can be as large as 1.8 cm and 1 to 8 cm apart on the rhizomes in this exceedingly variable species. The leaves can be as large as 7 cm long and 2 cm wide, and the inflorescence is about 3 cm tall. The single flower is 1 to 2 cm wide, and the most noticeable features are the widely spreading, glossy lateral sepals which may be any shade of yellow, orange, or red. The dorsal sepal is less than 1 cm long, hooded, and striped red, and the labellum is ligulate. The species is endemic to Australia's trees and rocks from sea level to 1200 m altitude. Cultivation requires good-sized pots or baskets with a well-draining mix or, preferably, large slabs on which the plants may roam, as well as warm temperatures, some shade, and high humidity.

Bulbophyllum kainochiloides Perrier (1937)

The pseudobulbs of this member of the section *Loxosepalum* are more than 3 cm tall and about the same distance apart on the rhizomes. The leaf is 10 cm long and only 1 cm wide. The inflorescence is about 30 cm long with many small flowers that are less than 1 cm in size. The plant grows on forest trees in Madagascar at 1300 m altitude. Pots or baskets with a well-draining mix at intermediate temperatures and with light shade would be appropriate conditions.

Bulbophyllum kermesinum Ridley (1886)

SYNONYM
Hapalochilus kermesinus (Ridley) Garay & Kittredge (1986)

In this member of the section *Hyalosema* the pseudobulbs are not close together, the leaves are 7 cm long, and the scape is shorter than the leaves. The spreading flowers are yellow white with dark red suffusions on the sepals. The petals taper to a filiform section which terminates in a white globose mass. The plants grow in Papua New Guinea and can be cultivated in warm, moist conditions with light shade. PLATE 23

Bulbophyllum klabatense Schlechter (1911)

This remarkable species was discovered in Sulawesi at about 900 m above sea level and is a member of Rudolf Schlechter's section *Lepidorhiza*. It is a large epiphyte, growing to 30 cm tall. The pseudobulbs are 5 cm tall and close together on the rhizomes. The leaves are oval, to 25 cm long by 6 cm wide, and the inflorescence is 20 cm long with two or three flowers which open successively. The dorsal sepal is 3.2 cm long, the lateral sepals are 4.5 cm long, and the petals about 2 cm long. The labellum is a bit longer than 1 cm, fleshy, keeled, and with finely serrate margins. It can be found in India and Malaya and needs intermediate temperatures, a bit of shade, and pots or baskets with a mix that drains well.

Bulbophyllum lageniforme Bailey (1904)

SYNONYM
Bulbophyllum adenocarpum Schlechter (1910)

The specific name of this plant, which belongs to the section *Adelopetalum*, refers to the pseudobulbs and means "flask-shaped." The pseudobulbs are depressed, ovoid, about 1 cm in diameter, and are close together on the rhizomes. The leaf is linear, about 5 to 10 cm long. The inflorescence can be 7 cm tall and has one to four flowers. The flowers are somewhat bell shaped, less than 1 cm long, and are pale green or pink with brownish veins. They have an unusual labellum with two pairs of keels, the outer pair less prominent than the inner pair. The plants grow in Australia either as epiphytes or lithophytes and above 750 m altitude. Cultivation could be in pots or baskets or on slabs under warm conditions, light shade, and with moderate humidity.

Bulbophyllum latisepalum Ames & Schweinfurth (1920)

Like other species in the section *Monilibulbon*, this one also is characterized by small size, closely held pseudobulbs, and a single flower displayed well above the plant. The very attractive flowers are pale orange with purple veins, and the labellum is bright orange. The lateral sepals are relatively large and broad, hence the specific name. This plant is endemic to Borneo at about 2000 m altitude, and it can be grown in light shade on small mounts at intermediate temperatures with frequent watering.

Bulbophyllum laxiflorum (Blume) Lindley (1830)

SYNONYMS

Bulbophyllum laxiflorum var. *celebicum* Schlechter (1911), *Diphyes laxiflora*
   Blume (1825)
Bulbophyllum luzonense Ames (1912)
Bulbophyllum syllectum Kraenzlin (1921)

The one species of the section *Corymbosia* as described by Louis Pfeiffer in
1870 that is most often seen in cultivation is *Bulbophyllum laxiflorum*. It also is
the type of that section. The flowers are held on long, filiform pedicels in
clusters of 15 or more and have thin segments that are white or slightly yellow. The plant grows throughout Southeast Asia and adapts readily to warm
greenhouse conditions. The clone 'Emly' was awarded a CBR/AOS in St.
Louis, Missouri, in 1983; it had 124 pure white flowers on six inflorescences.

Bulbophyllum leandrianum Perrier (1937)

This plant belongs to the section *Loxosepalum* and has 1-cm globular pseudobulbs that are sometimes wider than they are tall and are close together on
the rhizomes. The leaf is sometimes more than 20 cm long and is almost
round in cross section and very narrow, only 0.15 cm at the most. The inflorescence is at least as tall as the plant and has many small yellow-green flowers on short pedicels. The species is endemic to Madagascar's forests above
900 m altitude. Slight shade, containers with a quickly draining mix, daily
moisture, and warm to intermediate conditions are suitable.

Bulbophyllum leopardinum (Wallich) Lindley (1830)

SYNONYMS

Dendrobium leopardinum Wallich (1824), *Phyllorchis leopardina* (Wallich)
   Kuntze (1891), *Sarcopodium leopardinum* (Wallich) Lindley (1850)

This species is the type of the section *Leopardinae* which was described by
George Bentham in 1883 and is quite similar to *Bulbophyllum dayanum*, but it
lacks the hirsute sepals and petals that are so distinctive in the latter. The
flowers occur in pairs and are about 4.5 cm long and 3.5 cm wide with dark
spots on the sepals and petals and a distinctive dark red labellum. The plant
grows at rather high altitudes, usually about 2000 m above sea level, in India,
Nepal, Bhutan, Myanmar, and Thailand. It requires cool to intermediate
conditions with semishade and a potting mix that holds some moisture.

Bulbophyllum leptanthum Hooker fil. (1890)

SYNONYM

Bulbophyllum cylindricum King and Pantling (1895)

The pseudobulbs of this species are approximately 2.5 cm tall, cylindric,
and about 3 cm apart on the rhizome. The leaf is 7 or 8 cm tall, and the scape

emerges from the rhizomes as well as from the base of the pseudobulbs and is only 2.5 cm tall. The very small flowers are greenish yellow, subracemose, and there are only two to four of them in an umbel. The species grows in India at about 1500 m above sea level and can be cultivated on slabs or in pots at intermediate temperatures with shade and high humidity.

Bulbophyllum leptopus Schlechter (1905)

This species, the type of the section *Leptopus* which was described by Rudolf Schlechter in 1905, has hanging pseudobulbs that are a bit more than 2 cm long and lie against the rhizomes. The roots emerge from the pseudobulbs all along the rhizomes. The flowers are yellow with red-brown spots on the petals and with a dark reddish brown labellum. Since the flowers are held on bracts 2 to 3 cm long, they are more visible than many other flowers. The plants grow on the trunks of large forest trees in New Guinea at about 1000 m above sea level and need to be mounted on large slabs of tree fern or cork with padding under the roots to hold moisture. Warm to intermediate temperatures and shade assure good growth and flowering.

Bulbophyllum levanae Ames (1915)

This species and *Bulbophyllum nymphopolitanum* Kraenzlin (1916) as well as *B. trigonosepalum* Kraenzlin (1916) are sometimes considered the same as they resemble each other in many ways. They are all members of the section *Lepidorhiza* that is endemic to the Philippines and seem to differ mainly in the coloration of the flowers. The flowers of *B. levanae* are about 4 to 7.5 cm long, borne successively, and opening widely with long sepals and petals and a prominent, very dark red labellum. They range in color from all yellow sepals and petals to all red with many variations in between. The pseudobulbs are crowded, making these easy to grow in pots in warm to intermediate conditions with adequate water and light shade.

Bulbophyllum levyae Garay, Hamer & Siegerist (1995)

This large plant, often 40 cm tall, was collected by Wolfgang Bandisch in Papua New Guinea and grown by Mrs. Ralph Levy of Memphis, Tennessee, after whom it was named. It is a member of the section *Pachyanthe* which Rudolf Schlechter described in 1912. The pseudobulbs are only 1 cm apart, the leaves are 28 cm long and 3.5 cm wide, and the inflorescence is 40 cm tall with three or four yellow-orange flowers which have orange-red labellums. The dorsal sepal is 4 cm long and 1.2 cm wide, the lateral sepals 4 cm long and 1 cm wide, and the tiny petals are less than 0.5 cm long. The papillose labellum is flat, without keels or tubercles, and is 3 cm long by 1 cm wide. The plants grow well in intermediate temperatures with light shade and require large pots or baskets for good balance. PLATE 24

Bulbophyllum lilacinum Ridley (1896)

SYNONYM

Bulbophyllum careyanum var. *roseum* Rolfe (1904)

The flowers of this species are, naturally, a lovely lilac color which contrasts with the color of other species of the section *Careyana* which are darker and brighter. *Bulbophyllum lilacinum* can be found in peninsular Thailand and Malaysia and is best cultivated in pots or on mounts in intermediate, slightly shaded areas with a regular supply of moisture and fertilizer. This lovely plant shows off the light-colored flowers best when allowed to grow on a slab of tree fern and will in time completely encompass it. PLATE 25

Bulbophyllum lilianae Rendle (1917)

SYNONYM

Bulbophyllum revolutum Dockrill & St. Cloud (1957)

The pseudobulbs of this member of the section *Adelopetalum* are slightly more than 1 cm tall and about 2 cm apart on the rhizomes. The leaf can be 2.5 cm long and is less than 1 cm wide. The inflorescence is between 1.5 and 2.5 cm long with one to three flowers, but usually two flowers whose pedicels arise from almost the same place on the peduncle. The flowers are less than 1 cm in size, red with darker stripes, and do not open widely, but all the flowers open at one time. The plant grows below 900 m altitude in the cloud forests of Australia, usually as an epiphyte and only rarely as a lithophyte. It requires bright light and warm temperatures and would do well mounted on twigs as it prefers to grow in strands and does not form thick masses.

Bulbophyllum limbatum Lindley (1840)

SYNONYM

not *Bulbophyllum limbatum* Parish & Reichenbach fil. (1874) which is
    B. rufilabrum Parish ex Hooker fil. (1888)

The interesting pseudobulbs are very flat, almost 2 cm in diameter, and 8 cm apart on the rhizomes. The leaf can be more than 12 cm long and the inflorescence 18 cm, erect, with about a dozen flowers. The dorsal sepal is less than 1 cm long with white hirsute edges, and the lateral sepals and petals are tiny, all yellow with dark red veins and edges. The labellum is about 0.5 cm long, the central portion smooth and the rest densely papillose, basally dark yellow, apically brown. *Bulbophyllum limbatum* grows in peninsular Thailand, Myanmar, Sumatra, Borneo, Malaya, and Singapore. In deference to its very spreading growth habit, the plant should be cultivated on large mounts with padding around the roots, and warm, moist conditions. The flowers are held well above the leaves and are easily enjoyed, with only the widely spaced pseudobulbs keeping this plant from being amenable to pot culture.

Bulbophyllum lindleyanum Griffith (1888)

SYNONYMS
Bulbophyllum caesariatum Ridley (1924)
Bulbophyllum rigens Reichenbach fil. (1865)
Phyllorchis lindleyana (Griffith) Kuntze (1891)

This species grows in India and Thailand and has small (3 cm tall) pseudobulbs that are close together, and leaves that are from 7 to 15 cm long. The flowers are held on a recurved scape that is 10 to 20 cm tall. There are many small pale green flowers with purple stripes in the raceme, and they are unusual in that they are tomentose. The species can be cultivated in small pots or baskets in intermediate conditions.

Bulbophyllum lingulatum Rendle (1921)

This creeping little plant is a member of the section *Pygmaea*. It has pseudobulbs that are less than 1 cm tall, ovoid, and often 1.5 cm apart on the thin creeping rhizomes. The leaves can be 3.5 cm long and about 0.5 cm wide. The inflorescence is 3 cm tall and bears one or two tiny flowers that open at the same time. The flowers do not open widely and are either white or pale yellow. The species is endemic to New Caledonia where it grows as an epiphyte in forests at 600 to 1400 m above sea level. Cultivation would require warm to intermediate temperatures, small pots or slabs, partial shade, and high humidity.

Bulbophyllum lobbii Lindley (1847)

SYNONYMS
Bulbophyllum lobbii var. *siamense* (Reichenbach fil.) Reichenbach fil. (1882),
   Phyllorchis lobbii (Lindley) Kuntze (1891)

Most well known of the section *Sestochilos* is *Bulbophyllum lobbii* which was discovered in Java by Thomas Lobb in 1846. It has many varieties, among which are var. *breviflorum* J.J. Smith (1908), var. *claptonense* Rolfe (1904), var. *colosseum* Ridley (1895), var. *henshallii* Henfrey (1851), and var. *nettesiae* Cogniaux (1901). The pseudobulbs can be 5 cm tall and about 8 cm apart on the thick rhizome with a leaf to 25 cm long. The stalk is 10 cm long with one widespreading flower that can open to 7 cm. The dorsal sepal is 5 cm long, and the lateral sepals are slightly longer and curved downward. The petals are less than 4 cm long and they are very narrow, while the labellum is less than 1 cm long. The entire flower is pale yellow with purple-brown markings. *Bulbophyllum lobbii* has a large, distinctive flower. Perhaps the best-known cultivar of the many awarded clones is 'Kathy's Gold' AM/AOS which was awarded in 1988 in San Antonio, Texas, and owned by Robert and Sharon Thayer of the same city. The flower had a natural spread of 8 cm and was gold with maroon markings. This beautiful plant has been propagated and is widely available. *Bulbophyllum lobbii* grows in Thailand, Malaya, the Philippines, and Borneo. Plants originating in the Philippines seem to have the largest flowers with most of the others being at least somewhat smaller. Pots or baskets with a good mixture of well-draining materials, light shade, warm to intermediate temperatures, and a good supply of moisture are all that are needed to enjoy this delightful plant. PLATE 26

Bulbophyllum longicaudatum J. J. Smith (1914)
SYNONYM
Bulbophyllum blumei var. *longicaudatum* J. J. Smith (1911)

This plant is a member of the section *Ephippium* and in most respects is very similar to *Bulbophyllum cuspidilingue*, differing only in slightly larger flowers of more intense color. It grows in New Guinea on trees in the lightly shaded areas near sea level. The roots hold the plant slightly above the surface of the host plant, and they grow well on long pieces of tree fern. Naturally, a good deal of moisture is necessary for optimum growth as well as bright light but not direct exposure to noonday sunshine.

Bulbophyllum longipedicellatum J. J. Smith (1910)

This member of the section *Papulipetalum*, which was defined by Rudolf Schlechter in 1912, comes from New Guinea and has 12-cm long leaves and but one flower per long inflorescence. The dorsal sepal is almost 2 cm long and cupped, and the margins are covered with white papillae. The lateral sepals are more than 2 cm long, the petals are minute, apically papillose, and the small labellum has hirsute edges. The flower is green with reddish markings at the apex of the labellum. It grows well in pots or baskets at intermediate to warm temperatures with protection from direct sunlight. PLATE 27

Bulbophyllum longiscapum Rolfe (1896)
SYNONYM
Bulbophyllum praealtum Kraenzlin (1909)

This member of the section *Intervallatae* has 5-cm tall pseudobulbs about 4 cm apart on the rhizomes, and leaves that are more than 20 cm long. But, true to the specific name, the inflorescences can be almost 80 cm tall with the flowers developing sequentially on the short rachis which increases in length as it slowly produces more flowers. The flowers are less than 1 cm in size, project from the large sheaths nicely, and are yellow green with dark purple markings. The plant grows in mangrove swamps or open forest at very low elevations from the Solomon Islands to Tonga, Samoa, and Fiji. This species should be cultivated in large pots filled with a mix that retains moisture, in partial shade, and with a steady supply of water and fertilizer.

Bulbophyllum macphersonii Rupp (1934)

SYNONYMS

Bulbophyllum purpurascens F. M. Bailey (1884), *Osyricera purpurascens*
(F. M. Bailey) Dean (1893)

This member of the section *Polyblepharon* is a miniature species from
North Queensland, Australia. It grows as an epiphyte or lithophyte and forms
very dense clumps. The pseudobulbs are about 0.1 cm tall and crowded, and
have 2-cm long leaves that lie close to the ground on alternate sides of the
pseudobulbs. The rhizomes often become pendulous. The inflorescence can
be 5 cm long and has only a single 1.5-cm diameter, dark red-purple flower
which opens widely. The parts of the flower are minute, and the labellum is
slightly hirsute. *Bulbophyllum macphersonii* grows in rain forests or slightly
exposed areas at moderate elevations. It is often a bit difficult to grow but
does best mounted on cork or some similar slab, and kept rather cooler than
usual, with constant air movement in shaded areas. Perhaps most importantly, it should be given frequent doses of fertilizer and high humidity.
PLATE 28

Bulbophyllum macranthoides Kraenzlin (1904)

Friedrich W. L. Kraenzlin named this species based on material Odoardo
Beccari collected from Irian Jaya. It is a member of the section *Stenochilus*
and had not been seen for many years until a plant collected by Wolfgang
Bandisch in Morobe Province, Papua New Guinea, flowered in the collection of the Missouri Botanical Garden. It had pretty yellow flowers suffused
with pink that were about 5 cm wide on very short peduncles. The leaves
were 20 cm long on pseudobulbs 10 cm apart. Intermediate to warm conditions and good humidity are necessary for successful cultivation.

Bulbophyllum macranthum Lindley (1844)

SYNONYMS

Bulbophyllum cochinchinense Gagnepain (1950)

Bulbophyllum purpureum (Reichenbach fil.) Naves (1880), *Sarcopodium*
    purpureum Reichenbach fil. (1856)

Phyllorchis macrantha (Lindley) Kuntze (1891), *Sarcopodium macranthum*
    (Lindley) Lindley (1850)

This species is the type of the section *Stenochilus* which was described by
J. J. Smith in 1914 and has a very wide range, having been found in Thailand,
Malaysia, Singapore, Vietnam, Sumatra, Borneo, Myanmar, Java, Indochina,
Philippines, India, and New Guinea. The pseudobulbs are 3 cm tall and
about 10 cm apart on the thickened rhizome and have a single 10- to 25-cm
long leaf. The flowers have a natural spread of 4 cm or more and they open

flat. The dorsal sepal and petals are pale cream with dark brownish markings, and the lateral sepals are free but curved inward and are pale with a few spots. Henry N. Ridley's comment on this species was, "The flowers smell of cloves." The plants grow epiphytically in low forests, usually not over 500 m elevation. Large slabs, shade, and warm temperatures assure good growth. PLATE 29

Bulbophyllum macrobulbon J. J. Smith (1910)

The three species of Rudolf Schlechter's section *Macrobulbon* that are most commonly found in cultivation are this one, *Bulbophyllum phalaenopsis* J. J. Smith (1937), and *B. spiesii* Garay, Hamer & Siegerist (1990). These all have pseudobulbs that are densely packed together and good-sized flowers that are held close to the pseudobulbs. The smallest of these is *B. macrobulbon* with pseudobulbs about 8 cm tall and 6 cm across (what Schlechter calls "as large as a medium-sized apple"). The 10-cm flowers are yellow green with dark brown spots, and the petals are dark red at the base, while the labellum is light purple. This species can be found in Papua New Guinea on moss-covered rocks or on trees at low elevations. The leaves are more than 20 cm long and often can be as long as 60 cm. *Bulbophyllum macrobulbon* was described by J. J. Smith in 1910 and has been erroneously called *B. balfoureanum* by gardeners. This species, as well as others in this section with long leaves, must be grown in pots or baskets and suspended either from the ceiling or a frame so that the leaves do not lie on the bench or table surface, thereby causing them to rot. Warm temperatures, a bit of shade, and high humidity help the plants attain their best growth.

Bulbophyllum macrochilum Rolfe (1896)

This species is a member of Henry N. Ridley's section *Intervallatae* and is similar in many ways to *Bulbophyllum longiscapum* but differs mainly in the inflorescence being only 30 cm long. It grows from Singapore to Borneo and can be cultivated in warm conditions with high humidity and partial shade.

Bulbophyllum maquilingense Ames (1932)

This member of the section *Megaloglossum* has pseudobulbs that are often 1.5 cm tall and crowded on the rhizomes. The leaves are as long as 4.5 cm and about 1.5 cm wide, often slightly recurving apically. The inflorescences arise from the bases of the pseudobulbs, and there are often as many as eight from each pseudobulb holding the single flowers well above the leaves. The cucullate dorsal sepal is 1 cm long and 5 cm wide, and the lateral sepals are slightly smaller, oblong, and acute. The petals are less than 1 cm long, and the labellum is ligulate, only 0.6 cm long. The sepals are pink with purple markings, and the petals are dull green with purple markings. The species grows on tree trunks in the Philippines and can be cultivated in warm, moist conditions, preferably on wooden or husk mounts, in partial shade.

Bulbophyllum masdevalliacium Kraenzlin (1904)

This species comes from the northern part of New Guinea where it grows on forest trees at altitudes up to 500 m above sea level. It is a member of the section *Ephippium*. The flowers resemble those found in the genus *Masdevallia* and are quite striking. The scape is 20 cm long and the flowers are a good size with the hirsute dorsal sepal 3.5 cm long and the lateral sepals 8 cm long. The dark red-brown flower is completely edged a lovely shade of pale cream. Either pots or slabs would be appropriate with warm temperatures, slight shade and, of course, a good supply of moisture and gentle air movement. PLATE 30

Bulbophyllum masonii (Senghas) Wood (1986)

SYNONYM
Cirrhopetalum masonii Senghas (1978)

Karlheinz Senghas named this species in honor of Maurice Mason of Talbot Manor, Fincham, Norfolk, the owner of a fine orchid collection. It is a member of the section *Polyblepharon* and has pseudobulbs that are approximately 1 cm tall, with leaves that can be almost 8 cm long and 2.5 cm wide. The 8-cm tall inflorescence has one purple flower that is flushed green and is truly spectacular. The dorsal sepal is 21 cm long, very thin and twisted, with the edges minutely hirsute on the apical half. The fused lateral sepals are also about 21 cm long, very thin and twisted, but have glabrous margins. The petals are about 3.5 cm long, densely ciliate, and the labellum is almost 2 cm long. This species grows as an epiphyte in New Guinea at altitudes between 1500 and 2500 m. It can be cultivated in intermediate to cool conditions in pots or baskets with good drainage and ample moisture and light.

Bulbophyllum maxillare (Lindley) Reichenbach fil. (1861)

SYNONYMS
Cirrhopetalum maxillare Lindley (1843), *Phyllorchis maxillaris* (Lindley)
    Kuntze (1891)

This species is quite similar to *Bulbophyllum masdevalliacium*, but the dorsal sepal is noticeably ciliate, making it even more striking. It can be grown in slightly shaded areas with warm temperatures and high humidity and would be a most admirable addition to any collection. In some instances it has been called *B. blumei* (Lindley) J. J. Smith (1905), but that entity is correctly *B. cuspidilingue* Reichenbach fil. (1861).

Bulbophyllum mearnsii Ames (1913)

SYNONYM
Bulbophyllum carinatum Ames (1912)

   This species grows only in the Philippines and it is a typical member of the section *Lepidorhiza*, a delightful successive flowering plant with a vivid red papillose labellum. It can be grown in pots in slightly shaded areas at intermediate temperatures and requires a good deal of moisture to thrive.

Bulbophyllum meridense Reichenbach fil. (1850)

SYNONYM
Didactyle meridense Lindley (1852)

   This Venezuelan species, named for the province in which it grows, is a member of the section *Didactyle*. It has sharply angled pseudobulbs a few centimeters apart, and a long arching inflorescence that rises well above the 12- to 13-cm long leaves. The flowers are arranged in a raceme, are less than 1 cm wide, and are very pale yellow brown or lavender with darker markings. The fimbriate labellum is dark lavender with white margins and has a large, heavy rib. As in all members of this section, there are a pair of extra staminodes below the normal pair on the column. Intermediate temperatures, moisture, and partial shade are required for successful cultivation. PLATE 31

Bulbophyllum minutipetalum Schlechter (1913)

   Deep shade near the forest floor and elevations as high as 2000 m are the natural habitat of this small species which belongs to the section *Peltopus*. The white flowers open widely and are held on pedicels about 5 to 7 cm tall. The specific name, of course, refers to the extremely small petals. This plant requires a cool to intermediate environment, pots with a medium that retains moisture and, of course, shade is essential. PLATE 32

Bulbophyllum minutissimum (F. von Mueller) F. von Mueller (1878)

SYNONYMS
Bulbophyllum moniliforme F. von Mueller (1878), not *B. moniliforme* Parish &
   Reichenbach fil. (1874) also of the section *Minutissima*
Dendrobium minutissimum F. von Mueller (1865), *Phyllorchis minutissima*
   (F. von Mueller) Kuntze (1891)

   This well-named orchid is the type species of the section *Minutissima* as defined by Ernst Pfitzer in 1888. It has pseudobulbs that are only 0.3 cm in diameter, flattened, and green with red suffusions. The pseudobulbs are quite close together on the rhizomes and form large masses. The leaves are less than 0.1 cm long, and the inflorescence is 0.3 cm long. The ovary is hirsute, and the single flower is about 0.3 cm long and opens widely to show off its dark red stripes on a pale background. The species grows on trees or rocks and can be mounted on small pieces of cork at intermediate temperatures in light shade and with only moderate humidity. An eye loupe or other type of magnification is strongly advised to see the charming flowers.

Bulbophyllum minutulum Ridley (1924)

This tiny species of the section *Monilibulbon* has flattened oblong pseudo-bulbs that are less than 1 cm with a leaf 0.5 cm tall. The scape is 2 to 3 cm tall with flowers that open during the day and close at night. The dorsal sepal may be 0.7 cm long, and the recurved lateral sepals are only slightly longer. The sepals are a light orange at the base, shading to pale yellow at the apex, and have raised orange keels. The petals are 0.2 cm long, acute, and pale yellow. The labellum is recurved, elliptic, papillose, and yellow and orange. This species grows in Borneo and Malaya on tree trunks in shaded areas from 700 to almost 2000 m above sea level. It is unusual in that it grows with moss as well as on bare tree bark, so it should do well in either pots of some sort or on pieces of bark. It is a dainty little plant with the flowers standing well above the interesting pseudobulbs and would be a nice addition to a collection of unusual small orchids. There are many others in this section, all of which are quite similar and would be excellent additions to a group of miniature orchids.

Bulbophyllum moniliforme Parish & Reichenbach fil. (1874)
SYNONYM
Phyllorchis moniliforme (Parish & Reichenbach fil.) Kuntze (1891)

The pseudobulbs of this minute species, which is a member of the section *Minutissima*, are 0.5 cm in diameter, round, very wrinkled, and close together on the rhizomes. The inflorescence is about 2 cm tall and has a single yellow flower that is less than 1 cm in size. It is interesting that leaves have never been reported. In *Flora of British India* (5: 757), J. D. Hooker commented, "A remarkable little species, like a small eria." The plant grows in Laos, Cambodia, Vietnam, India, Myanmar, and Thailand at about 800 m above sea level. It can be cultivated on small mounts in intermediate to warm conditions with moderate humidity and protection from direct sun.

Bulbophyllum multiflorum Ridley (1885)

This very appropriately named species of the section *Loxosepalum* has pseudobulbs that are about 3 cm tall and 1 cm apart on the rhizome. The leaf is 8 cm tall and 1.5 cm wide. The 25-cm long inflorescence is curved and well displayed above the leaves and has many white flowers. This plant grows on tree trunks in Madagascar at 1500 m above sea level. Cork or bark slabs in light shade and intermediate temperatures are required for good cultivation. There are many more seldom seen species of this section, all quite similar. Most of them are endemic to Madagascar, but some have also been reported in the central areas of Africa.

Bulbophyllum myolaense Garay, Hamer & Siegerist (1995)

This plant is a species of the section *Polyblepharon* and was collected by Owen Stanley in an area of Papua New Guinea called Myola, after which it was named. The pseudobulbs are close together, and the leaf is 4.5 cm long and 1.7 cm wide. The inflorescence is about 6 cm long and carries one flower which is slightly larger than 2 cm in diameter. All the petals and the labellum have partially ciliate edges, while the small petal edges are completely ciliate. The labellum has an elevated median keel-like lamella. This species can be grown in intermediate to warm temperatures with frequent watering, light shade, and good air movement.

Bulbophyllum nabawanense Wood & Lamb (1944)

Described by J. J. Wood and Anthony Lamb, this pretty plant was found in Borneo near Nabawan, its namesake, growing as a terrestrial or occasionally as an epiphyte. It is a member of the section *Pahudiella*. The pseudobulbs are cylindrical and are not crowded on the rhizomes. The leaves can be 10 cm long, and there are only one or two flowers per 10-cm long inflorescence. The flowers open widely and are very pale yellow with red-purple spots and apices. The sepals are broad but the margins do not roll inward. This most attractive plant can be grown successfully at warm temperatures, in dappled shade, in either pots or baskets with a large proportion of peat moss in the mix, and needs abundant humidity.

Bulbophyllum nasica Schlechter (1913)

SYNONYM
Bulbophyllum blumei var. *pumilum* J. J. Smith (1910)

In the section *Ephippium* there is another single-flowered, easily grown species called *Bulbophyllum nasica*. In 1910 it was called *B. blumei* var. *pumilum* J. J. Smith, but Rudolf Schlechter correctly pointed out that it is totally different from what was then known as *B. blumei*, a species from Java. *Bulbophyllum nasica* comes from Papua New Guinea where it grows on tree trunks in primary rainforest at about 750 m elevation. The space between pseudobulbs is very small, and the plant is easily handled on cork or tree fern pieces. The plant is small, only about 7 cm high, and the inflorescence is slightly taller. The lateral sepals are the focal point, about 0.7 cm long, broad at the base, then quite narrow and long with swollen, verrucose tips. The flower is yellow to deep red with a reddish dorsal sepal that is striped with purple. The plant flowers more than once a year and needs frequent watering, fertilizing, and warm temperatures with light shade. It makes a most pleasant addition to any collection because of the colorful flowers and the manageable size of the plant.

Bulbophyllum nebularum Schlechter (1913)

This species is a member of the section *Epibulbon*, which consists of epiphytic plants, about 30 cm long, with pseudobulbs 1 cm tall that are held close to the rhizome. The single leaf can be as large as 6 cm long. The solitary flowers occur on short pedicels that are a little more than 1 cm long. The flowers are white with a red streak on the petals, the sepals are long and pointed, and the labellum has a glabrous surface that is red with white on the base and apex. This plant grows as an epiphyte on trees in New Guinea at an elevation of about 2500 m above sea level. Successful cultivation demands intermediate to cool temperatures and mounting on pieces of tree fern or bark. Moderate shade and good air movement are also necessary.

Bulbophyllum nematopodum F. von Mueller (1873)

SYNONYM
Phyllorchis nematopoda (F. von Mueller) Kuntze (1891)

This species is a member of the section *Nematorhizis*. The clustered pseudobulbs can be 2 cm tall, oval, tapering to a narrow apex, and are encased in the stringy remains of the bracts. The erect leaves can be 13 cm tall and 2 cm wide, with 3-cm petioles. The inflorescence is often 7 cm tall with a single flower on a declined peduncle. These flowers are about 1 cm in size and cream colored or yellow green with red markings and a red labellum. The dorsal sepal is less than 1 cm in size and cucullate, and the lateral sepals are about 1 cm long, 0.5 cm wide, and ovate. This species is endemic to Australia at altitudes above 750 m in cloud forests where it grows as an epiphyte. It can be handled in small pots or baskets or on mounts with intermediate temperatures, light shade, and regular watering.

Bulbophyllum newportii (F. M. Bailey) Rolfe (1909)

SYNONYMS
Bulbophyllum trilobum Schlechter (1910)
Sarcochilus newportii F. M. Bailey (1902)

The leaves of this species of the section *Adelopetalum* are about 4 cm long and the flowers number three to six per inflorescence. They are held above the leaves and are a very pale pink or white overlaid with burgundy or mahogany spots, while the labellum is pale yellow and spotted with burgundy. Individual flowers are less than 1 cm in size but are very nicely displayed. The natural habitat is the Australian rain forests or cloud forests either as an epiphyte or lithophyte at moderate altitudes. This species can be grown in pots or baskets or on medium-sized mounts. It needs intermediate temperatures and frequent misting with slight shade. The clone 'Emly' CBR/AOS was awarded in St. Louis, Missouri, in May 1993. Other species in the section *Adelopetalum* are worthwhile adding to a collection if possible, such as *Bulbophyllum boonjee* Gray & Jones (1984) and *B. wilkianum* Hunt (1947).

Bulbophyllum nigrescens Rolfe (1910)

The pseudobulbs of this species are ovoid, about 1.5 cm tall, and 1.5 cm apart on the rhizomes. The leaf is about 11 cm long and 1.5 cm wide. The raceme is much longer than the leaf and carries many small pendulous flowers. The sepals are pale yellow, heavily lined and dotted with black purple, and are apically and marginally hirsute. The petals and labellum are black purple, and the anterior and margins are hirsute. These plants grow in southern China, Myanmar, Thailand, and Vietnam at altitudes of 500 to 1300 m above sea level. They can be cultivated in small pots or baskets in warm to intermediate conditions with fairly high humidity.

Bulbophyllum nigropurpureum Carr (1932)

The pseudobulbs of this tiny member of the section *Polyblepharon* are minute, only 0.2 cm wide, globular, and crowded together on the rhizomes. The leaf is 4 cm long, and several inflorescences arise from each tuft of dry sheaths at the bases of the pseudobulbs. The scape is only 2 cm long and has one dark purple flower that opens widely. *Bulbophyllum nigropurpureum* grows near rivers on old mangrove trees in the low elevations of Malaya and Singapore and should be cultivated on small cork, tree fern, or similar mounts in shade with warm temperatures and high humidity.

Bulbophyllum nymphopolitanum Kraenzlin (1916)

The pseudobulbs of this member of the section *Lepidorhiza* are about 4 cm long and 2 cm wide, and the leaf is approximately 12 cm long and 4 cm wide. The raceme is shorter than the leaf with four or fewer flowers spaced slightly apart and flowering successively. The dorsal sepal is 3 cm long, and the lateral sepals are 3.5 cm with the margins apically incurved. The petals are 1.5 cm long and are reflexed, while the trilobed labellum is 2.5 cm long. The flowers are dark red-purple and the labellum is a dark, shiny puce. This species is also from the Philippines and requires some shade and warm, humid growing conditions.

Bulbophyllum obtusum (Blume) Lindley (1839)

SYNONYM
Diphyes obtusa Blume (1825)

This species is a member of the section *Fruticicola* and has the typical hanging, sheathed rhizomes with the pseudobulbs appressed to it. The flowers are orange, and the labellum is not papillose but is hirsute on the underside. *Bulbophyllum obtusum* grows in Malaya, Sumatra, Java, and Borneo at elevations as high as 1700 m above sea level. It prefers to be grown on mounts in intermediate to warm temperatures with light shade and high humidity.

Bulbophyllum obyrnei Garay, Hamer & Siegerist (1995)
SYNONYM
Osyricera ovata Bailey (1907), not *Bulbophyllum ovatum* Seidenfaden (1979)

Despite the connate lateral sepals, this plant is referred to section *Polyblepharon*. The specific epithet was originally spelled with an apostrophe, as "*o'byrnei.*" The species has been found in Papua New Guinea and is named in honor of Peter O'Byrne of the United World College of Southeast Asia in Singapore.

Bulbophyllum ochroleucum Schlechter (1905)

This species, the type of the section *Uncifera* as described by Rudolf Schlechter in 1912, is a rambling, often pendent plant with pseudobulbs sometimes 10 cm apart on the rhizomes. The single leaf is 12 cm long, and the inflorescence is very short, often with many of them together, each bearing up to nine tiny flowers. The flowers are pale, usually shades of yellow or orange. This species grows as a terrestrial or epiphyte in damp areas of Indonesia and New Guinea, about 1200 m above sea level. It can best be cultivated on large slabs of tree fern in moist, shaded, warm to intermediate conditions. There are a number of other species in this section, but they are all quite similar. Most of them are endemic to New Guinea, but *Bulbophyllum hatusimanum* Tuyama (1940) has been found in Guam and a few are from Australia.

Bulbophyllum odoratissimum (J. E. Smith) Lindley (1830)
SYNONYMS
Phyllorchis odoratissima (J. E. Smith) Kuntze (1891), *Stelis odoratissima*
J. E. Smith (1816), *Tribrachia odoratissima* (J. E. Smith) Lindley (1826)
Stelis caudata D. Don (1825)

The habit of this member of the section *Medusa* is very similar to that of *Bulbophyllum congestum* with pseudobulbs that are 2.5 cm tall, subcylindric, at least 3.5 cm apart on the rhizomes, and with a 7.5-cm long leaf. The flowers, however, are larger, the lateral sepals are yellow at their apex, and the labellum is reddish brown. This orchid has the unusual distinction of being one of the very few in the genus that has a pleasant odor. Distribution is throughout India, Nepal, China, Thailand, Myanmar, Laos, and Vietnam, and culture is best in baskets or pots with a loose mix, dappled shade, warm temperatures, and regular watering and fertilization. PLATE 33

Bulbophyllum odoratum (Blume) Lindley (1830)

SYNONYMS
Bulbophyllum elatius Ridley (1896)
Bulbophyllum tylophorum Schlechter (1912)
Diphyes odorata Blume (1825), *Phyllorchis odorata* (Blume) Kuntze (1891)

This species, the type of the section *Aphanobulbon* as described by Rudolf Schlechter in 1911, has minute pseudobulbs that are close together on the rhizomes, large leaves up to 40 cm tall, and an inflorescence sometimes more than twice as long as the leaves. There are many pale flowers, usually yellow or green, and they often have yellowish apices on the sepals and petals. These tiny flowers are less than 0.5 cm in size and even though the flowers are small, they open widely and appear almost triangular. Since there are so many of them and they are well spaced on the inflorescence, they make a very nice showing. The habitat is large, ranging from Malaya, Sumatra, Borneo, Sulawesi, and throughout the Philippines, where the plants grow as epiphytes at low altitudes on trees that are near rivers. The plants can be grown in pots if they (the plants) are large enough to support the massive leaves. Warm temperatures with some shade and a lot of moisture and good air circulation are necessary.

Bulbophyllum orbiculare J. J. Smith (1913)

SYNONYM
Bulbophyllum verrucirhachis Schlechter (1913)

This interesting, small plant of the section *Ischnopus* has 2-cm rounded pseudobulbs as far apart on the rhizomes as 7 cm and leaves that can reach 12 cm long. The inflorescence may be 32 cm long with a fractiflex rachis to 11 cm which can carry as many as 30 flowers. These flowers may open a few at a time or have many open at once. They range in size from 1 cm to about 1.5 cm long and have a distinctively ciliate labellum. The species grows as an epiphyte in forests at 650 to 2500 m above sea level in Indonesia, Papua New Guinea, and the Solomon Islands. Cultivation could be on slabs with moss under the roots or in shallow baskets or pots with any medium that holds moisture. The plants need semishade and intermediate to warm temperatures.

Bulbophyllum orectopetalum Garay, Hamer & Siegerist (1992)

This plant was called *Bulbophyllum lobbii* by Seidenfaden and Smitinand, but when fresh material was examined it was deemed to be a new species and so described. It is similar to *B. lobbii* but the flowers are much smaller (2.5

cm wide) and pale cream suffused purple within, and the petals are out-stretched, erect, and dominate the flower, hence the specific name. *Bulbophyllum orectopetalum* is known only from Thailand and is best grown in pots or baskets with an open potting mix, light shade, and intermediate temperatures. PLATE 34

Bulbophyllum ornithoglossum Schlechter (1913)

The pseudobulbs of this member of the section *Ephippium* are four angled, 1.5 cm tall, and about 1 cm apart on the rhizome with a leaf 6 cm long and 1 cm wide. The single flower is held on a 5-cm tall inflorescence and has sepals slightly less than 2 cm long, a minute petal, and a labellum that is only 0.7 cm long. As is true for other species in this section, the labellum is basally widened, then tapers abruptly, and extends into a long, narrow apex. The flowers are pale tan and are dotted and striped in a darker shade. The plants grow on trees in New Guinea at about 400 m altitude and can be cultivated in pots or baskets or on slabs in warm environments with regular moisture and fertilizer. All the plants in this section are admirable additions to an orchid collection and all are easy to grow in warm, humid, lightly shaded areas.

Bulbophyllum ornithorhynchum (J. J. Smith) Garay, Hamer & Siegerist (1992)

SYNONYM
Cirrhopetalum ornithorhynchum J. J. Smith (1903)

This species, endemic to Java, is very similar to the others in the section *Hyalosema*, but the flower is cream colored with brown-red markings on the back of the dorsal sepal. The petals are triangular with long, slender apices that end in a wonderful small teardrop which hangs down over the outer edges of the lateral sepals. Cultivation can best be accomplished in warm, humid, lightly shaded areas in pots or baskets with a mix that drains well. PLATE 35

Bulbophyllum orthoglossum Wendland & Kraenzlin (1896)

Another member of the section *Lepidorhiza* that comes from the Philippines and Borneo is this bright yellow-green species which is quite similar to the others in this section but the labellum is unique. It has three lobes, with the side lobes rather small, papillose, and curved down, while the midlobe is basally thickened. The column wings are tapered into a long, bristly tooth. Warm and humid conditions with partial shade are needed to insure good growth. PLATE 36

Bulbophyllum oxychilum Schlechter (1901)

SYNONYMS

Bulbophyllum buntingii Rendle (1913)

Bulbophyllum ellipticum De Wildeman (1921), not *B. ellipticum* Schlechter (1913) of the section *Epibulbon*

The pseudobulbs of this member of the section *Cocoina* are slightly larger than 2 cm tall and 1.5 cm wide, angled, and 2 cm apart on the rhizome. The leaf can be as long as 12 cm and has an acute apex. The inflorescence is sometimes more than 30 cm long with 100 flowers. The flowers are less than 1 cm in size and white or pale pink; many of the flowers in the raceme open simultaneously, making a lush display. The plants grow from sea level to about 500 m elevation in central Africa in moist conditions and should be cultivated in slightly shaded warm areas. Pots with a generous amount of moss or some such moisture-retentive material give the best results.

Bulbophyllum papilio J. J. Smith (1910)

This large but very interesting species is a member of the section *Intervallatae* with leaves about 24 cm long and an inflorescence that can be 75 cm long, drooping down below the pseudobulbs. Each inflorescence displays only one 5-cm purple-and-yellow flower at a time but produces many of them over a season. This orchid grows in forests at rather high elevations in Irian Jaya and Papua New Guinea and should be grown on slabs or in hanging baskets in cool, moist conditions with shade. If its size can be accommodated, this plant will give a long period of very satisfactory bloom.

Bulbophyllum pardalotum Garay, Hamer & Siegerist (1995)

This small species also has the rambling habit typical of the section *Nematorhizis*, but the delightful flowers make it highly desirable in the orchid collection. It is not as rampant a grower as some others in the section with 1 cm or so between the four-sided pseudobulbs. The leaves are about 3 cm long and the inflorescence is only slightly longer, but the flowers open widely, are 4 cm long and bright yellow-orange with red dotted stripes, and have a bright orange labellum with hirsute edges. The flowers have the interesting characteristic of opening in the morning and closing each day in the late afternoon. This species grows in the Philippines, not Papua New Guinea as has been frequently stated, and can be cultivated on tree fern slabs or poles in warm conditions. A well-grown plant will almost always be in flower.

Bulbophyllum parviflorum Parish & Reichenbach fil. (1874)

SYNONYM

Phyllorchis parviflora (Parish & Reichenbach fil.) Kuntze (1891)

This species has 2-cm pseudobulbs that are 5 cm apart on the rhizomes. The leaves are about 12 cm long and 2 cm wide, and the inflorescence is about 18 cm tall with many white flowers. The lateral sepals, petals, and labellum are somewhat hirsute. The species grows in Myanmar and Thailand at 400 m elevation and requires warm, moist conditions.

Bulbophyllum patens King ex Hooker fil. (1890)
SYNONYM
Phyllorchis patens (Hooker fil.) Kuntze (1891)

In the section *Stenochilus* is *Bulbophyllum patens* which differs from *B. macranthum* only in having wider leaves and a much smaller and darker flower. It grows in India, Thailand, Malaya, Borneo, and Sumatra on trees at sea level or slightly higher. Warm temperatures, shade, and ample humidity are required for good results.

Bulbophyllum pavimentatum Lindley (1862)
SYNONYMS
Bulbophyllum dorotheae Rendle (1913)
Bulbophyllum papillosum Finet (1903)
Bulbophyllum yangambiense Louis & Mullenders ex Geerinck (1976)
Phyllorchis pavimentata (Lindley) Kuntze (1891)

This attractive species is a member of the section *Pendula*. The pseudobulbs are smaller than 4 cm tall by 2 cm wide and are clustered together on the rhizome. The leaves can be more than 20 cm long and the inflorescence more than 30 cm long. The rachis is graceful, arching, to 20 cm long. There are many flowers about 1.5 cm wide that only partially open, but they are quite colorful with pale sepals that are suffused with purple and their tips are thickened and papillose. The petals are white and the labellum has lateral lobes which are densely ciliate. This species grows in Nigeria, Cameroon, Gabon, and Zaire and can be cultivated in pots or baskets with moss or fiber on the surface to hold moisture or on well-padded slabs at warm to intermediate temperatures with no direct sunlight.

Bulbophyllum pectinatum Finet (1897)
This attractive species of the section *Sestochilos* has pseudobulbs about 1 cm tall that are clustered together and leaves that are 6 cm long and 1.5 cm wide. The flowers are close to 4 cm long and more than 5 cm wide and are held upright on curving pedicels that are approximately the same length as the leaves. The sepals and petals are white or pale green with dark red dots that form stripes. The column is pure white, and the labellum is pale yellow with very dark red papillae on the turned-down apex and erose edges of the median portion. The underside of the labellum is white and is held on a very

long (over 2 cm) thin, red-striped column foot. The species grows in Thailand, Vietnam, India, southern China, Taiwan, Indochina, and Myanmar at 1500 m above sea level. It can be grown in intermediate conditions in either a pot or basket or mounted on a slab, but a bit of shade and a lot of moisture are needed. This is a nice plant for coffee tables when grown in a pot because the flowers are very attractive and sure to be a subject of conversation. A very similar species, *Bulbophyllum spectabile* Rolfe (1898), grows in Myanmar, China, and Thailand.

Bulbophyllum penicillium Parish & Reichenbach fil. (1874)
SYNONYM
Bulbophyllum inopinatum W. W. Smith (1915)

The pseudobulbs of this species are about 2.5 cm tall and close to one another on the rhizome, and the leaves are 15 cm long. The raceme is more than 30 cm long, with the peduncle slightly thickened and decurved, and it bears numerous small, lax flowers. The flowers are yellow with the petals and labellum heavily edged with long purple hairs. This species grows at an altitude of about 2000 m in India and Myanmar and requires intermediate temperatures to grow well.

Bulbophyllum petiolare Thwaites (1861)

The pseudobulbs of this small epiphyte resemble an elongated pea and are arranged like a chain with 5-cm long leaves on 2.5-cm petioles. The erect inflorescence can be 7.5 cm long with four or five greenish-orange flowers that have a red labellum. The sepals are about 0.5 cm long, and the petals half that size. The species is endemic to the wet evergreen forests of Sri Lanka as high as 1300 m above sea level. The plants should be cultivated in pots or baskets or on slabs in intermediate temperatures with high humidity and light shade.

Bulbophyllum phalaenopsis J. J. Smith (1937)

This species is a member of the section *Macrobulbon* and in horticulture has been called *Bulbophyllum giganteum*. It has enormous leaves, and the specific name undoubtedly refers to their resemblance to the leaves of *Phalaenopsis gigantea*. The flowers are dark blood red and have long yellow protuberances from the outside of the sepals and petals, making them resemble (at least to the flies) rotting flesh covered with maggots. The accompanying odor means that this plant must be housed outside when in flower, where it will be visited by every fly in the vicinity. It can be cultivated in pots filled with tree fern and, despite the obviously malodorous scent, has an extremely interesting flower. Warm temperatures, shade from intense light, and good air circulation are a must. PLATE 37

Bulbophyllum planibulbe (Ridley) Ridley (1907)

SYNONYM

Cirrhopetalum planibulbe Ridley (1893)

This small species has pseudobulbs that are 1.5 cm tall and less than 1 cm wide, and are flattened and appressed horizontally to the rhizome. They can be as far apart as 5 cm and carry a leaf that is 2.5 cm long. The scape is 9 cm tall and usually has two flowers but can carry as many as five flowers. The dorsal sepal is 1 cm long and 0.5 cm wide, concave, with a long pointed apex. The lateral sepals are 1.8 cm long and 0.3 cm wide, free, also with a long pointed apex, and all sepals are yellow and are heavily spotted with dark purple except on the edges. The petals are less than 0.5 cm long and bright yellow. The labellum is small, curved, and orange. Henry N. Ridley said of this species, "A very curious little plant, distinguished from all others known to me by the pseudobulbs lying flat on the very slender stems, which thus traverse them for their whole length and are adnate to them." This plant looks best when grown on a slab of coconut husk or tree fern or something similar because that gives the long inflorescence an opportunity to show off the bright flowers to best advantage. It grows in Thailand, Malaya, and Sumatra and can be cultivated in warm, moist conditions. Variety *sumatranum* J. J. Smith (1932) has flowers that are almost twice as large.

Bulbophyllum plumula Schlechter (1913)

This small plant from New Guinea is part of the section *Polyblepharon*, is only 6 cm tall, and has an inflorescence that is 10 cm long. The sepals are about 1.6 cm long and the minute petals are edged with cilia. The flower displays a remarkable labellum that can be almost 1.5 cm long, is very thin, and is almost completely covered with long hairs. The elongated sepals and the labellum are dark red. This species grows from 700 to 1000 m elevation and can be cultivated in pots or baskets in warm to intermediate temperatures and light shade. It is an easy plant to grow and attracts a lot of attention because of the extraordinary labellum. PLATE 38

Bulbophyllum polyrhizum Lindley (1830)

The most noticeable characteristic of this species of the section *Racemosae* is the crowded pseudobulbs which when young are glossy and covered with thin sheaths. When older, they develop a number of concentric rings and become very rugose. The leaves are 6 to 7 cm long and deciduous when flowering takes place. The scape is 8 to 13 cm tall, inclined, with six to eight pale green or yellow flowers that are less than 1 cm long. The species grows in Nepal at elevations up to 1000 m above sea level and can be cultivated in pots or baskets at intermediate to warm temperatures and slight shade. The interesting pseudobulbs and the easily seen flowers make this a very desirable species to grow.

Bulbophyllum ponapense Schlechter (1921)

This small epiphyte grows in the Caroline Islands at low elevations and is a member of the section *Fruticicola* with hanging rhizomes that have the pseudobulbs closely appressed to them. The flowers are quite attractive because they are red and yellow and a bit more openly displayed than are some of the other flowers in this section. Hanging slabs, frequent watering, warmth, and shade are necessary for optimum growth and flowering.

Bulbophyllum popayanense Lehmann & Kraenzlin (1899)

This species was named after the highlands of Popayán, Colombia, where it was discovered, and belongs to the section *Didactyle*. It grows as high as 1800 m above sea level and requires intermediate temperatures. The pseudobulbs have sharp angles and are only a few centimeters apart, and the long, arching inflorescence rises well above the 14-cm long leaves. The flowers are racemose, are about 1 cm wide, are very pale yellow brown or lavender with darker markings, and the labellum has a large, heavy rib. There are a pair of extra staminodes below the usual pair on the column. Cultivation requires intermediate temperatures, a moist environment, and moderate shade.

Bulbophyllum posticum J. J. Smith (1911)

The pseudobulbs of this species of the section *Diceras* are about 6 cm apart on a pendent rhizome that can be 60 cm long. Leaves are about 6 cm long, and there are many single-flowered inflorescences. The flowers are cream colored with maroon veins and labellum, and the horns on the basal portion of the labellum are quite distinct. This species grows on trees below 2500 m altitude in Indonesia and New Guinea. The plants should be grown on a piece of wood, tree fern, or cork and hung in an area where they will have intermediate to cool temperatures, light shade, and good humidity and air circulation.

Bulbophyllum psittacoglossum Reichenbach fil. (1853)

SYNONYMS

Phyllorchis psittacoglossa (Reichenbach fil.) Kuntze (1891), *Sarcopodium psittacoglossum* (Reichenbach fil.) Hooker fil. (1863)

This is another species of the section *Leopardinae* with a somewhat different growing habit because the pseudobulbs are quite close together, making it easier to confine to the pot. The flowers are lovely, pale yellow with dark red stripes. The plant comes from India, Myanmar, and Thailand, sometimes as high as 1800 m, and adjusts well to intermediate conditions, either in pots or baskets or on mounts, as long as it is well supplied with moisture, light shade, and good air circulation.

Bulbophyllum pumilum (Swartz) Lindley (1830)

SYNONYMS
Bulbophyllum calabaricum Rolfe (1906)
Bulbophyllum drallei Reichenbach fil. (1885)
Bulbophyllum flavidum Lindley (1840)
Bulbophyllum gabonis Lindley & Reichenbach fil. (1865)
Bulbophyllum herminiostachys (Reichenbach fil.) Reichenbach fil. (1861)
Bulbophyllum leucopogon Kraenzlin (1912)
Bulbophyllum moliwense Schlechter (1906)
Bulbophyllum nanum De Wildeman (1903)
Bulbophyllum porphyroglossum Kraenzlin (1895)
Dendrobium pumilum Swartz (1805), *Genyorchis pumila* (Swartz) Schlechter (1901)

The pseudobulbs of this popular plant that belongs to the section *Cocoina* are about 4 cm tall, slightly less than 2 cm wide, and 2 cm apart on the rhizomes. The leaf can be longer than 20 cm and is about 4 cm wide. The inflorescence is often 30 cm long with about 60 flowers that open simultaneously in a spreading raceme. The flowers are less than 1 cm in size and are pale cream or green and often have purple suffusions. The plant usually grows as an epiphyte on large trees but sometimes as a lithophyte in the central portions of Africa at altitudes up to 1900 m above sea level. Cultivation should be in moist, intermediate to warm conditions in pots or baskets and with partial shade.

Bulbophyllum purpureum Thwaites (1861)

The pseudobulbs of this small epiphyte are ovoid, 0.5 cm long, and very close together on the rhizomes. The leaf is at most 2.5 cm long and 0.7 cm wide. The inflorescence is less than 2.5 cm long, with an umbel of 0.2-cm wide purple flowers on a sharply deflexed pedicel. The dorsal sepal is 0.3 to 0.4 cm long, subulate, and declined. The lateral sepals are connivent, and the petals and labellum are minute. The plants grow on trees in wet evergreen forests of Sri Lanka at altitudes of 500 to 1300 m above sea level. They should be cultivated on twigs or small slabs in warm, shaded areas and with high humidity. This is one plant where it would be wise to supply eye loupes or other magnification for visitors to observe the flowers.

Bulbophyllum pygmaeum (J. E. Smith) Lindley (1861)

SYNONYMS
Bulbophyllum ichthyostomum Colenso (1894)
Dendrobium pygmaeum J. E. Smith (1808)

This descriptively named species is the type of the section *Pygmaea* which was described by Heinrich Gustav Reichenbach in 1861 and forms dense mats on trees and rocks in New Zealand. The pseudobulbs are about 0.3 cm in diameter and the leaf may be 1.7 cm long. There is a single, minute, white flower on a very short inflorescence. Plants can be grown in intermediate temperatures on small slabs with constant high humidity. A magnifying glass or eye loupe is recommended to fully appreciate the tiny flowers.

Bulbophyllum quadrangulare J. J. Smith (1911)

This species has conical pseudobulbs about 2 cm tall and 3 cm apart on the branching rhizomes. The leaf is lanceolate, about 7 cm long and 1.5 cm wide. The inflorescence arises from the rhizome and can be erect or pendent, almost 20 cm long, and has one colorful flower which is often 3 cm tall and 2 cm wide. The narrow dorsal sepal is more than 3 cm long with edges that roll inwards, and the lateral sepals are about the same size as the dorsal, striped red on a pale ground, and reflexed at the base. The minute petals are papillose and the three-lobed labellum is less than 1 cm long. This species belongs to the section *Megaloglossum* and grows in Irian Jaya as well as Papua New Guinea from sea level to over 300 m altitude. It prefers very wet areas and tree branches that are covered with moss. The flowers open widely for a few hours each morning and then close. It can be grown under warm, very moist conditions either on slabs or in pots or baskets. A layer of spaghnum on top of the potting media helps to conserve the necessary moisture, and protection from direct sunlight is essential to good growth.

Bulbophyllum radiatum Lindley (1830)

SYNONYM
Phyllorchis radiata (Lindley) Kuntze (1891)

The pseudobulbs of this species of the section *Corymbosia* are about 2 cm tall, subcylindric, and 1 cm apart on the rhizomes. The leaf is 5 cm long, and the inflorescence is 6 cm long with a cluster of yellowish or white flowers that have thin segments. This species is native to China, Hong Kong, Myanmar, Thailand, and Malaya at relatively low elevations. It can be grown in pots or baskets in warm areas with a bit of shade and regular watering.

Bulbophyllum radicans F. M. Bailey (1897)

SYNONYM
Bulbophyllum cilioglossum Rogers & Nicholls (1935)

This species has the typical pendent, apically upcurved rhizomes of the section *Fruticicola* with leaves that can be 8 cm long. The inflorescence is at most 1 cm long with one 0.5-cm flower that does not open widely. The flowers are pale white or pink with dark red margins and stripes, while the labellum is yellow and has red cilia on the reverse side. The plant is indigenous to Australia where it grows on trees or rocks from sea level to 1000 m elevation. Warm to intermediate temperatures and protection from direct sunlight should result in flowering several times a year.

Bulbophyllum recurvum Lindley (1830)
SYNONYMS
Phyllorchis recurva (Lindley) Kuntze (1891)
Tribrachia pendula Lindley (1825)

This species is a member of the section *Pendula* and is quite similar to *Bulbophyllum pavimentatum* with densely clustered pseudobulbs and a long inflorescence which can be even more pendulous. The flowers are quite colorful with sepal tips that are suffused purple and are only slightly papillose. The plant grows in Sierra Leone and Nigeria and can be cultivated in warm, semishaded, humid areas on padded mounts or in pots or baskets with a layer of moss or coconut fiber on top to help keep the plants moist.

Bulbophyllum reflexum Ames & Schweinfurth (1920)

This species was named by Oakes Ames and Charles Schweinfurth in 1920 and is part of the section *Globiceps*, but is sometimes confused with *Bulbophyllum coniferum* which was discussed earlier. The pseudobulbs are about 1 cm apart on the rhizome and are 1 to 2 cm tall. The leaves are as tall as 15 cm and are elliptic, and the inflorescence is more than 20 cm long with many flowers in a dense raceme. The flowers are small, less than 0.5 cm, pale with dark purple markings, and all sepals and petals, as well as the labellum, are shortly hirsute on the edges. Unfortunately, this flower, as is the case with so many in this genus, has a rather unpleasant odor. It grows as an epiphyte on mossy trees in forests at 1000 to 2000 m altitude in Malaya, Sumatra, Borneo, and Java. Successful cultivation requires an intermediate temperature and ample moisture with mottled shade and planting in either pots or baskets.

Bulbophyllum repens Griffith (1851)
SYNONYM
Bulbophyllum khasyanum Reichenbach fil. (1874)

This attractive orchid belongs to the section *Globiceps* and has small pseudobulbs that are close together, leaves that are about 1.3 cm long, and flowers that are held on a short scape. The flowers form a dense, globose, conical head and are deep reddish brown with dark purple lines on the sepals and a yellow edge to the dorsal sepal and labellum. In some clones the entire flower is lighter in color and the labellum is a lovely pale yellow. Despite being held on a scape that is shorter than the leaves, the flowers are easily seen. The awarded clone 'Emly' CBR/AOS was grown on a cork raft in an intermediate to warm greenhouse, in light shade, with daily misting and frequent fertilization. This species is native to Thailand, Myanmar, and India at moderate elevations. PLATE 39

Bulbophyllum restrepia (Ridley) Ridley (1907)

SYNONYM
Cirrhopetalum restrepia Ridley (1893)

Henry N. Ridley named this species after the South American genus *Restrepia* which the flower resembles. The pseudobulbs are about 1 cm tall and 1 cm apart on the rhizome, and have a leaf that can be 7 cm long and 2.5 cm wide at the apex. The inflorescence is 6 cm tall with an ovary more than 2 cm long which carries the flower above the leaves. The dorsal sepal is narrow, 1.5 cm long, pale green edged with red. The lateral sepals are 2.5 cm long and about 0.5 cm wide at the base. Their narrow apices join and they are yellow with red dots on the lower portions and edges. The petals and labellum are minute. This species grows in the lowlands of the Malay Peninsula and Borneo and requires warm temperatures to thrive. It can be grown in pots or baskets with a mix that retains moisture.

Bulbophyllum reticosum Ridley (1896)

In 1991 a very nice clone of *Bulbophyllum reticosum* was awarded a CBR/ AOS as *B. dearei* 'Berryessa'. *Bulbophyllum reticosum* is almost identical to *B. dearei*, but the two can be distinguished from one another by the pubescent labellum of *B. dearei* and the dorsal sepal of *B. reticosum* that reaches over the lateral sepals. Each has a pretty flower that is often carried above the leaves, making it very easy to enjoy. The plants can be cultivated in intermediate temperatures, mottled shade, and moist conditions.

Bulbophyllum rhodostictum Schlechter (1913)

This species is a member of the section *Papulipetalum* and grows on moss-covered trees near rivers at elevations of 350 to 450 m above sea level in New Guinea. The pseudobulbs are less than 0.5 cm tall and are crowded together on creeping rhizomes which are often covered with moss. The single leaf is about 10 cm tall, and the inflorescence is 6 cm long and drooping. It bears one small flower that is approximately 1 cm in diameter and pale yellow or green with lilac suffusions. The very small petals have long papillae at their apices. Unfortunately, the flowers last only a few days, but nevertheless this is a congenial plant that does not stray too far, has interesting pseudobulbs that are arranged alternately on the rhizome, and is not difficult to grow. It requires ample moisture, half shade, and warm conditions.

Bulbophyllum rubiferum J. J. Smith (1918)

Another member of the section *Globiceps*, *Bulbophyllum rubiferum* has pseudobulbs that are close together and tiny, and it has one leaf about 7 cm long. The pendent inflorescence can be 8 cm long with a few unusual flowers held in a semiumbel. The sepals are less than 0.5 cm long and pinkish with darker veins, and the petals are minute. The center of attraction is the dark, thick, papillose labellum. This plant grows in Borneo and Java near the bases of tree trunks at about 1500 m elevation. Cultivation should be on padded mounts of bark or cholla at intermediate temperatures with shade and consistent high humidity.

Bulbophyllum rufilabrum Parish ex Hooker fil. (1888)

SYNONYM
Bulbophyllum limbatum Parish & Reichenbach fil. (1874)

This species is a member of the section *Careyana*, and the pseudobulbs as well as the leaves are each about 5 cm long and the scape is 6 cm tall. The flowers are less than 0.5 cm long and are brown purple with cream-colored bracts. The plant grows in Thailand and India and can be cultivated in pots or baskets or on slabs in warm and lightly shaded areas.

Bulbophyllum rupicola Barbosa Rodrigues (1822)

In Brazil we find this most interesting small orchid which is a member of the section *Micrantha*. The crowded pseudobulbs are less than 2 cm tall, the semiterete leaves are about 3.5 cm long, and the flowers grow on a long, arching inflorescence. The white flowers are tiny but beautifully displayed when mounted on tree fern or some other slab. Again, warm conditions, light shade, and ample water are necessary for optimum growth and flowering.

Bulbophyllum salaccense Reichenbach fil. (1857)

This species of section *Cochlia* is pendent with narrow pseudobulbs less than 1 cm long that are appressed to the rhizome. The leaves are 8 cm long by 4 cm wide and distichous, and the inflorescence is 3 cm long with as many as 20 very small, dark purple flowers held in a globular head. The obtuse lateral sepals are free at the base. The plants grow on trees in Java, Malaya, Sumatra, and Borneo at elevations of 1200 to 2000 m above sea level. They can be grown on slabs in intermediate conditions, with slight shade and with frequent applications of water.

Bulbophyllum saltatorium Lindley (1837)

SYNONYM
Phyllorchis saltatoria (Lindley) Kuntze (1891)

This member of the section *Ptiloglossum* is very similar to *Bulbophyllum barbigerum*. When the name was published in the *Botanical Register* by Lindley, a fine drawing of the plant with enlargements of the various flower parts was included. The pseudobulbs are 3 cm apart and less than 3 cm tall, and the narrow leaves can be as long as 10 or 11 cm. The inflorescence is frequently as long as 7 or 8 cm, and the many-flowered rachis is about 4 cm long. The individual flowers are small, they all open at the same time and have a labellum with fine but fluffy and very mobile hairs. The entire flower is various shades of purple, including the hairs. The species grows in trees in lowland forests in the African countries bordering the Atlantic Ocean just north of the equator. Culture should include potting in a rich, moisture-retentive mixture and supplying high humidity, some shade, and warm temperatures.

Bulbophyllum samoanum Schlechter (1911)

SYNONYM
Bulbophyllum christophersenii L. O. Williams (1939)

The pseudobulbs of this species are about 1.5 cm tall and 0.8 cm wide, and crowded on the rhizome. The leaves are about 14 cm long. The inflorescence is single flowered, approximately 12 cm tall. The dorsal sepal is erect, 1 cm long and 0.5 cm wide, the lateral sepals 1.5 cm long and 0.5 cm wide, spreading, and the petals and labellum are minute. The flowers are pale yellow green with red-purple markings. The species is found in New Caledonia, New Hebrides, Fiji, and Samoa from 300 to 900 m above sea level. It, too, needs warm and moist conditions to grow well.

Bulbophyllum saronae Garay (1999)

This plant from Papua New Guinea belongs to the section *Hyalosema*. The pseudobulbs are about 3 cm tall and 1.5 cm wide, and the leaf can be 11 cm long. The single flower is borne on an inflorescence about 10 cm long. The dorsal sepal can be 6.5 cm long and only 0.7 cm wide, the fleshy lateral sepals 5 cm long and 0.5 cm wide, the petals 0.5 cm long and 0.2 cm wide, and the labellum even smaller. The flower is pale yellow green with brownish markings and shading. Wolfgang Bandisch discovered this new orchid and named it in memory of his daughter Sharon, who died tragically in a freak accident when only two years old. Culture should be in a basket or pot with the usual loose potting medium, frequent watering, and intermediate temperatures.

Bulbophyllum saurocephalum Reichenbach fil. (1886)

SYNONYMS
Bulbophyllum ebrachteolatum Kraenzlin (1916)
Bulbophyllum erythrostachyum Rolfe (1903)

A very appropriately named species is *Bulbophyllum saurocephalum* (*sauro*, meaning "snake," and *cephalum*, "meaning head"), the type of the section of the same name as described by Rudolf Schlechter in 1911. The species is endemic to the Philippines at medium altitudes. The pseudobulbs are spaced 1 to 2 cm apart and have one leaf that can be 17 cm long. The peduncles are purple, cylindrical, swollen, with more than 30 small flat flowers distributed around it on a mature plant. These flowers, when viewed from the side, resemble the heads of snakes, hence the name of the species. The flowers are white, striped purple with a greenish-white sheath. By far the best way to display the inflorescences is to mount the plant on a slab. Warm temperatures and moist conditions guarantee good growth. The species has received several awards, including the clone 'Emly' CCM/AOS awarded in St. Louis, Missouri, in May 1991 when it had approximately 250 flowers and 100 buds on seven inflorescences with an additional 7 immature inflorescences. PLATE 40

Bulbophyllum savaiense Schlechter (1911)

This species is quite similar in all respects to the others in the section *Pelma* with the exception of the plant habit which can be patent as well as pendulous. The tiny white flowers open widely and can number as many as nine per inflorescence. The plant grows in Vanuatu, Fiji, and Samoa on moss-covered branches in open forests from 300 to 700 m elevation. It is said to have the smallest flowers of any bulbophyllum that grows in Fiji. Warm temperatures, constant humidity, and only very light shade are necessary for cultivation.

Bulbophyllum schillerianum Reichenbach fil. (1860)

SYNONYMS

Bulbophyllum aurantiacum F. von Mueller (1862), *B. aurantiacum* var. *wattsii* Bailey (1913), *Dendrobium aurantiacum* (F. von Mueller) F. von Mueller (1870), *Phyllorchis aurantiaca* (F. von Mueller) Kuntze (1891), not *B. aurantiacum* Hooker fil. (1864) of the section *Cocoina*

This pendent epiphyte of the section *Sphaeracron* can grow to 40 cm long with pseudobulbs that are less than 1 cm in size, are spaced about 1.5 cm apart on the rhizomes, and are closely appressed to them. The leaves are variable in size, from 2 to 10 cm long, and the peduncles are usually in clusters of as many as 10, but are only 0.3 to 0.4 cm long. The flowers are less than 1 cm in size, open only slightly, and are bright orange, as the synonym *Bulbophyllum aurantiacum* F. von Mueller (1892) implies. The species is endemic to Australia and grows over a wide range of variable conditions. It has been found growing in mangrove swamps and as high as 1000 m above sea level. It can be cultivated in intermediate to warm conditions but requires shade and high humidity and, of course, ample room beneath the plants for the rhizomes to hang down unhindered. The brilliant color of the flowers makes this orchid quite attractive.

Bulbophyllum schimperianum Kraenzlin (1902)

SYNONYM
Bulbophyllum acutisepalum De Wildeman (1916)

This species belonging to the section *Cocoina* was named after the collector, Mr. Schimper, who found it in the forests of Cameroon at 1850 m above sea level. The pseudobulbs are about 2.5 cm tall with a leaf that can be as long as 13 cm. The inflorescence is often as tall as 30 cm and carries many very small pale flowers that are frequently suffused with pink. The plant grows in Uganda, Liberia, Nigeria, Republic of the Congo, and Congo (Zaire) in forests from 800 to 1800 m elevation. Warm, lightly shaded, moist conditions are necessary for good culture.

Bulbophyllum scotiifolium J. J. Smith (1918)

This species is quite similar to the others in the section *Sphaeracron* with small pseudobulbs that are closely appressed to the rhizomes. The leaves are usually about 3 cm long, and their cross section is almost round with a shallow indentation. The flowers occur either singly or in pairs on very short peduncles along the rhizomes and they all bloom at one time. The sepals are less than 1 cm long, filiform, and pale yellow. The plants are endemic to Java at elevations of 250 to 1000 m above sea level. They can be cultivated on branches or slabs in warm conditions with high humidity and moderate protection from direct sunlight.

Bulbophyllum secundum Hooker fil. (1888)

SYNONYM
Phyllorchis secunda (Hooker fil.) Kuntze (1891)

The pseudobulbs of this species are globose, about 1.5 cm in diameter, and close together on the rhizomes. The leaves can be 4.5 cm long and 0.8 cm wide, and the inflorescence is more than 12 cm tall with many beautiful small red flowers. The apices of the petals and the lobes of the labellum are hirsute. The plants grow in India, Vietnam, Nepal, southern China, Myanmar, Thailand, and Laos from 2000 to 2500 m above sea level and can be cultivated in intermediate conditions.

Bulbophyllum semiteretifolium Gagnepain (1930)

The pseudobulbs of this member of the section *Corymbosia* are globose, less than 1 cm in diameter, and about 2 cm apart on the rhizomes. As the specific name indicates, the 5-cm long leaves are semiterete. The erect inflorescence is also 5 cm tall and has several small whitish flowers. The species is endemic to open forest in Vietnam at about 2000 m altitude. It can be grown in intermediate conditions in small pots or baskets, light shade, and high humidity.

Bulbophyllum semperflorens J. J. Smith (1907)

SYNONYMS
Bulbophyllum flavescens var. *triflorum* J. J. Smith (1905)
Bulbophyllum simulacrum Ames (1915)

This plant is smaller than the others mentioned in the section *Aphanobulbon* and has pseudobulbs about 1 cm apart on the rhizome and leaves and inflorescences each 11 cm tall. There are only a few flowers per inflorescence, but they are more than 1 cm in size with inrolled, marginally hirsute sepals and yellow, reflexed labellums that are also densely hirsute on the margins. The plant grows in Java and the Philippines and can be cultivated in pots or baskets in warm, shady, and moist areas. It would be a nice addition to an orchid collection because the flowers are quite attractive.

Bulbophyllum serra Schlechter (1916)

This species is a member of the section *Intervallatae* and has pseudobulbs that are 6 cm tall and only about 1 cm apart on the rhizome and a leaf that can be 30 cm long. The inflorescence is about 70 cm long, drooping, with 30 or more lax flowers that bloom successively on the fractiflex rachis. The sepals are lanceolate, about 5 cm long, and the petals are 0.5 cm long. The labellum is 5 cm long, with nodular and wavy edges. The flowers are creamy white with red suffusions at their bases and a dark red labellum. These large plants grow in New Guinea forests at about 150 to 400 m above sea level. Although the flowers last only a few days, the plants flower continuously all year and are a good addition to the collection if there is space to house them. They should be grown in large pots with a bark and fiber potting mix, liberal water, light shade, and warm temperatures. There are many others of this section that are desirable additions, such as *Bulbophyllum mamberamense* J. J. Smith (1915), *B. micronesiacum* Schlechter (1921), *B. nieuwenhuisii* J. J. Smith (1926), *B. orsidice* Ridley (1916), and *B. pristis* J. J. Smith (1913).

Bulbophyllum siamense Reichenbach fil. (1867)

Those orchids from Thailand that are called *Bulbophyllum lobbii* are often actually *B. siamense*, and, while attractive, lack the long, thin sepals and wavy, twisted petals that give *B. lobbii* the Fu Manchu look that is so charming. Nevertheless, they are nice plants to add to the collection since they are easy to grow and the flowers are pretty, if not spectacular. These, too, respond well to intermediate conditions and slight shade.

Bulbophyllum sillemianum Reichenbach fil. (1884)

Heinrich Gustav Reichenbach named this member of the section *Sestochilos* after Augustus Sillem of Sydenham, England, who imported it from Myanmar. The small round pseudobulbs are a short distance apart on the rhizome, and the inflorescence is not as tall as the leaves. The flower is a lovely lemon yellow with greenish veins and a labellum that is white with a dark maroon apex and maroon spotting. The petals reflex and wrap around the dorsal sepal in a most becoming manner. The plants can be grown in intermediate temperatures in pots or baskets, with semishade and abundant moisture. PLATE 41

Bulbophyllum singaporeanum Schlechter (1911)

This orchid had been called *Bulbophyllum densiflorum* by Henry N. Ridley in 1896, but Robert A. Rolfe had already used that specific epithet in 1892 for a different species so it cannot be used here. *Bulbophyllum singaporeanum* is a member of the section *Densiflora*. The 5-cm tall pseudobulbs are about 10 cm apart on the rhizome, and the leaf can be 30 cm long. The inflorescence is only 5 to 6 cm long, but it has many small green-and-purple flowers which, unfortunately, do not have a pleasant odor. The plant grows on trees near water in the lowlands of Borneo, Singapore, and Malaya. It requires a large slab of wood on which to mount it, warm temperatures, good air circulation, moderate shading, and an outdoor location when in flower.

Bulbophyllum spectabile Rolfe (1898)

This member of the section *Sestochilos* is often considered conspecific with *Bulbophyllum pectinatum*, but the side lobes of the labellum are less erose in this species. In other respects it is the same. It grows in India, China, Thailand, and Myanmar and also prefers intermediate temperatures. This, too, is a nice plant for moving to the living quarters when in flower as it is a good size for a small table and has most interesting large flowers.

Bulbophyllum spiesii Garay, Hamer & Siegerist (1990)

A member of Rudolf Schlechter's section *Macrobulbon*, *Bulbophyllum spiesii* has a many-flowered inflorescence that is dark blood red. It was first encountered at an orchid show in mid-America where it was noted not only because of its large leaves (86 cm long) but also because of its distinctive odor. This plant and *B. phalaenopsis* give credence to the saying that nothing in nature occurs accidentally. They both have dark red flowers and an odor that has been likened to that which is emanated by a multitude of dead elephants lying in the sun for a week. This odor quickly draws every green bottle fly in the neighborhood to feast on the supposed carrion, but actually they help (quite unintentionally) to transport the pollen from plant to plant. These are not plants to grow in the home or even in a greenhouse unless they can be moved outdoors when they are in flower. The species was named in honor of Armyn Spies of Belleville, Illinois, who collected the plants in Vanuatu. They were not in flower at the time. PLATE 42

Bulbophyllum stenobulbon Parish & Reichenbach fil. (1874)

SYNONYM

Phyllorchis stenobulbon (Parish & Reichenbach fil.) Kuntze (1891)

The pseudobulbs of this orchid are less than 2 cm tall, cylindric, and about 3 cm apart on the rhizomes. The leaf is almost 4 cm long and 1 cm wide, and the scape is about 2.5 cm long. The one or two flowers are less than 1 cm in size but nonetheless quite attractive. The sepals and petals open widely and are white with yellow-orange apices. The species grows in Laos, Vietnam, Myanmar, and Thailand and can be cultivated in warm to intermediate temperatures with high humidity and moderate shade. Small pots or baskets with a potting mix that drains well and daily watering are appropriate.

Bulbophyllum stictosepalum Schlechter (1913)

This robust epiphyte is the only member of the section *Stictosepalum*, which Rudolf Schlechter described in 1913. It can grow to 35 to 45 cm tall with pseudobulbs that are cylindric, 1 to 2 cm high, and a single leaf as long as 40 cm and 5 cm wide. The scape can be 30 cm tall and carries 5 to 10 flowers that are yellow brown with red veins. The dorsal sepal is almost 3 cm long, the lateral sepals slightly longer, and the petals less than 1 cm long. This species grows in misty forests of New Guinea at elevations of 1000 m above sea level. Schlechter enthused about this species, as he felt the lovely color, long inflorescences, and long-lived flowers would make it very worthy of cultivation. It can be grown in pots with frequent misting, light shade, and intermediate temperatures.

Bulbophyllum stolzii Schlechter (1915)

The pseudobulbs of this small creeping plant are as tall as 3 cm and often are more than 10 cm apart on the thin rhizomes. The leaves can be as long as 7 cm and are 1 cm wide. The inflorescence is about 10 cm long with a fractiflex rachis that often has as many as 10 flowers. These flowers are less than 1 cm in size, greenish with purple markings, and many of them open simultaneously. The plants grow in very moist areas of Tanzania and Malawi from 1300 to 2500 m altitude. The relatively large distance between pseudobulbs would indicate that the plants are most successfully housed on slabs of tree fern, cork, or wood. A moss layer in which the roots can retain the necessary moisture, and intermediate conditions help to assure good growth.

Bulbophyllum streptosepalum Schlechter (1913)

This species is very similar to *Bulbophyllum contortisepalum* except that the petals do not have a threadlike median lobe and the labellums are a bit different. Cultivation is the same for both species: mounting on bare slabs or in pots at warm to intermediate temperatures, in slight shade, and with frequent applications of water and fertilizer. This species flowers freely and would be a nice addition to an orchid collection.

Bulbophyllum striatum (Griffith) Reichenbach fil. (1861)

SYNONYMS

Bulbophyllum striatitepalum Seidenfaden (1982)

Dendrobium striatum Griffith (1851), *Sarcopodium striatum* (Griffith) Lindley (1853)

The pseudobulbs of this member of the section *Racemosae* are globular, 1.5 cm in diameter, and 1 to 3 cm apart on the rhizomes. The flowers are yellow green with a purple labellum. The species is endemic to Sikkim and Khasia (India) and grows at about 1500 m above sea level. Intermediate temperatures, frequent watering, light shade, and pots or baskets with a potting mix that contains some moss are necessary for these plants to grow well.

Bulbophyllum subcubicum J. J. Smith (1913)

SYNONYMS

Bulbophyllum foveatum Schlechter (1913)

Bulbophyllum quadratum Schlechter (1913)

Bulbophyllum savaiense subsp. *subcubicum* (J. J. Smith) J. J. Vermeulen (1993)

The growth habit of this species is similar to the growth habit of other members of the section *Pelma*, but rhizomes are only 40 cm long and they occasionally are branching. The pseudobulbs are almost 2 cm tall, appressed to the rhizomes, and are a dull yellow green to orange. The leaf is 4 cm long and acute. There are many inflorescences that have from two to nine flowers each. These flowers are minute, pale green or yellow green, with a red to orange labellum. Since there are so many colorful flowers at one time and they sometimes last for three weeks, they make a nice showing. The species grows throughout the Philippines, Irian Jaya, Papua New Guinea, Vanuatu, Fiji, and Samoa from sea level to 2000 m elevation. It can be grown on slabs in slightly shady, humid, warm to intermediate areas.

Bulbophyllum subumbellatum Ridley (1896)

The pseudobulbs of this species, the type of the section *Pahudiella* as defined by Leslie Garay, Fritz Hamer, and Emly Siegerist in 1993, are cylindric and can be as large as 3.5 cm tall and 0.5 cm wide, and sometimes are 7 cm apart on the rhizomes. They have one leaf that is about 15 cm long and 4 cm wide. The scape is 10 cm tall with two or three flowers that are 2 cm in size. The cucullate dorsal sepal is less than 2 cm long, the lateral sepals are basally involute with their apices reflexed, and the petals are less than 1 cm long and are aristate. The labellum is curved and very small. The sepals and petals are green with red spots and suffusions, and the labellum is dark red. The plants are found in Borneo and Java and can be cultivated in warm, moist conditions, preferably on moss-covered slabs to accommodate the spreading habit. They need to be protected from direct sunlight.

Bulbophyllum sulawesii Garay, Hamer & Siegerist (1996)

In this plant of the section *Lepidorhiza*, the pseudobulbs are close together on the rhizomes, the leaves are about 7 cm long, and the inflorescence is perhaps 60 cm tall with five or six flowers which bloom successively. The dorsal sepal is from 5 to more than 8 cm long and a bit more than 1 cm wide, the lateral sepals can be as large as 12 cm long and 1.2 cm wide, and the petals are almost 3 cm long and 1.2 cm wide. The labellum is fleshy, compressed laterally with erose margins, and is less than 2 cm long. This species is from Palu, Sulawesi. Despite its pale yellow color, it is a commanding flower and a great addition to any collection. Warm to intermediate temperatures with light shade and regular applications of water and fertilizer are suitable. PLATE 43

Bulbophyllum sumatranum Garay, Hamer & Siegerist (1996)

This orchid was called *Bulbophyllum lobbii* var. *breviflorum* J. J. Smith (1908), but it actually has nothing in common with *B. lobbii* beyond being members of the same section, *Sestochilos*. The specific name, naturally, indicates the country of origin, Sumatra. The pseudobulbs are about 4 cm tall and 3 cm wide and have one leaf that is 15 cm long and 4 or 5 cm wide. The inflorescence is only 4 or 5 cm tall, to which J. J. Smith alluded in his choice of a varietal name. The flat dorsal sepal is a bit longer than 3 cm and about 1 cm wide at the base. The lateral sepals are about 3 cm long and 2 cm wide and sharply recurved, and the petals are about 3 cm long and 1 cm wide, with the apices recurved. The labellum is cordate and is also curved. The sepals are all yellow or ivory with dark red-brown spots, and the petals are yellow to cream with red-brown stripes. The labellum is dark red-purple edged in yellow with a lacquered appearance, and the column is bright yellow. Cultivation should be in slightly shaded intermediate temperatures with good drainage in the pots and high humidity.

Bulbophyllum tenerum Ridley (1903)

This plant is very similar to *Bulbophyllum planibulbe* but is roughly half the size. It, too, grows on the Malay Peninsula and can also be cultivated in warm, moist conditions on a slab of some sort.

Bulbophyllum tentaculiferum Schlechter (1913)

This species of the section *Polyblepharon*, like others in the section, has an unusual long, thin, hirsute labellum and also comes from New Guinea at about 2300 m elevation. The flowers are pale beige to white and greenish on the interior. The specific name is derived from the petals that resemble tentacles. The plants are best grown in shaded, cool to intermediate temperatures, in small pots. PLATE 44

Bulbophyllum thomsoni Hooker fil. (1890)

This species is quite similar in growth habit and other features to *Bulbophyllum parviflorum*. It has 2-cm tall pseudobulbs that are 5 cm apart on the rhizomes, leaves 12 cm tall, and an inflorescence that exceeds that in length. The flowers, however, are pale greenish white with a yellow labellum. The species is native to India and also can be grown in intermediate to warm conditions on large mounts.

Bulbophyllum tollenoniferum J. J. Smith (1916)

This species is native only to Papua New Guinea and is quite similar to the others in the section *Stenochilus* but has a very large greenish-yellow flower. It grows at altitudes of 40 to more than 700 m above sea level and also requires warmth, slight shade, and high humidity. This plant is a good addition to a greenhouse or outdoor growing area but could be difficult to maintain in a home environment because it requires large mounts and daily moisture.

Bulbophyllum tortuosum (Blume) Lindley (1830)

SYNONYMS
Bulbophyllum indragiriensis Schlechter (1906)
Bulbophyllum listeri King & Pantling (1895)
Diphyes tortuosa Blume (1825)

This member of the section *Polyblepharon* is a rather unusual plant with pendulous, readily branching rhizomes that sometimes reach 30 cm long. The terete pseudobulbs are held parallel to the rhizomes and are only about 1.5 cm long and 1 cm apart. The pendent rhizomes are attached to the branches only at the base of the plant and can be as long as 30 cm. The leaves are 5 cm long and 1 cm wide, and there are many very short single-flowered inflorescences that are nestled right up to the rhizomes. All flower parts are less than 0.5 cm, are yellow and red, and despite the closeness to the pseudobulbs they do show up well because of the color. The plants can be found hanging from trees in Bhutan, Thailand, Malaya, Laos, Vietnam, Sumatra, and Java at elevations of 300 m and only occasionally as high as 2000 m above sea level. Cultivation is easiest on a tree fern pole or slab as the plants must hang from a support of some kind. If it is absolutely impossible to supply enough moisture to make tree fern mounting tenable, a small pot with the medium up to the very top and the pot tipped over a bit on its side so the plant could dangle down would be satisfactory. Temperature should be warm to intermediate, and there should be a steady supply of water and fertilizer as well as free air movement and shade from direct sunlight.

Bulbophyllum trachyanthum Kraenzlin (1894)

SYNONYM
Bulbophyllum klossii Ridley (1916)

   This member of the section *Hyalosema* is large, 20 cm tall at least, with the inflorescence a bit shorter. The dorsal sepal is about 7 cm long, the lateral sepals about 5 cm long, and the petals 2 cm long and aristate. The flowers are spotted very deep red on the dorsal and the base of the lateral sepals, the apices of the lateral sepals are cream, and all sepals are slightly pubescent covered with short trichomes. The petals are red with a white basal area. This New Guinea species is quite similar to *Bulbophyllum fritilariiflorum*. It grows at rather high elevations in forests and is cultivated best in intermediate temperatures, slight shade and, as usual, a considerable amount of moisture. It has a very attractive flower and is certainly worthy of space in any group of orchids.

Bulbophyllum transarisanense Hayata (1916)

SYNONYMS
Bulbophyllum pectinatum var. *transarisanense* (Hayata) Ying (1990)
Bulbophyllum viridiflorum Hayata (1912), not *B. viridiflorum* Schlechter
   (1910)

   The 2-cm tall pseudobulbs of this species, which is a member of the section *Sestochilos*, are close together on the rhizome, and the single leaf is as long as 6 cm. The inflorescence is often as long as 7 cm and has widely cupped, large sheaths. The pale yellow-green flower is solitary and marked with tiny dots that are arranged in longitudinal lines. The dorsal sepal and petals are 2 cm long, and the lateral sepals are slightly longer and wide, narrowing at the apex. The labellum is large, 2.5 cm long and 2 cm wide, sharply reflexed midway, thickened, and has small spots. It is endemic to the forests of Taiwan at elevations of 1500 to 2500 m above sea level. It can be cultivated in pots or on slabs in intermediate, lightly shaded conditions. This is a nice species to grow as the flowers are very large for the size of the plant.

Bulbophyllum tremulum R. Wight (1851)

   The pseudobulbs of this member of the section *Ptiloglossum* are about 1 cm in diameter, and the leaf is ovate and about 5 cm long. The inflorescence can be 20 cm long with 6 to 10 large yellow flowers that become purple at the margins of the sepals. The sepals are about 2 cm long and pubescent, and the lateral sepals are reflexed. The petals are very much smaller and are fringed. The labellum is purple, linear-oblong, and covered with long, tremulous hairs, hence the specific name. The species is found in the hills of India at about 1000 m above sea level. It can be cultivated in warm to intermediate temperatures with a good supply of moisture, light shade, and good air circulation.

Bulbophyllum tricanaliferum J. J. Smith (1913)

This member of the section *Hyalosema* is indigenous to Papua New Guinea and Irian Jaya and has been collected at 1900 m above sea level. It is interesting because not only is the flower a nice size with dorsal sepals 7 cm long, but because the lateral sepals, which are 5 cm long, grow alongside one another and are often twisted. This gives the unusual presentation of an elongated, narrow dorsal sepal and long, narrow laterals curling beneath it. The petals project forward like antennae with slightly enlarged tips. The flower is truly a memorable sight. This species can be grown at intermediate temperatures with light shade and high humidity and does quite well on a slab of some sort as it has about 5 cm between pseudobulbs and could outgrow a pot rather quickly.

Bulbophyllum tricarinatum Petch (1923)

This very small species has pseudobulbs that are 0.4 cm tall and 0.3 cm wide, very close together on the rhizome. The leaves are a bit more than 3 cm long and ovate, and the inflorescence is only 2.5 cm tall with two to four subumbellate flowers. The flowers are yellow green and minute, only 0.5 cm long. These plants grow in Sri Lanka as epiphytes on trees as high as 1500 m above sea level. They can be cultivated in small pots in warm conditions, with shade, good air circulation, and moderate humidity.

Bulbophyllum tricornoides Seidenfaden (1979)

This Thai species in the section *Careyana* is interesting because it appears to be identical to *Bulbophyllum tricorne* Seidenfaden & Smitinand (1965) until it is given a close inspection. In this species the petals are longer than the column, but in *B. tricorne* the column exceeds the petals. In all other respects the species are the same, and they can also be grown in pots or on slabs at intermediate temperatures and in light shade. Other readily available species in this section are *B. cupreum* Lindley (1838), *B. dissitiflorum* Seidenfaden (1979), *B. elassonotum* Summerhayes (1935), *B. morphologorum* Kraenzlin (1908), *B. orientale* Seidenfaden (1979), *B. propinquum* Kraenzlin (1908), *B. rufinum* Reichenbach fil. (1881), *B. sicyobulbon* Parish & Reichenbach fil. (1881), and *B. xanthum* Ridley (1924). The most obvious difference in these species is the color of the flowers although, of course, there are small structural differences, too. They are all easily grown and display their congested, long inflorescences best when they are hung on slabs of cork, tree fern, wood, cholla, and so forth. This position allows the plants to roam completely around the mount and eventually grow some leads in a pendent manner, making an interesting display even when not in flower. For those growers not comfortable with slabs, a good-sized basket or pot with an open medium that allows good drainage is satisfactory. These plants also adapt well to a wire basket lined with sheets of spaghnum moss, then filled with a loose medium such as tree fern or bark chunks. In this manner the plants are free to grow on the outside of the basket as well as within it while retaining more moisture than is possible on a slab. As noted above, these plants come mainly from Thailand, with some from Malaysia, Laos, Vietnam, Myanmar, and India. They require warm to intermediate temperatures with frequent watering, fertilization, and protection from direct sunlight.

Bulbophyllum uniflorum (Blume) Hasskarl (1844)
SYNONYMS
Bulbophyllum galbinum Ridley (1896)
Bulbophyllum uniflorum var. *rubrum* (Ridley) Carr (1932), *Ephippium uniflorum*
    Blume (1825), *Phyllorchis uniflora* (Blume) Kuntze (1891)
Bulbophyllum variable var. *rubrum* Ridley (1907)

The pseudobulbs of this species which belongs to the section *Pahudiella* can be 10 cm tall and 1 cm wide, and are 10 cm apart on the heavily sheathed rhizomes. The leaves are about 30 cm long. Despite the specific name, the inflorescence can have more than one flower. The dorsal sepal is a bit more than 4 cm long and 1.5 cm wide, tapering to a long point. The lateral sepals are only slightly shorter than the dorsal sepal and a bit wider, narrowing abruptly and pointing outwards. The petals are slightly longer than 2 cm and taper to a narrow apex. The labellum is cordate, deflexed, and about 1 cm long. The flowers are yellow green with dark red stripes, and the labellum is red with a yellow apex. This species can be found in Malaya, Sumatra, Borneo, Java, and the Philippines at 800 to 1500 m above sea level. Cultivation is most easily accomplished on large chunks of cork or tree fern or some similar material with shade, warmth, and high humidity.

Bulbophyllum unitubum J. J. Smith (1929)

This spectacular member of the section *Hyalosema* is from Papua New Guinea, Irian Jaya, and Borneo. The plant has tall, thin, angular pseudobulbs fairly close together, each with one leaf about 10 cm long. The inflorescence is 14 cm long and bears a single commanding flower. The dorsal sepal can be 9 cm long and curves inward to form an elongated tube. The lateral sepals are about 7 cm long, narrow, curved, and drooping like a Fu Manchu mustache; these parts are pale yellow overlaid in red to maroon. The most interesting parts of the flower are the petals which taper to a long, thin thread ending in a dark red ball that is covered with sharp, spiny protuberances. These petals are held upright and arc gracefully over the lip, which has long hairs on the disc. Warm, shady conditions suit this plant quite well, as does a pot or basket with a loose, well-draining medium. PLATE 45

Bulbophyllum vanvuurenei J. J. Smith (1917)

This species was discovered in Sulawesi by L. van Vuuren in 1913. It is quite similar to others in the section *Lepidorhiza* but has a distinctive shape and proportion to its labellum which is rather undulate and slightly papillose on the lower section. It has a somewhat pale purple color overlaid on the yellowish background, and it grows in New Guinea as well as in Sulawesi. Intermediate conditions with light shade and gentle air circulation are needed.

Bulbophyllum virescens J. J. Smith (1900)

This plant is considerably larger than *Bulbophyllum pahudia*, also of the section *Pahudia*, with 14-cm tall pseudobulbs that are sometimes 20 cm apart, leaves 30 cm long and 12 cm wide and, again, a flower scape slightly shorter than the leaves. The flowers form a circle, and the dorsal sepal is 12 cm long and the lateral sepals also 12 cm, but not crossed over each other. The flowers are much the same color as in *B. carinatum*, yellow with dark purple spots. This species comes from Malaya and Sumatra, but while there is no information available about any odor, it is probably safe to assume that the flowers are also malodorous.

Bulbophyllum viridescens Ridley (1908)

This miniature species of the section *Aeschynanthoides* has creeping rhizomes that root at every node, and the pseudobulbs are spaced 12 cm or more from one another. The leaves are thick and fleshy, about 3.5 cm long and 1.7 cm wide. The inflorescence can arise from a leaf base or anywhere along the rhizome and is about 6.5 cm long with a 4-cm scape. There are approximately eight flowers that are each less than 1 cm long and yellow green with a brown labellum. The species grows in Borneo and Malaya at about 1100 m above sea level and can be raised on large slabs or very large and shallow pots so the plant can roam. Warm to intermediate temperatures, light shade, and good air circulation are necessary for proper growth and flowering. These flowers, too, are easily seen and enjoyed. Others of this section that are quite similar and make an attractive appearance whether in flower or not are *Bulbophyllum drymoglossum* Maximowicz (1887), *B. somai* Hayata (1920), and *B. tokioi* Fukuyama (1935).

Bulbophyllum wadsworthii Dockrill (1964)

This species is quite similar to *Bulbophyllum gadgarrense* of the section *Oxysepala*, but the rhizomes are a bit thicker and longer, and do not branch as readily as do those of *B. gadgarrense*. The flowers are white with a small orange labellum. The species is endemic to tropical rainforests of Australia above 750 m and can be cultivated on slabs in a warm, shady, and moist environment.

Bulbophyllum weddelii (Lindley) Reichenbach fil. (1861)

SYNONYMS

Bulbophyllum bolivianum Schlechter (1922)
Didactyle weddelii Lindley (1852), *Phyllorchis weddelii* (Lindley) Kuntze (1891), *Xiphizusa weddelii* Reichenbach fil. (1852)

One of the most attractive species of the section *Didactyle* is *Bulbophyllum weddelii*. The pseudobulb is only 3 cm tall and many angled, and the leaf is about 4 cm long. The scape is 26 cm tall, with the flower spike about 8 cm, sharply pendent, and bearing numerous flowers that open widely. The flowers are pale green with the sepals spotted brown red, while the labellum is white with a purple base and spots and has a heavy rib. The flowers open successively, and their natural spread is approximately 2 cm. The species is native to Brazil and Bolivia, and the plants can be grown in intermediate conditions with light shade and a good supply of moisture. A CBR/AOS was granted in 1991 in San Francisco to a clone named 'Sonoma' which was owned by Petite Plaisance of Valley Ford, California. PLATE 46

Bulbophyllum weinthalli Rogers (1933)

The 1- or 2-cm round pseudobulbs are held closely together on the rhizome, forming dense thick mats, and they each have one leaf that is 2.5 cm long. The inflorescence is 2.5 to 3 cm long and has one attractive flower that is often 2.5 cm in diameter. The flowers open widely and are pale yellow or green with bright red-purple spots. The species grows on pine trees in Australia's rain forests and wet areas at sea level or slightly higher. This small, creeping plant can be grown on pieces of wood or other material with a lot of water and moderate shade in warm to intermediate temperatures.

CHAPTER 6

Bulbophyllums Formerly in the Genus *Cirrhopetalum*

Many plants have been assigned to the genus *Cirrhopetalum* at one time or another, some of which are genuinely of that genus as it was originally described. Unfortunately, many true bulbophyllums are also being called cirrhopetalums today. In 1994 Leslie Garay, Fritz Hamer, and Emly Siegerist published a taxonomic paper in the *Nordic Journal of Botany* addressing this problem and that outline will be followed here. Briefly, the primary character of the genus *Cirrhopetalum* is the convex blade formed by the lateral sepals when they are adnate on both sides to the base of the column foot and twist once to bring the outer sides of the sepals together. In the past, many species have erroneously been referred to this genus merely because they had pseudoumbellate or capitate inflorescences.

Bulbophyllum acutiflorum A. Richard (1841)

SYNONYM
Cirrhopetalum acutiflorum (A. Richard) Hooker fil. (1890)

This species belongs to the section *Elatae*. The pseudobulbs are about 2.5 cm tall and 5 cm apart on the rhizomes. The leaf is oblong, 5 cm tall and 2 cm wide. The scape is approximately 7 cm tall with an umbel of six to eight white flowers. The dorsal sepal is 1.6 cm long and acuminate, the lateral sepals are 2.2 cm long, lanceolate, and acuminate, and the petals are 0.7 cm long and ovate. The labellum is 0.6 cm long, fleshy, and recurved. The plants grow in India at about 1500 m elevation and can be cultivated in pots in intermediate temperatures with shade, frequent watering, and good air movement.

Bulbophyllum albidum (Wight) Hooker fil. (1890)

SYNONYM
Cirrhopetalum albidum Wight (1852)

This orchid is typical of the section *Elatae* with pseudobulbs about 2 cm tall and the leaf about 7 cm long. The scape has six to eight flowers that are each 2 cm long, and, as the specific name indicates, they are cream colored, but they have brown flecks. The species comes from in India and grows well with subdued light, warm temperatures, and moist conditions.

Bulbophyllum aureum (Hooker fil.) J. J. Smith (1912)

SYNONYMS

Cirrhopetalum aureum Hooker fil. (1890), *Phyllorchis aurea* (Hooker fil.) Kuntze (1891)

This orchid is a member of the section *Umbellatae*. The pseudobulbs are about 1.5 cm tall, 4 cm apart on the rhizomes, and the leaf is 4.5 cm long. The inflorescence is 4 cm long with two flowers on 1.5-cm pedicels. The yellow flowers face upwards, and the lateral sepals are 1.5 cm long, incurved, and at first are adherent. Joseph Hooker described this species from a drawing made by Mr. Jerdon of Madras who had a large collection of Indian orchid drawings. After Jerdon's death, the Royal Botanic Gardens, Kew, purchased the collection in 1873. One of Hooker's observations was, "It must be a beautiful plant." The species grows in the Nilgiri Hills of India. Cool to intermediate temperatures, shade, and regular applications of water and fertilizer are necessary for good cultivation.

Bulbophyllum bicolor Lindley (1830)

SYNONYMS

Cirrhopetalum bicolor (Lindley) Rolfe (1903), not *Bulbophyllum bicolor* (Lindley) Hooker fil. (1890) which is *Ione bicolor* (Lindley) Lindley (1853), and not *B. bicolor* Jumelle & Perrier (1912) which is *B. bicoloratum* Schlechter (1924)

This plant belongs to the section *Umbellatae* and has a ciliate dorsal sepal that is a little more than 1 cm long and inrolled lateral sepals that are about 2.5 cm long. The entire flower is pale tan with dark red stripes, and the apices of the dorsal sepal and the petals are dark red. There are usually three or four flowers per inflorescence, and they are quite attractive. The species is known from China and Hong Kong and can be grown in warm to intermediate conditions, preferably in a pot or basket with the usual quick-draining mixture, enough moisture, and good air circulation, in lightly shaded areas.

Bulbophyllum biflorum Teijsmann & Binnendijk (1853)

SYNONYMS

Cirrhopetalum biflorum (Teijsmann & Binnendijk) J. J. Smith (1903), *Phyllorchis biflora* (Teijsmann & Binnendijk) Kuntze (1891)

Bulbophyllum biflorum, the type species of the section *Biflorae* as defined by Leslie Garay, Fritz Hamer, and Emly Siegerist in 1994, has pseudobulbs that are four angled, about 4.5 cm tall and 2 cm wide, close together. The leaves are 10 cm or more long by 3 cm wide. The scape is 9 to 10 cm long and, as the name implies, bears two large flowers. The flowers are sometimes 10 cm long but are usually somewhat smaller. The lateral sepals are greenish yellow to wine colored, 7 or 8 cm long, and often are joined for at least part of this length. The dorsal sepal is much smaller, dull purple, and has a fine thread-like appendage from the tip which is equally as long as the dorsal itself. The petals are quite small with a short threadlike appendage, and the labellum, too, is less than 1 cm long and is yellow with purple spots. The species has been reported from Thailand, Malaya, Sumatra, Java, Bali, Borneo, and the Philippines. This plant grows nicely in a pot or basket with a medium that drains well, but the plant does need to be watered regularly. It also requires gentle air movement and protection from direct sun. PLATE 47

Bulbophyllum binnendijkii J. J. Smith (1905)

SYNONYM
Cirrhopetalum leopardinum Teijsmann & Binnendijk (1862)

This species belongs to the section *Pahudia* and grows in Java and Borneo at about 1000 m above sea level where it seems to prefer high light levels and an area rich in humus. The pseudobulbs are large and widely spaced on the rhizomes. The leaves are very large, sometimes as long as 40 cm. The flowers are on a 15- to 20-cm long inflorescence and make a very dramatic appearance. There are at least eight or nine flowers that form a circle with the lateral sepals radiating outward. All the sepals are similar, about 8 cm long and 1 cm wide, light green with dark reddish markings and curled apices. The petals are shorter and narrower with the same coloration. The overall impression one gets of this grotesque flower cluster is that an octopus-like creature is hovering amid the leaves. The plants must be grown in bright light and in pots with a moisture-retentive potting mix. The species adds quite a bit of interest to any collection of orchids, but the flower odor is not pleasant.

Bulbophyllum breviscapum (Rolfe) Ridley (1907)

SYNONYMS
Cirrhopetalum breviscapum Rolfe (1905)
Cirrhopetalum lasiochilum (Parish & Reichenbach fil.) Hooker fil. (1890),
    Phyllorchis lasiochilum (Parish & Reichenbach fil.) Kuntze (1891),
    Bulbophyllum lasiochilum Parish & Reichenbach fil. (1874)

This attractive species of the section *Umbellatae* has pseudobulbs that are 2 cm tall and about 3 cm apart on the rhizome. The sepals are all similar in size, about 2.5 cm long, and are yellow with large dark red-purple spots. The lateral sepals are slightly longer and beautifully inrolled but not crossing one another; in fact, they have been referred to as bowlegged. The petals are almost 1 cm long and the labellum is 1 cm long with dark red hairs on the edges. There are a number of color variations, and one of the most striking has dark reddish brown dorsal sepal and petals and a much lighter, almost white, background to the lateral sepals. The plant grows in India, Myanmar, Thailand, and Malaya. This is a very lovely orchid, easy to grow, and can quickly become a specimen plant if grown on a coconut husk or tree fern log that is hung in a warm, lightly shaded, moist area. With frequent fertilization and good air movement a spectacular plant can be enjoyed despite the fact that there is only one flower per inflorescence. Be sure to allow the plant to completely encompass the mount, and refrain from removing those pseudobulbs that stray off the mount.

Bulbophyllum carinatum (Teijsmann & Binnendijk) Naves (1880)
SYNONYMS
Bulbophyllum javanicum Miquel (1859)
Cirrhopetalum capitatum (Blume) Lindley (1843), *Ephippium capitatum* Blume
    (1825)
Cirrhopetalum carinatum Teijsmann & Binnendijk (1853)
Cirrhopetalum pahudii De Vriese (1854)

The pseudobulbs of this species, the type of the section *Pahudia* as described by Rudolf Schlechter in 1911, are at least 10 cm tall with leaves that are 41 cm long and 12 cm wide, very firm, and rugged. The inflorescence is less than half the length of the leaves and holds the dozen or so flowers in an umbel. The dorsal and lateral sepals are about 8 cm long and narrow, and the lateral sepals cross over each other. The petals are slightly shorter than the sepals, and all are yellow with deep red spots. The labellum is about 2 cm long and dark purple. This plant grows in Java as an epiphyte in wet areas and does well on large wooden or cork slabs in warm areas with high humidity. The flower, though large and showy, has a very unpleasant odor, which makes it unsuitable for indoor culture.

Bulbophyllum chondriophorum (Gagnepain) Seidenfaden (1974)
SYNONYM
Cirrhopetalum chondriophorum Gagnepain (1931)

This lovely small plant of the section *Elatae* grows in Sichuan, China, at about 1200 m elevation and has only rarely been found in Thailand. The entire plant is only 3 cm tall, with pseudobulbs about 1 cm apart. The inflorescence of five or more flowers is held slightly above the leaves. The most interesting thing about this tiny species is the profusion of thick, purple caruncles along the edges of the dorsal sepals and the petals. This species should do well in intermediate temperatures and is most attractive on small slabs rather than pots because of its relatively free-roaming nature.

Bulbophyllum delitescens Hance (1878)

SYNONYMS
Cirrhopetalum delitescens Rolfe (1882)
Cirrhopetalum mirificum Hance (1931), not *B. mirificum* Schlechter (1918)

This species of the section *Macrostylidia* was described by Henry Hance in the *Gardener's Chronicle.* The pseudobulbs are about 3 cm tall and 8 cm apart on the rhizomes, and the leaf is approximately 20 cm long and 4 cm wide. The inflorescence can be 26 or more cm tall and has two or three very striking flowers. The lateral sepals are more than 5 cm long, which is more than three times as long as the dorsal sepal, and are quite narrow. The dorsal sepal and the petals have long wiry projections from the blunt apices, and the stelidia are long and flat with two horns. The flower is a beautiful crimson red and quite attractive with the very long lateral sepals and long wiry apices of both the dorsal sepals and the petals. The species is found in Vietnam, Hong Kong, Thailand, and India and should do well in intermediate temperatures, light shade, high humidity, and gentle air movement. It is best to forego pots and use slabs of some sort because of the great distance between pseudobulbs.

Bulbophyllum elatum (Hooker fil.) J. J. Smith (1912)

SYNONYMS
Cirrhopetalum elatum Hooker fil. (1890), *Phyllorchis elata* (Hooker fil.) Kuntze (1891)

This orchid is native to India and Nepal at about 1500 m elevation and is the type of the section *Elatae* as defined by Leslie Garay, Fritz Hamer, and Emly Siegerist in 1994. The tall, ovoid pseudobulbs are close together, the leaves are about 20 cm long, and the scape about 25 cm tall. There are many flowers in an umbel with the dorsal sepal 1 cm long, the petals less than 1 cm, and the lateral sepals 3 cm long. The flowers are a gray yellow with purple spots. These plants can be grown in lightly shaded areas at intermediate temperatures and develop best in pots with a medium that gives good drainage.

Bulbophyllum emarginatum (Finet) J. J. Smith (1912)

SYNONYMS
Bulbophyllum brachypodum var. *geei* Rao & Balakrishnan (1968)
Cirrhopetalum emarginatum Finet (1897)

This species is the type of the section *Emarginatae* as defined by Leslie Garay, Fritz Hamer, and Emly Siegerist in 1994. The pseudobulbs are approximately 2 cm tall and 8 cm apart on the rhizome with leaves that are 4.5 cm tall. There are from one to five flowers (usually two) on a scape that is 4 cm tall. The flowers are about as long as the scape, and the labellum is notable for its very fleshy, papillose surface. This species grows in northeastern

India, Bhutan, Myanmar, Tibet, southern China, Thailand, and North Vietnam at 2000 m elevation and higher. It can be cultivated on slabs in cool areas with dappled shade and moderate humidity.

Bulbophyllum flaviflorum (Liu & Su) Seidenfaden (1972)

SYNONYM
Cirrhopetalum flaviflorum Liu and Su (1971)

This species belongs to the section *Cirrhopetaloides* as defined by Leslie Garay, Fritz Hamer, and Emly Siegerist in 1994 and has small wrinkled pseudobulbs that are close together and leaves that are 4 to 6 cm long. The flower scapes can be as long as 10 cm with about 10 flowers in an umbel. The yellow to reddish-yellow flowers are 3 cm long, the edges of the dorsal sepal are fringed, and the 2.5-cm long lateral sepals are incurved. The plants grow in China, Vietnam, Laos, and Thailand at about 1500 m elevation, and they would do well when cultivated in an intermediate temperature. Pots or baskets with the usual open mix are appropriate, and light shade, regular watering, and gentle air movement are necessary.

Bulbophyllum gracillimum (Rolfe) Rolfe (1907)

SYNONYMS
Bulbophyllum leratii (Schlechter) J. J. Smith (1912), *Cirrhopetalum leratii*
    Schlechter (1911)
Bulbophyllum psittacoides (Ridley) J. J. Smith (1905), *Cirrhopetalum psittacoides*
    Ridley (1896)
Cirrhopetalum gracillimum Rolfe (1895)
Cirrhopetalum warianum Schlechter (1913)

This small plant is a member of the section *Cirrhopetaloides* and less than 12 cm tall with pseudobulbs that are fairly close together. The inflorescence is approximately 30 cm long. There are usually less than 15 dark red flowers in the umbel, and the 1-cm long dorsal sepal as well as the petals are fimbriate and have long, thin tails. The lateral sepals are at least 4 cm long and only briefly connate at the base. The species has a very wide range, growing from Thailand to Indonesia, New Guinea, Fiji, Australia, the Solomon Islands, and New Caledonia. It is an epiphyte on tree trunks in deep shade near sea level in areas where there is good air movement. The plant does extremely well mounted on cork or other slabs when given the proper shade and air circulation with, of course, warm temperatures and high humidity.

Bulbophyllum guttulatum (Hooker fil.) Balakrishnan (1970)

SYNONYMS
Bulbophyllum umbellatum Lindley (1845), not *B. umbellatum* Lindley (1830)
    also of the section *Umbellatae*, *B. umbellatum* var. *bergmanni* Regel (1858)

Cirrhopetalum guttulatum Hooker fil. (1890), *Phyllorchis guttulata* (Hooker fil.) Kuntze (1891)

This species belongs to the section *Umbellatae*. It is a plant of comfortable size with the leaves about 25 cm long, the flower scape usually the same size or a bit longer, and an umbel that contains 8 to 10 attractive flowers. The ovoid dorsal sepal is about 0.5 cm long, the lateral sepals 0.7 cm and inrolled, and all floral parts are greenish to white with red dots. The column is interesting because it has very long, slender spurs. This species grows in the subtropical areas of the Himalayas in India and Vietnam. Wooden slabs or other types of mounts are most appropriate, but if the conditions are dry, a pot or basket may be substituted. Some shade and good air movement with warm temperatures and high humidity are required for proper growth and flowering.

Bulbophyllum hirundinis (Gagnepain) Seidenfaden (1974)

SYNONYM
Cirrhopetalum hirundinis Gagnepain (1931)

In this species of the section *Cirrhopetaloides* the 1-cm tall grooved pseudobulbs are close together and have a single 4-cm long leaf. The inflorescence is 6 cm long and carries an umbel of four to six graceful orange flowers. The 0.6-cm dorsal sepal is elongated apically with long cilia on the edges. The lateral sepals are 3 cm long, inrolled, and are very slightly hirsute on the edges. The petals are very small, falcate, and also are edged with cilia. The labellum is minute and dark red. The plants grow in Vietnam and Taiwan and can be cultivated in pots or baskets with a loose mix of bark and fiber or on mounts in warm to intermediate conditions with light shade and abundant moisture.

Bulbophyllum japonicum (Makino) Makino (1910)

SYNONYM
Cirrhopetalum japonicum Makino (1891)

This orchid is a true miniature, the whole plant not exceeding 7 cm in height. The wrinkled pseudobulbs are less than 1 cm tall and are close together on the rhizome with a leaf about 4 cm long. The inflorescence is less than 4 cm long and has three or four tiny flowers that form an umbel and are red with darker veins, giving the impression of being purple. As the name implies, this species is found in Japan but also in China and Taiwan. It can be grown in pots or on slabs in intermediate conditions with considerable amounts of moisture and slight shade.

Bulbophyllum lasiochilum Parish & Reichenbach fil. (1874)

SYNONYMS
Bulbophyllum breviscapum Rolfe (1905), not *B. breviscapum* J. J. Smith (1910)

which is *B. planifolium* Kittredge, name published without designation
of type, *Cirrhopetalum breviscapum* Rolfe (1905)
Cirrhopetalum lasiochilum (Parish & Reichenbach fil.) Hooker fil. (1890),
   Phyllorchis lasiochila (Parish & Reichenbach fil.) Kuntze (1891)

This lovely little plant is part of the section *Umbellatae* and has ridged
pseudobulbs that are 2 cm tall and spaced 3 cm apart on the rhizomes. The
one leaf is 5 cm long. The scape is approximately 4 cm long and has one very
attractive flower. The dorsal sepal is about 2 cm long and 0.5 cm wide, erect,
and usually dark purple. The lateral sepals are 2.5 cm long and incurved,
which gives them a rather bowlegged appearance, and they are very pale
cream or white with dark red spots. The petals are a bit smaller than the dorsal sepal and also are a dark, shiny purple. The labellum is 1 cm long, slightly
curved, and has two widely spreading wings that have very long dark purple
cilia on the edges. An attractive color variation exists that is a pale yellow
throughout with light red spots. This orchid grows in Myanmar, Thailand,
and Malaya and adapts well to culture on a tree fern in warm conditions with
daily waterings and frequent fertilization. It is an easily grown small species
and highly recommended for the collection.

Bulbophyllum longissimum (Ridley) Ridley (1911)
SYNONYM
Cirrhopetalum longissimum Ridley (1896)

A very spectacular member of the section *Cirrhopetaloides* as defined by
Leslie Garay, Fritz Hamer, and Emly Siegerist in 1994 is *Bulbophyllum longissimum*. It looks like a typical bulbophyllum with conical pseudobulbs close
together and so forth, until the flowers open and the exceptionally long lateral sepals make their appearance. The illustrations in old botanical plates
show beautiful upright flowers with sepals about 18 cm long curled up on the
top of the potting medium. The dorsal sepal has only a very few palae, and
the petals have ciliate margins. These orchids come from Thailand and
Malaya and do well in a warm environment in a pot or basket with an open
potting mix, light shade, and regular watering. *Bulbophyllum longissimum* has
contributed the wonderfully long lateral sepals to its famous hybrids, *B.* Elizabeth Ann and *Mastiphyllum* Louis Sander, which has been called *Cirrhopetalum* Louis Sander. This lovely species is endemic to Thailand at low elevations. PLATE 48

Bulbophyllum macraei (Lindley) Reichenbach fil. (1861)
SYNONYMS
Bulbophyllum autumnale (Fukuyama) Ying (1975), *Cirrhopetalum autumnale*
   Fukuyama (1935)

Bulbophyllum boninense Makino (1912), *Cirrhopetalum boninense* (Makino) Makino (1912)

Bulbophyllum makinoanum (Schlechter) Masamune (1930), *Cirrhopetalum makinoanum* Schlechter (1919)

Bulbophyllum urainse Hayata (1914), *Cirrhopetalum urainse* (Hayata) Hayata (1914)

Cirrhopetalum macraei Lindley (1830), *Phyllorchis macraei* (Lindley) Kuntze (1891)

Cirrhopetalum walkerianum Wight (1851)

This species, the type of the section *Macrostylidia* as defined by Leslie Garay, Fritz Hamer, and Emly Siegerist in 1994, differs only slightly from *Bulbophyllum delitescens* but perhaps most noticeably by the closely clustered pseudobulbs. It grows as an epiphyte in forests in Sri Lanka, India, Japan, and Taiwan at altitudes as high as 1500 m above sea level and requires a good bit of moisture to thrive. Unlike the petals of *B. delitescens*, those of this species do not have a long wiry point at the apex but a much shorter one, and the flowers are yellowish with a bit of purple. Pots, baskets, or slabs are suitable for growing this species as well as intermediate temperatures, light shade, and good air movement.

Bulbophyllum maculosum (Lindley) Reichenbach fil. (1861)

SYNONYMS
Cirrhopetalum annamicum (Finet) Tang & Wang (1951)
Cirrhopetalum maculosum Lindley (1841), *Cirrhopetalum maculosum* var. *annamicum* Finet (1910)

The leaf of this species belonging to the section *Umbellatae* is about 15 cm long and the scape only about half that length. The umbels can have as many as five small yellow-green flowers. The species comes from the western part of the Himalayas and can be grown in intermediate conditions, either on slabs or in pots or baskets, with the requisite light shade and high humidity.

Bulbophyllum medusae (Lindley) Reichenbach fil. (1861)

SYNONYMS
Cirrhopetalum medusae Lindley (1842), *Phyllorchis medusae* Kuntze (1891)

This species, the type of the section *Medusa* as described by Ernst Pfitzer in 1888, was named in honor of Gorgon Medusa, whose head sprouted snakes instead of hair. The pseudobulbs are 3 cm tall and 3 cm apart, and the leaf may be 20 cm long. The white or cream-colored flowers resemble a shaggy mop about 3.6 cm in diameter and up to 12 cm long. The plants grow on either limestone rocks or trees in Thailand, Malaya, Sumatra, Borneo, Singapore, and the Philippines. By far the most spectacular clone presented for AOS judging to date was 'Miami', which earned Jones & Scully of Miami,

Florida, a CCM/AOS of 90 points in 1981. It had 550 flowers on 110 inflorescences with a plant width of 87 cm; the plant had grown so rampantly that it covered the entire base of the basket that held it. An interesting clone from Thailand is called 'Spotty' and has reddish spots near the base of the flowers. This species grows well in warm, lightly shaded conditions in baskets or pots with regular applications of fertilizer and moisture, and makes a most interesting and attractive addition to an orchid collection. PLATES 49, 50, 51

Bulbophyllum melanoglossum Hayata (1914)

SYNONYM
Cirrhopetalum melanoglossum Hayata (1914)

    The pseudobulbs are about 2 cm tall and 4 to 6 cm apart on the rhizome of this member of the section *Elatae*. The single leaf is about 6 cm long. The inflorescence can be as long as 10 cm and have an umbel of 17 cream-colored flowers that have reddish dots. The dorsal sepal is less than 1 cm long, concave, and ciliate, and the lateral sepals are 1.5 cm long and joined for most of their length. The minute petals are slightly ciliate and the labellum is red. The species is endemic to Taiwan at about 1500 m elevation and can be cultivated in pots with a well-draining medium in lightly shaded, warm to intermediate areas with high humidity. The flowers are nicely displayed above the leaves and make a very pretty picture.

Bulbophyllum mysorense (Rolfe) J. J. Smith (1912)

SYNONYM
Cirrhopetalum mysorense Rolfe (1895)

    This plant is typical of the section *Umbellatae*, but the flower spike is a bit over 4 cm long, which is the same length as the leaves, thus making the plant very attractive. As might by surmised from the specific name, this species comes from the hills of the Mysore District in India. It benefits from intermediate growing conditions with some shade and a good supply of water.

Bulbophyllum purpurascens Teijsmann & Binnendijk (1862)

SYNONYMS
Bulbophyllum citrinum (Ridley) Ridley (1907), *Cirrhopetalum citrinum* Ridley (1896)
Bulbophyllum curtisii Ridley (1903)
Bulbophyllum klossii Ridley (1926)
Bulbophyllum perakense Ridley (1903)
Bulbophyllum peyerianum (Kraenzlin) Seidenfaden (1974), *Cirrhopetalum peyerianum* Kraenzlin (1893)
Bulbophyllum tenasserimense J. J. Smith (1912)
Cirrhopetalum compactum Rolfe (1895)

Cirrhopetalum lendyanum Reichenbach fil. (1887)
Cirrhopetalum pallidum Schlechter (1906)

Of the orchids belonging to the section *Elatae*, this is the one most often seen in collections. It is a well-behaved small plant with the pseudobulbs about 2 cm apart and the leaves rarely more than 8 or 9 cm long. The leaf margins and their obverse are purple when immature (hence the species name), and the flower scape rises above the leaves, displaying the flowers nicely. The flowers are small, white or pale yellow, about 10 or 12 in an umbel, and quite attractive. The plants grow in Thailand, Malaya, Sumatra, Java, Borneo, and so forth, and seem to do best in warm and shady conditions with ample moisture. Cultivating them in pots is easiest because of the moisture requirement. PLATE 52

Bulbophyllum rhombifolium (Carr) Masamune (1942)

SYNONYM
Cirrhopetalum rhombifolium Carr (1935)

Quite similar to *Bulbophyllum biflorum* and also a member of the section *Biflorae*, this species is slightly smaller in all parts. The pseudobulbs are four angled, about 4 cm tall and less than 2 cm wide, and close together, and the leaves are less than 10 cm long. The scape is about 9 cm long and has two large flowers that are less than 10 cm long. The lateral sepals are greenish yellow to wine colored, 7 cm long, and often joined for at least part of this length. The dorsal sepal is much smaller, dull purple, and has a fine thread-like appendage from the tip which is equally as long as the dorsal itself. The petals are tiny with a short threadlike appendage, there are dark maroon stripes on the sepals, and the minute labellum is yellow with purple spots. The species grows in Thailand, Malaya, Sumatra, Borneo, and the Philippines. It can be cultivated in pots or baskets with a loose potting mix, daily watering, warm temperatures, light shade, and good air circulation.

Bulbophyllum rothschildianum (O'Brien) J. J. Smith (1912)

SYNONYM
Cirrhopetalum rothschildianum O'Brien (1895)

Another of the section *Cirrhopetaloides* that is quite striking and very well known is *Bulbophyllum rothschildianum*, which was first published by James O'Brien as a cirrhopetalum in the *Gardener's Chronicle* in 1895. Perhaps the best-known clone of it was awarded as *Cirrhopetalum rothschildianum* 'Red Chimney' FCC/AOS, 91 points, in 1991 in Ohio. It had 25 flowers on four inflorescences and was exhibited by Owen Neils of East Lansing, Michigan. A 'Red Chimney' owned by Linda Buckley of Portland, Oregon, earned her an 83-point CCM/AOS in 1989 in Washington. It had 13 inflorescences which held 42 flowers and 19 buds. The flowers on these two plants had a natural spread of 2.4 to 2.6 cm and a vertical spread of 16.6 to 17 cm with the lateral sepals measuring a spectacular 13.2 to 15 cm. *Bulbophyllum rothschildianum* is easy to grow in an intermediate to warm setting, light shade, and preferably in a basket or pot with a normal potting mix and watering on a regular basis. It is indigenous to India and Thailand and caused a sensation when it was first exhibited to the Orchid Committee of the Royal Horticultural Society in London on 15 October 1895 by the Honorable Walter Rothschild. It was declared it to be "the handsomest of the plume-bearing section of *Cirrhopetalum*" and was awarded a First Class Certificate, an award granted only once before by the RHS to this genus. In addition to the very long lateral sepals, the flowers have beautiful mobile, heavily fringed palae on the petals and dorsal sepal which make it truly a wonderful addition to any collection. This species has sometimes, because of its size and similarity to *C. wendlandianum*, been referred to as a tetraploid version of that species, but it is definitely not that and is a valid species. PLATE 53

Bulbophyllum ruficaudatum Ridley (1909)

SYNONYMS
Bulbophyllum microbulbon (Ridley) Ridley (1907), *Cirrhopetalum microbulbon* Ridley (1896)
Bulbophyllum nanobulbon Seidenfaden (1974)

This species belongs to the section *Microbulbon*. It has tiny, rounded pseudobulbs that are about 2 cm apart, an elliptical leaf, and a scape that can be 12 cm tall. The dorsal sepal and petals have long hirsute edges and pointed apices. The narrow lateral sepals are conjoined except basally and are about 1.5 cm long. This species is found in Malaya and Borneo and can be cultivated in pots or baskets in warm conditions with light shade and ample moisture.

Bulbophyllum sarcophyllum (King & Pantling) J. J. Smith (1912)

SYNONYMS
Bulbophyllum panigraphianum Misra (1986)
Cirrhopetalum sarcophyllum King & Pantling (1895)

This species is the type of the section *Microbulbon* as defined by Leslie Garay, Fritz Hamer, and Emly Siegerist in 1994. It is about 22 cm tall with an inflorescence less than half that height. The flowers are borne in an umbel, are about 1.5 cm long, and are a pretty pale lemon color with dark red spots and lines. Most notable is the pale papillose labellum. The species is endemic to northeastern India and Myanmar and grows well on slabs with a heavy bed of moss in warm, shaded areas with daily misting to keep the humidity high.

Plate 1. *Bulbophyllum hirtum* 'Emly' CBR/AOS was awarded in St. Louis, Missouri, in October 1990. It is an easily grown, deciduous species from Asia. Photo by American Orchid Society.

Plate 2. *Bulbophyllum kanburiense* 'Emly' CBR/AOS was awarded in St. Louis, Missouri, in February 1992. Photo by American Orchid Society.

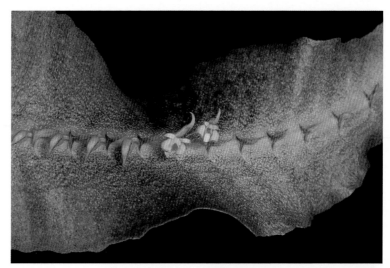

Plate 3. *Bulbophyllum maximum* has the typical wide rachis and tiny, successively opening flowers of the section *Megaclinium*. Photo by Marilyn M. LeDoux.

Plate 4. *Bulbophyllum purpureorachis* has a twisting rachis with small flowers marching up each side. Photo by Marilyn M. LeDoux.

Plate 5. *Bulbophyllum adenambon* is known for the unusual configuration of the dark red flowers. The plant shown was discovered by Wolfgang Bandisch at Ymas Lakes, Upper Sepik, West Irian Jaya. Photo by Mrs. Ralph Levy.

Plate 6. The type specimen of *Bulbophyllum agastor* 'Magnifico' CBR/AOS. Photo by Mrs. Ralph Levy.

Plate 7. Even the pseudobulbs of *Bulbophyllum ambrosia* are colorful. Photo by Clair Ossian.

Plate 8. *Bulbophyllum angustifolium* is a small species that grows on the exposed areas of mountains in Thailand. Photo by Tamlong and Heike Suphachadiwong.

Plate 9. *Bulbophyllum baileyi* is endemic to Australia and New Guinea. The attractive flowers are unusual in that they are nonresupinate. Photo by Mrs. Ralph Levy.

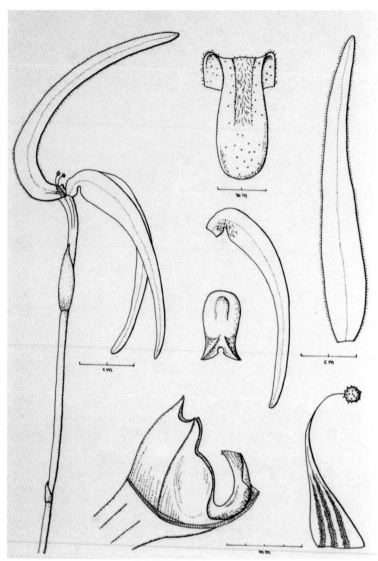

Plate 10. This drawing of *Bulbophyllum bandischii* by Fritz Hamer of Marie Selby Botanical Gardens, Sarasota, Florida, shows the type specimen. The clone 'Wolfgang's Gift' was grown by Marilyn M. LeDoux and awarded a CBR/AOS in St. Louis, Missouri, in October 1994.

Plate 11. *Bulbophyllum camero-nense* is from Malaysia with flowers only 2 to 2.5 cm in diameter. Photo by Mrs. Ralph Levy.

Plate 12. *Bulbophyllum carunculatum* has flowers that are almost 9 cm overall. Since the flowers open successively, the blooming season is prolonged. Photo by Mrs. Ralph Levy.

Plate 13. *Bulbophyllum cominsii* is native to Papua New Guinea. Shown here is a three-day-old, completely open flower with lateral sepals about 6 cm long. Photo by Mrs. Ralph Levy.

Plate 14. *Bulbophyllum congestum* grows from India and Thailand east to China and is best mounted so the rather distant pseudobulbs can roam freely. Photo by Tamlong and Heike Suphachadiwong.

Plate 15. *Bulbophyllum corallinum* 'Emly' CBR/AOS was awarded in St. Louis, Missouri, in December 1989. The tiny plant has interesting, waxy, lateral sepals. Photo by Walter L. Siegerist.

Plate 16. *Bulbophyllum cruentum*, also from Papua New Guinea, has petals whose edges are densely covered with raised papillae. Photo by Mrs. Ralph Levy.

Plate 17. *Bulbophyllum dayanum* is from Southeast Asia and is remarkable for the long hairs on the petals and sepals. Photo by Mrs. Ralph Levy.

Plate 18. *Bulbophyllum dearei* comes from Malaya, Borneo, and the Philippines. It is a well-behaved plant with pseudobulbs close together and attractive flowers that are well displayed. Photo by Mrs. Ralph Levy.

Plate 19. *Bulbophyllum facetum* is native to the Philippines. The elegant flower is about 7 cm in diameter. Photo by Mrs. Ralph Levy.

Plate 20. *Bulbophyllum fritilariiflorum*
'Tower Grove' CCM/AOS had 11 flowers
and five buds when awarded in Glencoe,
Illinois, in 22 1991. Photo by American
Orchid Society.

Plate 21. This specimen of *Bulbophyllum hahlianum* was discovered by Wolfgang Bandisch. Photo by Mrs. Ralph Levy.

Plate 22. *Bulbophyllum howcroftii* was discovered on the Sogeri Plateau in Papua New Guinea and named in honor of Neville Howcroft, who has contributed so much to the flora of that nation. Shown here is the type specimen. Photo by Mrs. Ralph Levy.

Plate 23. *Bulbo-phyllum kermesi-num* in Papua New Guinea. Photo by James Harper.

Plate 24. *Bulbophyllum levyae* comes from Lake Kutubu, Papua New Guinea. Shown here is the type specimen. Photo by Mrs. Ralph Levy.

Plate 25. *Bulbophyllum lilacinum* 'Cherokee' CBR/AOS was shown by Gene Crocker and awarded in Atlanta, Georgia, in November 1984. Photo by American Orchid Society.

Plate 26. *Bulbophyllum lobbii* 'Cass Lake' CBM/AOS was awarded in St. Louis, Missouri, in 1967 and is the variety *nettesiae*. Photo by American Orchid Society.

Plate 27. *Bulbophyllum longipedicellatum* was discovered by Wolfgang Bandisch at Lake Kutubu in Papua New Guinea. It has a very long inflorescence for which the species was named. Photo by Mrs. Ralph Levy.

Plate 28. *Bulbophyllum macphersonii*
'Kevin' CCM/AOS 84 points and CHM/AOS
82 points was awarded in November 1984 in
the city of New York. Photo by Clair Ossian.

Plate 29. *Bulbophyllum macranthum* growing at the Copenhagen Botanical Gardens. Photo by Leslie A. Garay.

Plate 30. *Bulbophyllum masdevalliacium* is from northern New Guinea. The lateral sepals are sometimes 8 cm long on a 20-cm inflorescence. Photo by Mrs. Ralph Levy.

Plate 31. *Bulbophyllum meridense* grows in Ecuador. The plant shown here is from the Gilberto Escobar Collection of Leslie A. Garay. Photo by Leslie A. Garay.

Plate 32. *Bulbophyllum minutipetalum* in situ in Papua New Guinea. Photo by Leslie A. Garay.

Plate 33. *Bulbophyllum odoratissimum* is quite similar to *B. congestum* and is unusual because it has a very pleasant odor. Photo by Tamlong and Heike Suphachadiwong.

Plate 34. *Bulbophyllum orectopetalum* is native to Thailand and resembles a small *B. lobbii* with erect, outstretched petals. Photo by Mrs. Ralph Levy.

Plate 35. *Bulbophyllum ornithorhynchum* is native to Java and New Guinea. The apices of the petals resemble tear drops. Photo by Mrs. Ralph Levy.

Plate 36. *Bulbophyllum orthoglossum* is endemic to Borneo. Photo by Charles Nishihira.

Plate 37. *Bulbophyllum phalaenopsis* is a huge plant with flowers that resemble maggot-infested meat in both appearance and odor. Bravely photographed without a telephoto lens by Walter L. Siegerist.

Plate 38. *Bulbophyllum plumula* obviously derives its specific name from the adornments to the labellum. Photo by James Harper.

Plate 39. *Bulbophyllum repens* 'Emly' CBR/AOS was awarded in St. Louis, Missouri, in November 1989. Photo by American Orchid Society.

Plate 41. *Bulbophyllum sillemi-anum* has a beautiful flower. Photo by Karlheinz Senghas.

Plate 40. *Bulbophyllum saurocephalum* 'Sea Breeze' CBR/AOS was awarded in March 1985 in Palm Beach, Florida, to Sea Breeze Orchids of Bayville, New York. The specific name refers to the flowers which resemble the heads of snakes. Photo by American Orchid Society.

Plate 42. *Bulbophyllum spiesii* owned by R. F. Orchids of Homestead, Florida, is shown here in March 1990. It has the same rotting-meat odor as others in the section *Macrobulbon*. Photo by Walter L. Siegerist.

Plate 43. *Bulbophyllum sulawesii* is native to Palu, Sulawesi. The inflorescence of this fantastic flower can be 60 cm tall with flowers 17 cm long that open successively. Photo by Mrs. Ralph Levy.

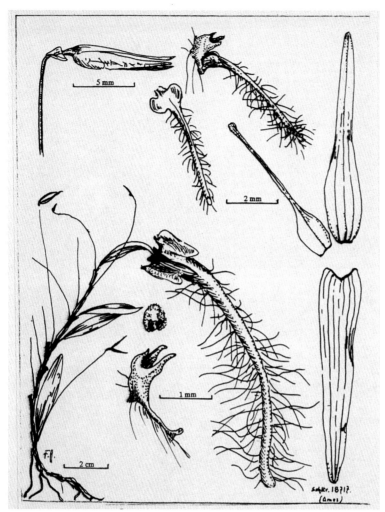

Plate 44. Drawing of *Bulbophyllum tentac-uliferum* by Fritz Hamer of Marie Selby Botanical Gardens, Sarasota, Florida. The petals are the "tentacles" referred to in the specific name.

Plate 45. *Bulbophyllum unitubum* 'Magnifico' CBR/AOS comes from New Guinea and Borneo. The tear drops on the petals are striking. Photo by Mrs. Ralph Levy.

Plate 46. *Bulbophyllum weddelii* 'Sonoma' CBR/AOS was awarded in November 1991 in the Pacific Central judging region and was shown by Petite Plaisance, Valley Ford, California. It is one of the comparatively few *Bulbophyllum* species from South America. Photo by American Orchid Society.

Plate 47. *Bulbo-phyllum biflorum*, a well-named plant, is from Southeast Asia. Photo by Mrs. Ralph Levy.

Plate 48. *Bulbo-phyllum longissi-mum* is a beautiful plant with long flow-ers up to 22.5 cm long. Photo by Mari-lyn M. LeDoux.

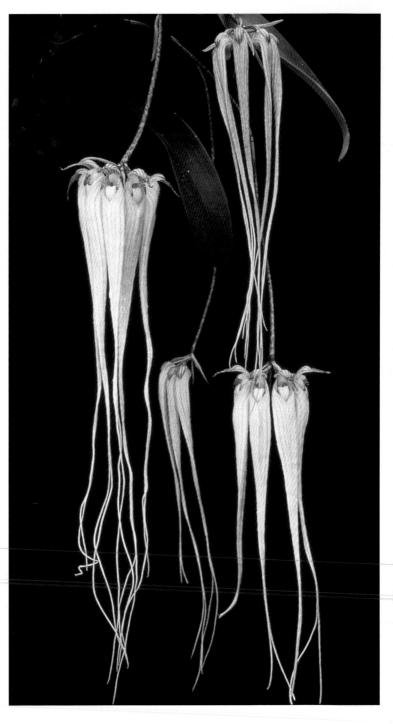

Plate 49. *Bulbophyllum medusae* 'Miami' CCM/AOS 90 points in October 1981, for Jones and Scully of Miami, Florida. This spectacular plant had 550 flowers on 110 inflorescences. The plant was 87 cm wide and had grown so rampantly that it entirely covered the base of the basket. Photo by American Orchid Society.

Plate 50 (above). *Bulbophyllum medusae* 'Spotty' is an unusual clone from Thailand. Photo by Tamlong and Heike Suphachadiwong.

Plate 51 (right). *Bulbophyllum medusae* clones (right) show the typical flower color. Variety *album* (left) has white flowers. Photo by Marilyn M. LeDoux.

Plate 52. The specific name of *Bulbophyllum purpurascens* refers to the shading on the back of the leaves, not the flower color. Photo by Wilbur A. Chang.

Plate 53. This unusual clone of *Bulbophyllum rothschildianum* shows why the species is a popular parent plant for hybridizers. Photo by Marilyn M. LeDoux.

Plate 54. *Bulbophyllum scabratum* is native to India and has at times been called *Cirrhopetalum caespitosum*. Photo by Clair Ossian.

Plate 55. *Bulbophyllum wendlandianum* is native to Myanmar and Thailand. The palae on the petals and dorsal sepal are eye-catching. Photo by Wilbur A. Chang.

Plate 56. *Cirrhopetalum dentiferum* 'Emly' CBR/AOS and CCM/AOS 84 points was awarded in St. Louis, Missouri, in December 1993. Photo by American Orchid Society.

Plate 57. *Cirrhopetalum minutiflorum* is a small but attractive species from Malaysia, Borneo, and the Philippines. Photo by Charles Nishihira.

Plate 58. *Cirrhopetalum pingtungensis* 'Memoria Kokie Millard' CBR/AOS was awarded in St. Louis, Missouri, in December 1994. It was shown by Marilyn M. LeDoux. Photo by Marilyn M. LeDoux.

Plate 59. *Cirrhopetalum pulchrum* 'Emly' CBR/AOS was awarded in St. Louis, Missouri, in September 1987. Photo by American Orchid Society.

Plate 60. *Drymoda siamensis* is a tiny deciduous plant from Laos and Thailand. Photo by Tamlong and Heike Suphachadiwong.

Plate 61. *Hapalochilus nitidus* is native to Papua New Guinea. Photo by Karlheinz Senghas.

Plate 62. *Mastigion ornatissimum* 'Lil' AM/AOS 81 points was awarded in San Francisco, California as *Cirrhopetalum ornatissimum* in September 1973. It was shown by Mr. & Mrs. Henry Severin of Cupertino, California. Photo by American Orchid Society.

Plate 63. *Rhytionanthos aemulum* 'Windy Hill' CBR/AOS was awarded in St. Louis, Missouri, in March 1999. It was owned by Marilyn M. LeDoux. Photo by Marilyn M. LeDoux.

Plate 64. *Sunipia grandiflora* is indeed a grand flower that is native to Myanmar and Thailand. Photo by Tamlong and Heike Suphachadiwong.

Plate 65. *Trias picta* comes from Myanmar and Thailand. Photo by Tamlong and Heike Suphachadiwong.

Plate 66. *Mastiphyllum* Louis Sander
(*Bulbophyllum longissimum* × *Mastigion
ornatissimum*). In November 1977, the
clone 'E. & R.' was awarded an 83 point
CCM/AOS in Baltimore, Maryland, as
Cirrhopetalum Louis Sander. It was exhib-
ited by Dr. Ralph W. Hodges. Photo by
American Orchid Society.

Plate 67. *Bulbophyllum
echinolabium,* a grace-
ful, exceptionally large
flower with a red label-
lum and long apex, was
crossed with *B. lobbii* in
1966, but the resulting
hybrid is not to be found
today. Photo by Mrs.
Ralph Levy.

Plate 68. *Bulbophyllum* Elizabeth Ann
(*B. longissimum* × *B. rothschildianum*) was
awarded in April 1986 in New York as
Cirrhopetalum Elizabeth Ann 'Buckleberry'
AM/AOS. It was exhibited by Rita Cohen of
Hewlett, New York. This very well known
clone has itself been a most successful
parent. Photo by Marilyn M. LeDoux.

Plate 70. *Bulbophyllum* Warren's Wizardry (*B. lobbii* × *B. digoelense*) was hybridized by Dr. Richard Warren. Photo by Mrs. Ralph Levy.

Plate 69. *Mastiphyllum* Kalimpong (*Bulbophyllum guttulatum* × *Mastigion ornatissimum*) has been in cultivation for a number of years and is not only easy to grow, but is easy to flower. Photo by Wilbur A. Chang.

Plate 71. *Triasphyllum* Emly's Delight (*Bulbophyllum* Emly Siegerist × *Trias disciflora*) was hybridized by Suphachadiwong Orchids of Thailand. Photo by Tamlong and Heike Suphachadiwong.

Plate 72. *Cirrhophyllum* Lion King (*Bulbophyllum medusae* × *Cirrhopetalum mastersianum*) was hybridized by Suphachadiwong Orchids of Thailand. Photo by Tamlong and Heike Suphachadiwong.

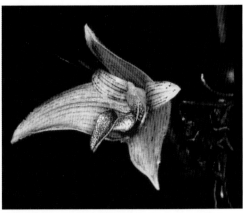

Plate 74. *Triasphyllum* Prasong (*Bulbophyllum lobbii* × *Trias vitrina*) was hybridized by Suphachadiwong Orchids of Thailand. It is another interesting and easy-to-grow hybrid, and as named in honor of the Supha-chadiwong's oldest son. Photo by Tamlong and Heike Suphachadiwong.

Plate 73. *Bulbophyllum* Nannu Nannu is (*B. trigono-sepalum* × *B. nabawanense*) was hybridized by Mrs. Ralph Levy. Photo by Mrs. Ralph Levy.

Plate 75. *Bulbophyllum* Crab Claw (*B. rothschildi-anum* × *B. dayanum*) was hybridized by Mrs. Ralph Levy. Photo by Mrs. Ralph Levy.

Plate 76. *Mastiphyllum* Magnifico (*M.* Louis Sander × *Bulbophyllum phalaenopsis*) was hybridized by Mrs. Ralph Levy. Photo by Mrs. Ralph Levy.

Plate 77. *Joara* Short Changed (*Mastiphyllum* Louis Sander × *Cirrhopetalum andersonii*) was hybridized by Mrs. Ralph Levy. Photo by Mrs. Ralph Levy.

Bulbophyllum scabratum Reichenbach fil. (1861)

SYNONYMS
Bulbophyllum caespitosum Wallich ex Lindley (1838), *Cirrhopetalum caespitosum* Wallich (1838)
Bulbophyllum confertum Hooker fil. (1890)

The note after the Latin description of this species that appeared in *Walper's Annals of Botany* (1861, p. 259) reads, "A little [epiphyte] from East Indies [imported] by the Duke of Devonshire now preserved at Chatsworth. It has small, pale yellow-ochre coloured flowers, without anything striking about them." The plant is small with crowded pseudobulbs and leaves to 15 cm long. The scape can be 7 cm long with three to six flowers per umbel. The lateral sepals are 2 cm long, the dorsal sepal 1.7 cm, and petals less than 1 cm. The dorsal sepal and petals droop forward and are finely ciliate. The flowers are pale yellow to yellow green. This species grows in India, Nepal, Thailand, and adjacent areas at altitudes of 1500 m. It is appropriate for the intermediate greenhouse with shade from direct sunlight. PLATE 54

Bulbophyllum setaceum Linn (1975)

SYNONYM
Cirrhopetalum lishanensis Cheng (1978)

The very pretty flowers of this species of the section *Cirrhopetaloides* are pale brownish green, the dorsal sepal is edged with cilia, and the lateral sepals are 3.5 cm long. The plants come from the forests of Taiwan and grow well in warm to intermediate temperatures in pots or baskets with an open mix, good air circulation, and not too much bright light. This very nice orchid makes an attractive addition to the collection.

Bulbophyllum sterile (Lamarck) Suresh (1988)

SYNONYMS
Bulbophyllum caudatum Lindley (1830), not *B. caudatum* L. O. Williams (1938) which is *B. williamsii* Hawkes (1956), *Cirrhopetalum caudatum* (Lindley) King & Pantling (1898), not *Cirrhopetalum caudatum* of some authors
Epidendrum sterile Lamarck (1783)

This species of the section *Medusa* is known only from Nepal and in many ways resembles *Bulbophyllum vaginatum* except that it is much smaller. The pseudobulbs are only 0.5 to 1 cm tall and are 2 cm apart on the rhizomes, forming dense mats. The leaf is 2.5 cm tall at most, and the flower scape is 1 cm long, just the height of the pseudobulbs. The flowers form an umbel and are also about 1 cm long. The lateral sepals are relatively long, very narrow, and threadlike. Mounting the plants on small pads of tree fern would an excellent choice, and intermediate temperatures, dappled shade, and a consistent supply of moisture would assure good growth and flowering.

Bulbophyllum thaiorum J. J. Smith (1912)

SYNONYMS

Bulbophyllum papillosum (Rolfe) Seidenfaden & Smitinand (1961), not
    B. papillosum Finet (1903) which is *B. pavimentatum* Lindley (1862),
    Cirrhopetalum papillosum Rolfe (1908)
Bulbophyllum thailandicum Seidenfaden & Smitinand (1965)

This attractive small species belongs to the section *Umbellatae*. The original name, *Bulbophyllum papillosum*, gives a clue to the most distinguishing feature of this species—the papillose lateral sepals which are well over 1 cm long. The pseudobulbs are tiny and close together, and the whole plant is less than 5 cm tall. There are about six flowers in an umbel which is held on a scape that is as long as the leaves. The background color of the flowers is off-white, and the petals and dorsal sepal have dark reddish-brown lines. This species comes from Myanmar and also from the area around Chiengmai (Thailand) commonly known as "The Golden Triangle," where it grows on deciduous trees in forests as high as 600 m above sea level. It can be cultivated in warm to intermediate conditions on small wooden slabs with light shade and abundant moisture.

Bulbophyllum thwaitesii Reichenbach fil. (1874)

SYNONYMS

Cirrhopetalum thwaitesii (Reichenbach fil.) Hooker fil. (1898)

The pseudobulbs are ridged, about 1.3 cm tall, and as far as 3.5 cm apart on the rhizomes. The leaves can be 6.6 cm long and 1.3 cm wide. The inflorescence is perhaps 5 cm tall with an umbel of two to six pale yellow-green flowers. The dorsal sepal is 0.5 cm long and ovate, and the lateral sepals are 1.2 cm long and falcate. The petals are 0.2 cm long and serrate, and the labellum is also minute. This species is endemic to Sri Lanka and grows as an epiphyte at altitudes up to 2000 m above sea level. It can be cultivated in pots or baskets in intermediate temperatures with high humidity and protection from direct sunlight. Gunnar Seidenfaden thought *Cirrhopetalum wightii* Thwaites (1861) might be a synonym of this species, but in this book it is treated as a separate entity.

Bulbophyllum tingabarinum Garay, Hamer & Siegerist (1994)

SYNONYMS

Bulbophyllum flaviflorum of some authors, not *B. flaviflorum* (Liu & Su)
    Seidenfaden (1973) also of the section *Cirrhopetaloides*
Cirrhopetalum miniatum Rolfe (1913)

The pseudobulbs of this member of the section *Cirrhopetaloides* are tetragonal, rugose, about 1.2 cm tall and 1 cm wide, and are close together on the rhizomes. The leaf is about 7 cm long and 1.5 cm wide, and the graceful inflorescence is 10 cm long and carries approximately eight beautiful flowers. The dorsal sepal is less than 1 cm long, cucullate, and fimbriate, and the petals are even smaller but are also fimbriate. The lateral sepals are connate, often as long as 10 cm, and very narrow. Robert A. Rolfe described the flowers as being "vermilion-colored, with bright yellow hairs on the margins of the petals and dorsal sepal." This orchid grows in Indochina and can be cultivated in pots or baskets or, preferably, on tree fern slabs in warm areas with protection from direct sunlight. Daily watering is necessary if the plant is grown on slabs. This orchid makes a beautiful display and is a fine addition to a collection.

Bulbophyllum trimeni (Hooker fil.) J. J. Smith (1912)
SYNONYM
Cirrhopetalum trimeni Hooker fil. (1898)

The asymmetrical pseudobulbs of this species of the section *Elatae* are less than 1 cm in size, rugose, and about 2 cm apart on the rhizomes. The leaves are lanceolate, to 2.3 cm long and 1.2 cm wide, and only rarely are there two per pseudobulb. The inflorescence is 4.5 cm tall with an umbel of six to eight pale beige flowers that are each less than 1 cm long. The plants are endemic to Sri Lanka in wet tropical forests above 750 m altitude. They can be grown in small containers or on slabs in warm, very humid, shaded conditions.

Bulbophyllum umbellatum Lindley (1830)
SYNONYMS
Bulbophyllum kontumense Gagnepain (1950)
Bulbophyllum morphologorum Reichenbach fil. (1852)
Bulbophyllum tortisepalum Guillaumin (1954)
Cirrhopetalum bootenensis Griffith (1851)

This species of the section *Umbellatae* has pseudobulbs that are about 4 cm apart with leaves as long as 12 cm. The scapes are always at least slightly shorter than the leaves, often much shorter, and bear only a few flowers each. The yellow-green dorsal sepal is less than 1 cm long and marked with dark red spots, and the lateral sepals are about 2 cm long, rolled, with yellow apices. The plants grow in India, Nepal, Vietnam, Taiwan, and China in forests as high as 1500 m above sea level. Intermediate temperatures, light shade, and ample moisture are necessary for healthy plants and flowers. Pots or slabs are appropriate, but pots are probably easier to maintain. The clone 'Evergreen' CBR/AOS, owned by Baker & Chantry, was awarded in Seattle, Washington, in 1981.

Bulbophyllum vaginatum (Lindley) Reichenbach fil. (1861)

SYNONYMS
Cirrhopetalum caudatum Wight (1851)
Cirrhopetalum stramineum Teijsmann & Binnendijk (1862)
Cirrhopetalum vaginatum Lindley (1830)

The pseudobulbs of *Bulbophyllum vaginatum* are 2 cm tall, about 5 cm apart on the rhizome, and have one leaf that is about 12 cm long. The scape is approximately 10 cm long and has an umbel of 12 to 15 pale yellow flowers. The ciliate dorsal sepal is less than 1 cm long, and the lateral sepals are about 7 cm long and are briefly connate near their base. The fringed petals and the labellum are minute. This orchid is a member of the section *Medusa* and in many ways it resembles *B. medusae*, but the flowers are ciliate and not spotted with pink as sometimes happens in *B. medusae*. *Bulbophyllum vaginatum* grows in Thailand, Sumatra, Java, Borneo, and Malaya, often on trees in open areas. The grace and charm of these beautiful "mops" of flowers make this a species well worth cultivating. It can be grown in pots containing a loose mix, with light shade from the sun and warm temperatures. High humidity and regular watering and fertilizing are also necessary to bring out the best in these plants.

Bulbophyllum wendlandianum (Kraenzlin) Dammer (1907)

SYNONYMS
Cirrhopetalum collettii Hemsley ex Hooker fil. (1890)
Cirrhopetalum collettianum Hemsley ex Collett & Hemsley (1890)
Cirrhopetalum wendlandianum Kraenzlin (1891)

Another orchid in the section *Cirrhopetaloides* is *Bulbophyllum wendlandianum*, which has sometimes been referred to as a smaller version of *B. rothschildianum*. An interesting characteristic of this species is that the inflorescence arises from the base of the new leaves before the full development of the pseudobulb; in other words, it is proteranthous. The natural habitat is Myanmar and Thailand, and the species flourishes under the same conditions as *B. rothschildianum*, giving the grower equal satisfaction. The length of the lateral sepals, the bannerlike palae on the dorsal sepal, and the tufted palae on the petals that move in every slight breeze give this lovely plant a charm that is hard to duplicate. Joseph Hooker, too, called this "a beautiful plant." Note the interesting flat, irregularly edged palae on the flower (see PLATE 55). Fortunately, this is an easy orchid to grow, needing only an open mix in a pot or basket, intermediate to warm temperatures, light shade, and frequent watering. PLATE 55

Bulbophyllum yoksunense J. J. Smith (1912)

SYNONYMS
Bulbophyllum brachypodum Rao & Balakrishnan (1968), *B. brachypodum* var.
   parviflorum Rao & Balakrishnan (1968)
Cirrhopetalum brevipes Hooker fil. (1890)

This species belongs to the section *Emarginatae* and is quite similar to *Bulbophyllum emarginatum* with 2-cm tall pseudobulbs 8 cm apart on the rhizomes and leaves 4.5 cm tall. It has, however, many more small rose-purple flowers. The plants grow from northern India to Myanmar at elevations of 2000 to 3000 m above sea level, again requiring cool temperatures, light shade, and moderate humidity for success in producing flowers.

CHAPTER 7

Cirrhopetalum

Cirrhopetalum Lindley (1824 nom.) (nom. conserv. 1935)

John Lindley established the genus *Cirrhopetalum* in the 1824 *Botanical Register* (10: sub t. 832). He stated that the pseudobulbs are often angular and that the inflorescence is terminated by a pseudoumbel with the flowers spread out in a semicircular pattern. The dorsal sepal is free, and the lateral sepals are porrect or recurved, adnate basally to the column foot and then twisted once to form a convex blade. The outer margins of the lateral sepals are then united, forming either a circular cavity around the labellum or a tunnel-like opening. The lateral sepals are much longer than the dorsal sepal, the petals are about the same size as the dorsal sepal and are usually hirsute, while the labellum is hinged and mobile. The genus name is derived from the Latin *cirrho*, meaning "tendril" or "curl of hair," and *petalum*, which means "petal," referring to the curved or curled petals. Type: *Bulbophyllum longiflorum* Thouars (1824)

There has been a great deal of confusion about the typification of the genus *Cirrhopetalum* because when Lindley published the name *Bulbophyllum longiflorum* as the type, he neglected to give a description, thereby invalidating the work. But when he published his description of the genus *Cirrhopetalum* in 1830 with six species but did not assign a holotype, we must refer to his original choice of *B. longiflorum*. To make things even more confusing, Caspar G. C. Reinwardt established his genus *Zygoglossum* for the same group of orchids in 1825, but since *Cirrhopetalum* was originally published in 1824 by Lindley, it must take precedence.

There is also a bit of confusion regarding the use of *Bulbophyllum longiflorum* as the type because it has accumulated a long list of synonyms, the first of which was *Epidendrum umbellatum* Forster fil. in 1786. This is merely a taxonomic synonym, not the basionym for the genus, and thus *B. longiflorum* Thouars remains the type of the genus *Cirrhopetalum*.

There are three sections in the genus and they are defined as follows:

Section *Cirrhopetalum* Lindley (1824)

In these orchids there is one leaf per pseudobulb, the lateral sepals twist once, and the outer margins unite, thus forming a tunnel-like passage around the labellum. The dorsal sepal and lateral sepals rarely are spatially separate, and the lateral sepals are convex and somewhat porrect. Type: *Bulbophyllum longiflorum* Thouars (1822)

Section *Recurvae* Garay, Hamer & Siegerist (1994)

These flowers are the same as those in the section *Cirrhopetalum* except that the dorsal and lateral sepals are always spatially separated and the petals occupy that space. The lateral sepals are recurved. Type: *Cirrhopetalum curtisii* Hooker fil. (1897)

Section *Wallichii* Garay, Hamer & Siegerist (1994)

The lateral sepals form a convex blade that is united through the outer margins, forming an opening around the labellum that is not a true tunnel-like passage. The lateral sepals may split into free segments near the end of the flowering period. Each pseudobulb has one leaf. Type: *Cirrhopetalum wallichii* Lindley (1830)

Cirrhopetalum albociliatum Liu and Su (1971)

SYNONYMS
Bulbophyllum albociliatum (Liu and Su) Nackejima (1973)
Bulbophyllum taichungianum Ying (1978)

This tiny species of the section *Cirrhopetalum* has pseudobulbs that are slightly taller than 1 cm and spaced about 2 cm apart on the creeping rhizomes. The leaves are less than 4 cm long and 1 cm wide with rounded apices. The inflorescence is 6 cm tall with an umbel of five or six flowers. The flowers are less than 1 cm long and have a dorsal sepal that is reddish with white, relatively long, hirsute edges. The lateral sepals are yellow red and connate, while the minute petals are reddish and also have white cilia on their edges. This species is endemic to the forests of central and southern Taiwan at approximately 1500 m above sea level. Cultivation should be in small pots or baskets with a potting mixture that drains well. Plants should be kept in areas with partial shade and medium humidity.

Cirrhopetalum amplifolium Rolfe (1913)

SYNONYM
Bulbophyllum amplifolium (Rolfe) Balakrishnan & Chowdhury (1967)

The pseudobulbs of this member of the section *Cirrhopetalum* are ovoid, between 4.5 and 5.5 cm tall, and enclosed in bracts, about 10 to 16 cm apart on the creeping rhizomes. The leaves can be 21 cm long and more than 5 cm wide on a 5-cm long petiole. The inflorescence is shorter than the leaves and carries three or four flowers in an umbel. These flowers are 5 to 6 cm long, a brownish yellow with purple markings. The dorsal sepal is concave, a bit more than 2 cm long, and the apex has a 1-cm long, filiform projection. The lateral sepals are about 3 cm long, connate but separating upon aging, and the petals are less than 1 cm long, triangular, ciliate, and have a 1-cm long, thin apical projection. The plants grow in Bhutan, Assam (India), Myanmar, and China at about 1800 m above sea level. Cultivation would require a large slab of any sort to accommodate the widely spaced pseudobulbs, and a thin layer of moss or fiber would be helpful to preserve some moisture around the roots. Intermediate temperatures and protection from direct sunlight encourage good growth.

Cirrhopetalum andersonii Hooker fil. (1890)

SYNONYMS

Bulbophyllum andersonii J. J. Smith (1912), not *B. andersonii* Kurz (1870)
which is *Cirrhopetalum flabelloveneris* (Koenig) Seidenfaden & Ormerad
(1995), *Phyllorchis andersonii* (Hooker fil.) Kuntze (1891)
Bulbophyllum henryi J. J. Smith (1912), *Cirrhopetalum henryi* Rolfe (1903)
Cirrhopetalum rivesii Gagnepain (1934)

Described by Joseph Hooker in the *Flora of British India*, this plant of the section *Recurvae* has about 7 or 8 cm between the 6-cm tall pseudobulbs, with leaves to 12 cm long, and a floral scape of widely varying heights. The umbel contains approximately six flowers, each of which has a dorsal sepal that is less than 1 cm long and has a small erose area near the apical threadlike projection. The lateral sepals are as long as 2 cm, conjoined, and recurved. The petals are distinctive, 0.4 cm long, with erose edges, and dark and papillose apices which have threadlike appendages. The column has long stelidia and a somewhat rounded projection at the back. The flowers are pale ivory overlaid with dark red dots. This plant comes from northeastern India, Vietnam, and southern China at elevations of 500 to 700 m above sea level. It can be grown in pots or baskets but will quickly outgrow them because of the large spaces between pseudobulbs. Mounting would be a good solution, allowing the plant to ramble up one side and down and around the other. Warm to intermediate conditions and excellent air circulation with some shade are necessary for success.

Cirrhopetalum asperulum (J. J. Smith) Garay, Hamer & Siegerist (1994)

SYNONYM

Bulbophyllum asperulum J. J. Smith (1909)

This species of the section *Cirrhopetalum* has a pretty flower, which is predominately white with dark red spots and a red labellum. The dorsal sepal has a long, acute apex and is hirsute, as are the petals. Its natural habitat is Borneo and it can be cultivated in warm to intermediate conditions with light shade, regular watering, high humidity, and good air movement. The plants can be grown in baskets or pots in any potting mix that provides good drainage.

Cirrhopetalum auratum Lindley (1840)

SYNONYMS

Bulbophyllum auratum (Lindley) Reichenbach fil. (1861), *Phyllorchis aurata* Kuntze (1891)

Bulbophyllum campanulatum Rolfe (1909), *Cirrhopetalum campanulatum* (Rolfe) Rolfe (1910)

Cirrhopetalum candelabrum Lindley ex Moore (1854)

The pseudobulbs of this beautiful member of the section *Recurvae* are 2 cm tall and only 1 cm apart, the leaves are approximately 12 cm long, and the flower scape is a few centimeters longer. The flowers form a whorl, and all the lateral sepals point straight down in a very distinctive fashion, making John Lindley's *Cirrhopetalum candelabrum* a very descriptive name for this taxon. The small dorsal sepal and the petals are yellow with dark red veins, hirsute edges, and long threadlike apices. The lateral sepals are pale pinkish white, deflexed, and about 3 cm long. This species is native to Thailand, peninsular Malaya, Sumatra, Borneo, and the Philippines where it seems to prefer growing on mangrove trees. It can easily be grown in baskets or pots in warm to intermediate conditions with mottled shade, moderate air movement, and high humidity.

Cirrhopetalum brienianum Rolfe (1893)

SYNONYMS

Bulbophyllum adenophorum (Schlechter) J. J. Smith (1912), *Cirrhopetalum adenophorum* Schlechter (1906)

Bulbophyllum brienianum (Rolfe) J. J. Smith (1912)

Bulbophyllum brunnescens (Ridley) J. J. Smith (1912), *Cirrhopetalum brunnescens* Ridley (1896)

Bulbophyllum makoyanum var. *brienianum* (Rolfe) Ridley (1907), *Cirrhopetalum makoyanum* var. *brienianum* (Rolfe) Ridley (1896)

In the original description of this plant that is part of the section *Cirrhopetalum* it was called *Bulbophyllum brienianum* by Robert A. Rolfe in honor of James O'Brien of Harrow-on-the-Hill, England, for whom it flowered. The pseudobulbs are 2 cm tall and only a few centimeters apart, the leaf is 12 cm long and at least 2 cm wide, and the flower scape can be 20 cm long and have eight lovely flowers. The dorsal sepal and petals are less than 1 cm long and are dark red with hirsute edges. The narrow lateral sepals are more than 2 cm long and their outer edges are connate, pale yellow with the basal area purple, and the labellum also is purple. The species grows in Borneo, Malaya, the Philippines, and Sumatra. It can be cultivated in pots or baskets with a potting mix that drains well, in warm to intermediate areas with light shade, high humidity, and a regular supply of water.

Cirrhopetalum cercanthum Garay, Hamer & Siegerist (1996)

The plants of this species, a member of the section *Cirrhopetalum*, are about 12 cm tall, the pseudobulbs are approximately 2.5 cm high, and the leaves are 11.5 cm by slightly less than 3 cm wide. The floral scape is 4.5 cm long with usually seven flowers in a subumbellate configuration. The dorsal sepal is less than 0.5 cm long, the lateral sepals are about 3.5 cm long and less than 0.5 cm wide, conjoined for at least part of their length, and all sepals are covered with muricate glands. The petals are very small and have a long ciliate apex. The dorsal sepal and petals are dark maroon and the lateral sepals are yellow fading to white with bluish red dots. The labellum is yellow or green with red markings. The specific name is from the Greek *kerkos*, which means "tail" and *anthos* or "flower," referring to the tail-like lateral sepals. The type specimen came from Borneo and was grown by Charles Nishihira of Hawaii. These orchids can be cultivated in warm, moist, lightly shaded areas with good air movement. Pots or baskets with a medium-sized mix and regular watering assure good growth.

Cirrhopetalum concinnum Hooker fil. (1890)

SYNONYM
Bulbophyllum pulchellum Ridley (1907)

The pseudobulbs of this species belonging to the section *Recurvae* are 1 to 2 cm apart, the plant is about 15 cm or more tall, and the scapes are much shorter, about 7 cm high. The fringed dorsal sepal is less than 1 cm long and the apex is pointed. The lateral sepals are a little more than 1 cm long and are connate, while the petals are long triangular and fringed. The flower is pale yellow with dark red spots, and the labellum is very dark red. This species frequently grows on old mangrove trees and has been found in the lowlands of the Philippines, Thailand, Vietnam, Malaya, Borneo, and Singapore as well as India. It grows well in pots or baskets in warm, slightly shaded, and moist conditions. Very similar to this species are *Cirrhopetalum sibuyanense* (Ames) Garay, Hamer & Siegerist (1994) and *C. zamboangense* (Ames) Garay, Hamer & Siegerist (1994), both from the Philippines.

Cirrhopetalum cumingii Lindley (1841)

SYNONYMS
Bulbophyllum cumingii (Lindley) Reichenbach fil. (1861), *Phyllorchis cumingii* (Lindley) Kuntze (1891)

John Lindley named this orchid after the collector, Cuming, who found it in the Philippines. It belongs to the section *Cirrhopetalum*, and the tetragonal pseudobulbs are about 2 cm tall and 2 cm apart on the rhizomes. The leaf is coriaceous, a little more than 7 cm long and 2 cm wide. The inflorescence is about twice as tall as the plant and has an umbel of approximately 10 beautiful, deep purple flowers. The dorsal sepal is acuminate and fimbriate, and the lateral sepals are almost completely conjoined. The petals are linear-lanceolate and fimbriate. This orchid grows in the Philippines from sea level to about 500 m elevation. It can be cultivated in pots or baskets with an open potting mix, warm temperatures, high humidity, light shade, and good air circulation.

Cirrhopetalum curtisii Hooker fil. (1897)

SYNONYMS
Bulbophyllum corolliferum J. J. Smith (1917), *B. corolliferum* var. *atropurpureum* J. J. Smith (1917)
Bulbophyllum curtisii (Hooker fil.) J. J. Smith (1912), *B. curtisii* var. *purpureum* J. J. Smith (1933)
Cirrhopetalum concinnum var. *purpureum* Ridley (1896)

The pseudobulbs of this orchid belonging to the section *Recurvae* are about 2 cm apart on the rhizomes, and the plant is 15 cm tall with scapes 7 cm tall. This species is quite similar to *Bulbophyllum concinnum* with the petal shape being the distinguishing feature. *Cirrhopetalum curtisii* has petals that are densely fringed but instead of being long and triangular, they are short and broad, narrowing abruptly into a point at the apex. The flowers are predominately dark red purple, but the labellum is bright yellow. The species grows in Malaya, Singapore, Thailand, Sumatra, and Borneo, frequently in mangrove swamps. It can be cultivated in warm conditions and preferably on tree fern or husk mounts with ample water and light shade. Mounting gives the plants the opportunity to show their flowers to the best advantage.

Cirrhopetalum cyclosepalon (Carr) Garay, Hamer & Siegerist (1994)

SYNONYM
Bulbophyllum cyclosepalon Carr (1932)

The pseudobulbs of this orchid of the section *Cirrhopetalum* are about 10 cm apart on the rhizomes and have a leaf that is approximately 15 cm long. The flower scape is considerably longer than 10 cm, and the dorsal sepal is notched, while the lateral sepals are quite small and the flowers are pale yellow with dark red markings. The species grows in Thailand, Malaya, and Java and can be cultivated in warm, moist environments with light shade. Considering the distance between pseudobulbs, it would be easiest to grow this species on large pieces of tree fern, cork, or some other mount, giving the plants room to wander. If slabs are not an option, try a large wire basket with moss lining and allow the rhizomes to wander over the edges, then gently attach them to the outside of the basket where they should grow happily.

Cirrhopetalum dentiferum (Ridley) Garay, Hamer & Siegerist (1994)
SYNONYM
Bulbophyllum dentiferum Ridley (1915)

The pseudobulbs of this species are more than 10 cm apart on the rhizome, and the leaf is between 10 and 20 cm long. The species belongs to the section *Cirrhopetalum*, and the flowers form a typical cirrhopetalum whorl and are displayed on a scape that is usually only 8 cm long but sometimes is longer. The dorsal sepal and the petals are apically pointed with dentate edges, and the lateral sepals are about four times as long as the dorsal sepal with the upper edges almost completely joined. The flowers are pale yellow with dark red-purple spots on the lateral sepals and stripes on the dorsal sepal and petals. This species comes from Thailand, Malaya, and Java. It grows well in warm temperatures and is content either in pots or baskets and it also grows well when mounted. Regular watering, semishade, and frequent fertilization are a must. PLATE 56

Cirrhopetalum farreri W. W. Smith (1921)
SYNONYM
Bulbophyllum farreri (W. W. Smith) Seidenfaden (1973)

William W. Smith named this plant after the collector, Reginald Farrer, when it flowered in Edinburgh, Scotland. The species belongs to the section *Cirrhopetalum* and has pseudobulbs that are almost 2 cm tall and less than 2 cm apart on the rhizomes. The leaves are 8 cm long and 2 cm wide, the inflorescence is at least 8 cm tall, often much taller, and there are usually five interesting flowers arranged in an umbel. The dorsal sepal and the petals are each about 0.4 cm long and have blunt apices. The lateral sepals are about 3 cm long, connate, and densely papillose. The plants come from Myanmar and can be grown in warm areas either on mounts or in containers as long as they are provided with light shade and considerable moisture.

Cirrhopetalum fibratum Gagnepain (1931)
SYNONYM
Bulbophyllum fibratum (Gagnepain) Seidenfaden (1973)

This small species of the section *Cirrhopetalum* has conical pseudobulbs that are 1 cm tall and about 2 cm apart on the rhizomes. These pseudobulbs are loosely held in long hairlike remnants of sheaths, and the leaf is about 5 cm long and 1.5 cm wide. The inflorescence is approximately 6 cm tall and has a whorl of flowers that are each 2.5 cm long. The dorsal sepal is less than

0.5 cm long and obtuse, and the lateral sepals are about 1.5 cm long with the basal half slightly pubescent. The petals are 0.6 cm long and 0.4 cm wide, almost quadrate. The species grows in Vietnam and can be cultivated in intermediate temperatures with a good supply of moisture and light shade. Pots or baskets with a loose mix or small slabs would be appropriate.

Cirrhopetalum flabelloveneris (Koenig) Seidenfaden & Ormerad (1995)

SYNONYMS

Bulbophyllum andersonii Kurz (1870), *Cirrhopetalum andersonii* (Kurz) Hooker fil. (1890)

Bulbophyllum gamosepalum (Griffith) J. J. Smith (1912), *Cirrhopetalum gamosepalum* Griffith (1851), *Phyllorchis gamosepalum* (Griffith) Kuntze (1891)

Bulbophyllum griffithianum Parish & Reichenbach fil. (1874)

Bulbophyllum lepidum (Blume) J. J. Smith (1905), *Cirrhopetalum lepidum* (Blume) Schlechter (1911), *Ephippium lepidum* Blume (1825)

Bulbophyllum rolfeanum Seidenfaden & Smitinand (1961)

Cirrhopetalum ciliatum Klinge (1898)

Cirrhopetalum gagnepanii Guillaumin (1964)

Epidendrum flabellum veneris Koenig (1791)

According to the current rules of botanical nomenclature, the specific epithet can be only one word and if two words are used they must be either hyphenated or united (that is, *flabello veneris* must become *flabelloveneris*). For many years the names *Bulbophyllum lepidum* or *Cirrhopetalum lepidum* have been widely used for this member of the section *Cirrhopetalum*. But once again, the rules must be followed, so *Ephippium lepidum* as described by Carl Ludwig von Blume in 1825, which was the source for the names used for so long, is reduced to synonymy because the epithet *flabelloveneris* was published 34 years earlier. Of course for a plant as attractive and easy to grow and flower as this one is, there are many other synonyms also. The pseudobulbs are 1.5 cm tall and are seldom more than 3 cm apart, the leaves are about 16 to 17 cm long, and the scape is slightly taller. The dorsal sepal is less than 1 cm long, has hirsute edges and an acuminate apex. The 2.5-cm long lateral sepals are connate almost completely, and the petals are tapered and hirsute and have an acute apex. The flower is usually a rose mauve, but there is a lovely pale yellow form also. The species can be found throughout India, Myanmar, Laos, Thailand, the Malay peninsula, Cambodia, Vietnam, and Indonesia. Given a warm to intermediate temperature, baskets or pots, regular watering and fertilizing, with good air circulation, this species should be an excellent addition to a collection.

Cirrhopetalum frostii (Summerhayes) Garay, Hamer & Siegerist (1994)

SYNONYMS

Bulbophyllum bootanoides (Guillaumin) Seidenfaden (1973), *Cirrhopetalum
    bootanoides* Guillaumin (1956)
Bulbophyllum frostii Summerhayes (1928)

Relatively new to the orchid scene, this is a most interesting little plant, a
member of the section *Cirrhopetalum*, with closely held pseudobulbs, clusters
of small flowers about 1 to 2 cm in size with a dorsal sepal that is round,
cupped, hirsute, and projects over the column and labellum. The lateral
sepals are turned inwards and joined, and the petals are a bit rounded and
also hirsute. The flower, which is pale yellow tan with dark reddish spots,
resembles a small boot, and it has been said that the wearer's toes could almost be seen wiggling inside. This plant grows best on small mounts in warm
and lightly shaded areas with ample water and light air movement. Of course,
small pots or baskets with an open potting mixture could be substituted for
slabs if necessary. The species comes from Vietnam, Thailand, and the
Malay Peninsula. The clone 'Evets' CBM/AOS was awarded in Atlanta,
Georgia, in July 1977 under the synonym *Bulbophyllum bootanoides*. It was
exhibited by FL Stevenson of Chamblee, Georgia.

Cirrhopetalum gamblei Hooker fil. (1890)

SYNONYMS

Bulbophyllum fischeri Seidenfaden (1973)
Cirrhopetalum thomsoni Hooker fil. (1890), *Phyllorchis thomsoni* (Hooker fil.)
    Kuntze (1891)
Phyllorchis gamblei (Hooker fil.) Kuntze (1891)

Joseph Hooker described this cirrhopetalum from India as well as a bulbophyllum, also from India, and gave them both the same specific epithet,
gamblei. When both genera were considered to belong to *Bulbophyllum*, these
names caused a bit of confusion but now that *Cirrhopetalum* is again recognized as a valid genus it should be more clear, especially since there are obvious differences between these two species. The small plant is a typical member of the section *Cirrhopetalum* with a few centimeters between pseudobulbs,
a scape about as long as the leaves, and the umbellate flowers each about 1.5
cm long, yellow with reddish markings. These orchids grow at altitudes of
2100 to 2400 m above sea level in India and require an intermediate to cool
area to grow and flower properly. Pots or baskets are appropriate, but the
main consideration is the temperature which precludes growing these
orchids in many areas where orchids normally do well. Regular applications
of water and fertilizer and a gentle circulation of air in somewhat shaded
locations are also necessary.

Cirrhopetalum grandiflorum Wight (1851)

SYNONYM

Bulbophyllum wightii Reichenbach fil. (1861)

This orchid of the section *Cirrhopetalum* is a large, wandering plant with internodes that are sometimes as long as 13 cm between pseudobulbs. The leaves are about 15 cm long, and the scapes are the same length with only two to four flowers each. The flowers are green to yellow with dark red markings and are about 6 cm long. The dorsal sepal and petals have long cilia on their edges, and the lateral sepals are about 5 cm long. This is a very attractive species whose native habitat is India, Sri Lanka, and China in wet forest areas where it grows on tree trunks at 1000 to 2000 m altitude. It can be cultivated in intermediate temperatures and requires high humidity to prosper. The distance between pseudobulbs would indicate that mounting the plant is the best approach, but if maintaining high humidity is a problem, perhaps a wire basket with moss lining it and allowing the plants to trail over the sides and grow into the moss would be the prudent solution. A shaded growing area is also necessary to prevent burned leaves.

Cirrhopetalum gusdorfii (J. J. Smith) Garay, Hamer & Siegerist (1994)

SYNONYM

Bulbophyllum gusdorfii J. J. Smith (1917)

A member of the section *Cirrhopetalum*, this species has leaves that are about 14 cm long on pseudobulbs that are only 1 or 2 cm apart on the rhizomes. The scape is 9 cm long and usually has eight flowers that are each 2.5 cm long. The small dorsal sepal is less than 0.5 cm, almost round, cupped, dark reddish brown, and fimbriate. The lateral sepals are about 2 cm long, coherent throughout most of their length, pale yellow with dark reddish purple at the base, similar to the sepals in *Cirrhopetalum flabelloveneris*. The petals are minute, blunt, apically papillose, dark brown, and fimbriate. The column is interesting in that it has three tiny projections at the back and also some on each side in the front. It grows in the Philippines, Sumatra, and Malaya and requires a warm, shaded and moist area to grow well. This would preclude mounting under most home conditions, but with a thick pad of moss under the roots and careful attention to watering it could be successful.

Cirrhopetalum makoyanum Reichenbach fil. (1879)

SYNONYM

Bulbophyllum makoyanum (Reichenbach fil.) Ridley (1907)

Heinrich Gustav Reichenbach described this appealing orchid in the *Gardener's Chronicle*. It is one of the section *Cirrhopetalum* and has 2-cm tall pseudobulbs that are fairly close together, with leaves 10 cm tall. The inflorescence is twice that length and has about 10 flowers. The dorsal sepal and petals are quite small, red brown, with threadlike apices, and edged with pale hairs at least 0.1 cm long. The real focal point of the flowers is the shape of the lateral sepals which are almost 4 cm long and have the upper edges connate for almost their entire length and the lower edges rolled under and sometimes partially joined. This makes the sepals appear extremely narrow. The lateral sepals radiate from the umbel, giving them the appearance of a sunflower. This species has been found in the Philippines, Borneo, Malaya, and Vietnam. It can be easily grown in warm to intermediate temperatures, either potted or mounted, and of course requires liberal amounts of moisture but should not be constantly wet. It is an excellent addition to a collection.

Cirrhopetalum mastersianum Rolfe (1890)
SYNONYMS
Bulbophyllum mastersianum (Rolfe) J. J. Smith (1912), *B. mastersianum* (Rolfe) Masamune (1942)

This impressive, large member of the section *Recurvae* has flowers that are about 5 cm long, and the dorsal sepal and the petals are all edged with fine cilia. The dorsal sepals have a short apical point, and the petals are long triangular with a narrow, tapering apex. The lateral sepals are at least 4 cm long, broad, conjoined, and recurved. The flowers are yellow with brownish shading and if well grown will bloom several times a year. Potting in a basket with a mix that holds some moisture in warm, lightly shaded conditions is best. High humidity and gentle air movement are conducive to flowering. This species is native to Borneo and the Moluccas as well as Vietnam.

Cirrhopetalum minutiflorum Garay, Hamer & Siegerist (1996)

This species of the section *Cirrhopetalum* is about 8 cm tall, the 2-cm tall pseudobulbs are close together, and the leaves are approximately 5.5 cm long. The biflowered inflorescence is shorter than the leaves. The dorsal sepal is about 0.5 cm long, the lateral sepals only 1 cm long and less than 0.5 cm wide, and the petals are minute. This species has the smallest flowers in the genus, but they are cream with a heavy overlay of small purple dots on the lateral sepals, purple veins on the dorsal sepals, and the labellum is orange. The specific name refers, of course, to the small flowers. The species comes from Borneo, and the type specimen was grown by Charles Nishihira of Hawaii. This is another species that requires an eye loupe or some sort of magnification to fully appreciate the tiny flowers. PLATE 57

Cirrhopetalum neilgherrense (Wight) Wight (1852)
SYNONYMS
Bulbophyllum kaitense Reichenbach fil. (1861)
Bulbophyllum neilgherrense Wight (1851)

This species is a member of the section *Recurvae* and has 4-cm tall pseudobulbs that are about 5 cm apart on the rhizome. The fleshy leaf is about 11 cm long with the scape a bit shorter. There are six to eight flowers in the umbel which are greenish with red markings that become darker with age. This orchid grows in the Nilgiri Hills of southwestern India at altitudes of 1800 m either as an epiphyte or a lithophyte in rather moist areas. It can be cultivated in large pots or, preferably, on heavy slabs, with considerable moisture, partial shade, and intermediate temperatures.

Cirrhopetalum nutans Lindley (1839)

SYNONYMS

Bulbophyllum nutans (Lindley) Reichenbach fil. (1862)
Bulbophyllum othonis (Kuntze) J. J. Smith (1912), *Phyllorchis othonis* Kuntze (1891)

This plant, named by John Lindley in the *Botanical Register*, has small pseudobulbs that are 2 cm apart, and the whole plant is only about 8 cm tall. It is part of the section *Cirrhopetalum*, and its outstanding feature is the very long inflorescence which is sometimes 23 cm tall. The flowers are many, each about 2 cm long with dorsal sepals and petals much the same size, less than 0.5 cm, and triangular with pointed apices. The lateral sepals are 2 cm long, very narrow, and conjoined. The species grows in the Philippines and can be cultivated in pots or baskets with a well-draining potting mix, intermediate to warm temperatures, high humidity, and dappled shade.

Cirrhopetalum ochraceum Ridley (1898)

SYNONYMS

Bulbophyllum ochraceum (Ridley) Ridley (1907), not *B. ochraceum* Cogniaux (1902) also of the genus *Bulbophyllum*
Bulbophyllum serratotruncatum Seidenfaden (1973)

The pseudobulbs of this attractive orchid of the section *Cirrhopetalum* are 2 cm tall and less than 1 cm apart on the rhizomes. The leaves are oblong, at most 16 cm long and 3 cm wide, and the inflorescence can be 20 cm tall with as many as 10 flowers. The dorsal sepal is cucullate, hirsute, 0.6 cm long and 0.3 cm wide, and is red with dark veins. The lateral sepals are almost completely conjoined with only the very tips free, 3 cm long and less than 1 cm wide, and are orange or yellow with darker markings basally. The petals are about 0.7 cm long, hirsute, and very dark red. The labellum is 0.3 cm long and olive green. This species grows in the low riverine areas of Malaya and is well suited to cultivation in pots or baskets with a potting mixture that retains a bit of moisture. Light shade, good air movement, and warm temperatures assure good growth.

Cirrhopetalum picturatum Loddiges (1840) ex Lindley

SYNONYMS
Bulbophyllum eberhardtii (Gagnepain) Seidenfaden (1992), *B. eberhardtii*
   (Gagnepain) Pham-Hoang (1972), *Cirrhopetalum eberhardtii* Gagnepain
   (1931)
Bulbophyllum picturatum (Loddiges) Reichenbach fil. (1861)

This plant from India is a member of the section *Cirrhopetalum* and was
introduced by Conrad Loddiges in 1836 and described by him in 1840. The
leaves are as tall as 13 cm and the scapes are about the same length. The dorsal sepal is 0.8 cm long and the petals are 0.4 cm, both with long threadlike
apices, while the lateral sepals are each 3.5 cm long and 0.6 cm wide. These
measurements are from the type specimen in the Paris herbarium. Besides
India, the natural habitat is Myanmar, Thailand, and Vietnam at roughly
1000 m elevation. The species has on occasion been found growing very
contentedly near waterfalls. An intermediate temperature with an abundant
supply of moisture suit it quite well and pots or baskets with a moisture-
retentive potting mix and light shade are the conditions of choice.

Cirrhopetalum pingtungensis (Ying & Chen) Garay, Hamer &
   Siegerist (1994)

SYNONYM
Bulbophyllum pingtungensis Ying & Chen (1988)

This very striking flower has been found only at Taiwan's lower altitudes
and is part of the section *Recurvae*. The plant is a good size, and the two to
three flowers per inflorescence are pale lime green with dark maroon lines
and edging on the slightly hirsute dorsal sepals. The dark maroon petals have
pale lemon edges with long dark maroon cilia, and the labellum is brownish
red. The dorsal sepal is about 2 cm long and the lateral sepals 3 cm long.
These plants can be grown in warm, lightly shaded conditions in large containers with enough moisture to simulate the natural forest conditions.
PLATE 58

Cirrhopetalum pseudopicturatum Garay

SYNONYM
Cirrhopetalum picturatum of some authors, not Loddiges (1840) ex Lindley

This plant has for more than 125 years been incorrectly called *Cirrhopetalum picturatum* despite differences in its petals and the size of its flowers.
The petals of this plant are broadly triangular-ovate, with a blunt apex, and
are never hirsute. The color can be yellow-green to yellow with purple dots.
Many plants in cultivation today are labeled *C. picturatum* but are correctly *C.
pseudopicturatum* and were imported from Myanmar. Intermediate conditions
with an ample supply of water are necessary for good cultivation.

Cirrhopetalum puguahaanense (Ames) Garay, Hamer & Siegerist (1994)

SYNONYMS
Bulbophyllum chekaense Carr (1932)
Bulbophyllum puguahaanense Ames (1915)

The specific name of this orchid of the section *Wallichii* refers to the area in which it grows in the Philippines. The pseudobulbs are close together and have a leaf that is about 7 cm long and 2 cm wide and a very short scape only 2.5 cm long with two nice flowers. The dorsal sepal is less than 0.5 cm long and pointed apically, the lateral sepals are about 1.5 cm long and 0.5 cm wide with only the apices free, and the petals are minute but visibly pointed. Pale yellow is the base color, with the dorsal sepal and petals spotted and veined with light red, while the lateral sepals are darker yellow toward the apices with light red spots. This species can be grown in pots or baskets in warm to intermediate areas with light shade and high humidity.

Cirrhopetalum pulchrum N. E. Brown (1886)

SYNONYM
Bulbophyllum pulchrum J. J. Smith (1912), not *B. pulchrum* Schlechter (1912) of the genus *Hapalochilus*

This, again, is a typical member of the section *Cirrhopetalum* with the long coherent lateral sepals, dorsal sepal with a long hairy projection that may widen at the tip into a small palae, and petals that are apically pubescent with hirsute edges and a threadlike projection. The most unusual aspect is the stelae on the column which are 0.2 cm or more long and arched. This species is found in Indonesia and the Moluccas and can be grown in warm to intermediate shaded areas, either in containers or mounted. It is not a difficult species to grow and rewards the grower with a fine crop of lovely flowers. PLATE 59

Cirrhopetalum retusiusculum (Reichenbach fil.) Hemsley (1882)

SYNONYMS
not *Bulbophyllum micholitzii* (Rolfe) Seidenfaden & Smitinand (1961) which is *Cirrhopetalum micholitzii* Rolfe (1912)
not *Bulbophyllum muscicolum* Reichenbach fil. (1872) which is *Cirrhopetalum wallichii* Lindley (1830)
Bulbophyllum retusiusculum Reichenbach fil. (1869)
not *Cirrhopetalum flavisepalum* Hayata (1914) also of the section *Cirrhopetalum*
not *Cirrhopetalum touranense* Gagnepain (1931) and not *C. touranense* var. *breviflorum* Gagnepain (1933), both of which are *C. skeatianum* (Ridley) Garay, Hamer & Siegerist (1994)

This very pretty member of the section *Cirrhopetalum* has at one time or another been called by several different names. The pseudobulbs are about 3 cm tall, ovoid, and 2 to 3 cm apart on the rhizomes. The leaf can be 10 cm long but is only about 1 to 1.5 cm wide. The inflorescence is usually the same length as the leaves or slightly longer and has an umbel of as many as a dozen flowers. The flowers vary in color, but usually the dorsal sepal and the petals are a nice shade of purple, the lateral sepals are tan or yellow, and the labellum is purple. The dorsal sepal and the petals are minute, and the lateral sepals are almost entirely connate and only 1.5 to 2.5 cm long. The plants grow from Nepal and India east to the Malay Peninsula, Laos, Vietnam, Taiwan, and Thailand from 300 to 2500 m above sea level. They can be cultivated in pots, baskets, or on slabs in warm to intermediate temperatures, with light shade and daily watering but must be in a potting medium that allows them to dry out each night.

Cirrhopetalum robustum Rolfe (1893)

SYNONYMS

Bulbophyllum graveolens (Bailey) J. J. Smith (1912), *Cirrhopetalum graveolens* Bailey (1896)

not *Bulbophyllum robustum* Rolfe which is *B. coriophorum* Ridley (1886)

This orchid is indeed a robust member of the section *Cirrhopetalum* with pseudobulbs as large as 10 cm tall that are spaced about 4 cm apart on the rhizomes. The leaves can be 66 cm long and 10 cm wide, and the scape as long as 20 cm or more with eight or nine flowers. The dorsal sepal is about 3 cm long and pale yellow green. The lateral sepals are approximately 5 cm long, conjoined for most of their length, and are also pale yellow green but with the area around the labellum a very dark red. The petals are about 1.5 cm long and heavily suffused dark red. This flower presents a striking appearance since the central portion of the pale sepals are dark red, and the labellum and the interiors of the lateral sepals also are dark red. This orchid is found only at the lower elevations of Papua New Guinea and requires lightly shaded, warm, and moist conditions for successful cultivation. Large and heavy containers are most suitable with perhaps a bit of broken clay pot or rocks in the bottom to balance the pots. These flowers are not only striking, but they are also long lasting.

Cirrhopetalum roseopunctatum Garay, Hamer & Siegerist (1995)

This species of the section *Cirrhopetalum* has pseudobulbs that are 3 cm tall, not closely adjacent to one another, and the single leaf is 16 cm long and 3 cm wide. The dorsal sepal is less than 1 cm long and almost round with three to five dentate apical projections. The petals are very much smaller with dentate apices, and the lateral sepals are 2.5 cm long and 1 cm wide.

This plant has a very pretty flower with its white lateral sepals that are spotted dark red and the dorsal sepals that are even more heavily spotted. The column is graced with long stelidia that have two projecting points. There may be as many as 17 flowers in each whorl. The type specimen probably came from Vietnam and was grown by Lucien Tempera of Copaigue, New York, and flowered in May 1990. The specific name refers, of course, to the rose-dotted lateral sepals.

Cirrhopetalum roxburghii Lindley (1830)
SYNONYMS
Aerides radiatum Roxburgh ex Lindley (1830)
Bulbophyllum roxburghii (Lindley) Reichenbach fil. (1861)

Strangely enough, this plant belonging to the section *Recurvae* had also been referred to the genus *Aerides* at one time. It grows on trees in the Ganges delta of India and is a plant of moderate size with leaves to 10 cm long and floral scapes about twice that length. The pseudobulbs are globose, and the barring on the umbel of yellow flowers seems to form a halo when viewed from above. The flowers are not greatly recurved, the petals are falcate, and the column is alate (that is, it has a straight wing). These are important distinctions because this species has very frequently been confused with *Cirrhopetalum sikkimense*. *Cirrhopetalum roxburghii* is best grown in pots or baskets in lightly shaded, warm areas with a moderate supply of water.

Cirrhopetalum sikkimense King & Pantling (1898)
SYNONYM
Bulbophyllum sikkimense (King & Pantling) J. J. Smith (1912)

This lovely plant also comes from India and is often confused with another member of the section *Recurvae*, *Cirrhopetalum roxburghii*, but there are recognizable differences: the inflorescence is equal to or slightly shorter than the leaves of the plant, the flowers are recurved, the petals are triangular, there is no telltale "halo" formed by the barring on the flowers, and the column wings are not straight and incurved. Cultivation is best accomplished in pots or baskets in warm conditions with moderate shade and regular watering and fertilizing.

Cirrhopetalum skeatianum (Ridley) Garay, Hamer and Siegerist (1994)
SYNONYMS
Bulbophyllum skeatianum Ridley (1915)
Cirrhopetalum touranense Gagnepain (1931)

This small orchid of the section *Cirrhopetalum* has pseudobulbs that are only 2 cm tall and 1 cm apart with leaves that are 6.5 cm long and 1 cm wide. The inflorescence is dark purple, approximately 10 cm tall, and has an umbel of 10 colorful flowers. The pedicels are less than 1 cm long and are bright orange. The small dorsal sepal is cucullate with purple markings. The lateral sepals are conjoined for almost their entire length, are slightly less than 2 cm long, and are bright orange with yellow apices. The round petals are almost the same size and color as the dorsal sepal, and the labellum is yellow with a red apex. The plants grow in Malaya at medium elevations. Cultivation can be in pots or baskets or on slabs in light shade with intermediate temperatures and high humidity.

Cirrhopetalum taeniophyllum (Parish & Reichenbach fil.) Hooker fil. (1890)

SYNONYMS
Bulbophyllum mundulum (Bull) J. J. Smith (1912), *Cirrhopetalum mundulum* Bull (1891)
Bulbophyllum simillinum Parish & Reichenbach fil. (1883), *Cirrhopetalum simillinum* (Parish & Reichenbach fil.) Hooker fil. (1890)
Bulbophyllum taeniophyllum Parish & Reichenbach fil. (1874)

Since the pseudobulbs of this species belonging to the section *Wallichii* are widespread, often as much as 9 cm apart, with leaves as tall as 16 cm and inflorescences only 9 cm tall, the plant needs room to expand. There are many flowers per inflorescence, and the dorsal sepal is cupped, finely serrate, and less than 1 cm long. The lateral sepals are about 1.5 cm long and are connate only on the apical portion. The petals are minute, triangular, and serrate, and the whole flower is greenish white with dark purple spotting. This entity grows in forests up to 1000 m elevation in Myanmar, Thailand, Laos, Malaya, Sumatra, Java, and adjacent areas. It should be cultivated on slabs of some sort so that it has room to meander. It requires a lot of moisture, therefore it would be well to pad the mount with spaghnum, coconut fiber, osmunda, or some other moisture-retentive material. Light shade and gentle air circulation are helpful in producing good growth and flowers.

Cirrhopetalum tigridum (Hance) Rolfe (1903)

SYNONYMS
Bulbophyllum retusiusculum var. *tigridum* (Hance) Tsi (1995)
Bulbophyllum tigridum Hance (1883)

This plant is very small, with an overall height of only about 3 cm and an inflorescence that is only slightly longer. It belongs to the section *Wallichii* and comes from China, Hong Kong, and Taiwan. It needs small pots or slabs with warm temperatures and light shade and a steady supply of moisture. The illustration of the type specimen is by Fritz Hamer of Marie Selby Botanical Gardens in Sarasota, Florida.

Cirrhopetalum umbellatum (Forster fil.) Hooker fil. & Arnold (1832)

SYNONYMS

Bulbophyllum clavigerum (Fitzgerald) Dockrill (1964), not *B. clavigerum* Perrier (1951) of the section *Ptiloglossum*, *Cirrhopetalum clavigerum* Fitzgerald (1883), *Phyllorchis clavigera* (Fitzgerald) Kuntze (1891)

Bulbophyllum layardii (F. von Mueller & Kraenzlin) J. J. Smith (1912), *Cirrhopetalum layardii* F. von Mueller & Kraenzlin (1894)

Bulbophyllum longiflorum Thouars (1822), not *B. longiflorum* Ridley (1896) which is *B. inunctum* J. J. Smith (1906), *Cirrhopetalum longiflorum* (Thouars) Schlechter (1915), *Phyllorchis longiflora* (Thouars) Kuntze (1891)

Bulbophyllum umbellatum J. J. Smith (1905), *Cymbidium umbellatum* (Forster fil.) Sprengel (1815), *Epidendrum umbellatum* Forster fil. (1786), *Phyllorchis umbellatum* (Forster fil.) Kuntze (1891)

Cirrhopetalum africanum Schlechter (1915)

Cirrhopetalum thomasinii Lindley ex Josst (1851)

Cirrhopetalum thouarsii Lindley (1824), *C. thouarsii* var. *concolor* Rolfe (1892), *Phyllorchis thouarsii* (Lindley) Kuntze (1891)

The number of synonyms for this species that belongs to the section *Cirrhopetalum* is incredible and confusing because at one time the plant was even referred to the genus *Cymbidium* and then in 1891 Carl E. O. Kuntze moved everything to the genus *Phyllorchis*. The plant is about 15 to 20 cm high, with approximately 5 cm between pseudobulbs. The inflorescence is at least as tall as the plant and has as many as a dozen flowers. The dorsal sepal is less than 1 cm long and has a very long thread projecting from its apex. It is usually pale off-white with various degrees of dark red spotting. The lateral sepals are conjoined for most of their length and are about 4 cm long. They may be pale ivory or spotted with dark red-brown. The small petals have many cilia and are heavily spotted dark red, and the column has long pointed stelidia. *Cirrhopetalum umbellatum* grows throughout Africa, Madagascar, east through the Malay Peninsula, Philippines, New Guinea, Australia, New Caledonia, Fiji, Tahiti, and Guam. The plants are found from low elevations to 1700 m in forests. Intermediate to warm temperatures and a large container suit them very well. They, too, are easy plants to grow and flower and reward the grower with many beautiful blossoms.

Cirrhopetalum wallichii Lindley (1830)

SYNONYMS

Bulbophyllum hookeri (Duthie) J. J. Smith (1912), *Cirrhopetalum hookeri* Duthie (1902)

Bulbophyllum muscicolum Reichenbach fil. (1892)

not *Bulbophyllum wallichii* Reichenbach fil. (1861) of the section
Tripudianthes, not *Cirrhopetalum wallichii* Lindley (1839) which is
Bulbophyllum wallichii Reichenbach fil. (1861)

This species of the section *Wallichii* also has a very confusing nomenclatural background. When John Lindley described it, he mentioned specimens
which did not match the description and this naturally led to many plants
being called *Cirrhopetalum wallichii* which were actually quite different. The
pseudobulbs are about 2 cm tall and close together, the leaf can be 10 cm tall
but is usually much shorter, with the floral bracts 12 cm or more long. There
are sometimes as many as 10 flowers per umbel, each about 4 cm long, and
they are a pleasing brick red color. This species comes from India, Nepal,
and China at elevations as high as 2400 m above sea level. It requires cool
temperatures and a somewhat shaded and moist environment in which to
grow.

Cirrhopetalum wightii Thwaites (1861)

SYNONYMS

Bulbophyllum elliae Reichenbach fil. (1861), *Cirrhopetalum elliae* (Reichenbach
    fil.) Trimen (1885)
Cirrhopetalum macraei Wight (1851), not *C. macraei* Lindley which is
    Bulbophyllum macraei (Lindley) Reichenbach fil. (1861)
Cirrhopetalum roseum Jayaweera (1963)

The pseudobulbs of this member of the section *Cirrhopetalum* are about 2
cm long and spaced 6.5 cm apart on the rhizomes. The leaves can be 14 cm
long and 2.7 cm wide. The inflorescence is about 6 cm long, decurved, with
five to eight flowers in an umbel. The dorsal sepal is spathulate, apically
erose, to 0.7 cm long and 0.4 cm wide. The lateral sepals are about 1.5 cm
long, and the petals are serrate and less than 0.4 cm long. The labellum is
ligulate and less than 0.5 cm long. The flowers are a nice greenish color with
red dots. This epiphyte grows in Sri Lanka in wet evergreen forests above
850 m altitude and can be cultivated in pots or baskets or on slabs in warm to
intermediate conditions with light shade, good humidity, and gentle air
movement.

CHAPTER 8

Allied Genera

B eside *Cirrhopetalum*, several genera are closely allied to the genus *Bulbo-phyllum*, many of which are desirable plants for hobbyists to grow. Some of them are old favorites that are now using a new scientific name, usually in an attempt to classify them more accurately. Often species and genera are shuffled around when more specimens are collected and a broader picture of the relationships is obtained. Many of these allied genera will readily interbreed with the bulbophyllums and cirrhopetalums as well as each other, thus opening up a whole new aspect of orchid breeding as well as hybrid nomenclature.

Some plants described in this chapter may not be considered good horticultural subjects for the average home orchid grower because they may have very tiny flowers, short blooming periods, and so forth, but they are all interesting species and well worth knowing about as possible additions to the orchid collection.

As with the genera *Bulbophyllum* and *Cirrhopetalum*, so too other genera described in this chapter go through a dry season that does not mean a total absence of water but only a greatly reduced amount. The plants should not be allowed to wither and dry out completely, but the water should be monitored closely. For instance, if you normally water every day, perhaps once every third or fourth day would be appropriate for the "dry season." Watch the plants very closely and if the leaves fall or the pseudobulbs wither, the plants may be too dry.

Acrochaene Lindley (1853)

In this genus the anther is one-celled with two pollinia, and the lateral sepals are fully adnate to the sides of the long column foot, while the petals are vertical at the base of the column. Type: *Acrochaene punctata* Lindley (1853)

Acrochaene punctata Lindley (1853)

SYNONYMS
Bulbophyllum kingii Hooker fil. (1888)
Monomeria punctata (Lindley) Schlechter (1915)

The raceme is dense and sharply pendulous, and the flowers are 2.5 cm long, olive green with small red dots. The petals are always longer than the column. This species comes from Sikkim, Darjeeling, and Bhutan and requires intermediate to cool conditions to grow well.

Chaseella Summerhayes (1961)

Only one species belongs to the genus *Chaseella*.

Chaseella pseudohydra Summerhayes (1961)

This small plant has pseudobulbs that are about 2.5 cm apart and approximately 0.6 cm tall and 0.5 cm wide with 6 to 11 leaves at the apex. The leaves are tiny, fleshy, about 1.2 cm long and 0.1 cm wide, and with the pseudobulbs reminded Victor Summerhayes of *Hydra*, a genus of invertebrate animals having a single internal cavity such as jellyfish and corals, hence the specific name. The inflorescence has one or two minute flowers that are bright red. The plants grow in Zimbabwe and Kenya in rain forests at approximately 2000 m elevation. To successfully grow these tiny but interesting plants, the grower must keep them in somewhat shady, intermediate conditions and give them copious amounts of water.

Codonosiphon Schlechter (1912)

The pseudobulbs are very close together on the rhizome, and the dorsal sepal is connate with the lateral sepals which are united into a bell-shaped tube. The column foot is firmly attached to the labellum, and the column is slender and almost without a foot. Type: *Bulbophyllum codoanthum* Schlechter (1914)

Codonosiphon campanulatum Schlechter (1914)

The pseudobulbs of this species are about 2 cm tall and are close together on the rhizomes. The leaf can be 13 cm long and almost 2 cm wide. The dark red flower is 1 cm long. The species grows on trees in the mist forests of Papua New Guinea at about 1000 m altitude and requires very moist conditions and shady intermediate temperatures.

Codonosiphon papuanum Schlechter (1914)

The pseudobulbs of this species are slightly smaller than the others of the genus, and the leaf is only 7.5 cm tall. The flowers are less than 1 cm in size and are dark red, while the apex of the labellum is bright yellow. The species, too, grows as an epiphyte in the forests of New Guinea at approximately 1000 m above sea level and needs intermediate temperatures, some shade, and very moist conditions to survive.

Drymoda Lindley (1838)

These are small plants with a single leaf and usually only one flower per inflorescence. The column is short with spreading wings, the lateral sepals are attached to the end of the very long column foot, and there are four pollinia. Type: *Drymoda picta* Lindley (1838)

Drymoda digitata (J. J. Smith) Garay, Hamer & Siegerist (1994)
SYNONYMS
Bulbophyllum digitatum J. J. Smith (1911), *Monomeria digitata* (J. J. Smith) Kittredge (1985)

This small species has more than one flower per inflorescence. It is native to Papua New Guinea and can best be cultivated on small pieces of bark or tree fern in moist, intermediate conditions.

Drymoda gymnopus (Hooker fil.) Garay, Hamer & Siegerist (1994)
BASIONYM
Bulbophyllum gymnopus Hooker fil. (1890)

This species has narrow pseudobulbs, leaves that may be as long as 20 cm, and many flowers on each long inflorescence. The flowers are greenish white with a yellow labellum and are widely spaced from the base to the tip of the inflorescence. The species grows in the Himalayas as high as 1200 m above sea level and can be cultivated on tree fern or bark slabs in intermediate conditions with light shade and high humidity.

Drymoda picta Lindley (1838)

The pseudobulbs are 1.3 cm wide, discoid, with a single leaf that is 1 cm long and fugacious. The inflorescence is 5 cm tall and has one yellow-green flower with purple stripes that can be 1.5 cm long. The labellum is dark maroon. The species grows in Myanmar, Thailand, and Laos from sea level to 1300 m and can be cultivated on tree fern or bark mounts in warm to intermediate conditions.

Drymoda siamensis Schlechter (1906)

This species greatly resembles *Drymoda picta* except that the young pseudobulbs are extremely wrinkled and covered with papillae of calcium carbonate crystals, and the labellum is larger than in the other species. The leaf is tiny and quickly deciduous. The plants grow in Thailand and Laos at 600 to 900 m elevation. Cultivation is best accomplished when the plants are mounted on bark or tree fern in warm to intermediate temperatures with light shade and high humidity. PLATE 60

Epicrianthes Blume (1825)

This slow-growing genus is pendent with a branching rhizome that is covered with silver-gray sheaths. It is noted for its unusual petals which are very tiny and have a number of extremely mobile ornaments. There is one flower per inflorescence, the flowers open widely, and the sepals are usually the same shape and size. Type: *Epicrianthes javanica* Blume (1825)

Epicrianthes cimicina (J. J. Vermeulen) Garay & Kittredge (1985)

BASIONYM
Bulbophyllum cimicinum J. J. Vermeulen (1982)

This species is found in Papua New Guinea and has a most unusual growth habit, forming branching strands that hang down from limbs of trees in rain forests at altitudes of 500 m above sea level. These forests have a dry season each year which must be reproduced in greenhouse culture if this species of *Epicrianthes* is to survive. The pseudobulbs are basally appressed to the rhizomes, and the apical portions recurve. The leaves are 3 cm long and 2 cm wide, thick, and acute. The inflorescence has a single flower which is held close to the pseudobulb, but there are many of them that open in succession. The flowers are small, yellow, and have long thin protrusions on the petals which are covered with black hairs. Each flower is open about a week. This species requires mounting on horizontal slabs, a definite dry period during the year, and good air movement for successful cultivation.

Epicrianthes decarhopalon (Schlechter) Garay & Kittredge (1985)

SYNONYM
Bulbophyllum decarhopalon Schlechter (1913)

The pseudobulbs of this species are about 1 cm tall and 2 to 3 cm apart on the pendulous rhizome, and they press against the rhizome for a portion of their length, then curve slightly outwards. The leaf is about 8 cm long with the apical portion slightly decurved. The inflorescence is short, and the single flower is about 1 cm across. The sepals are pale with purple spots as are the bases of the petals, but the rest of the petals consists of 10 lumpy, pendent, mobile appendages. The labellum also has purple spots and has shiny verrucose edges. The plants grow in deep shade in rainforests near rivers, but they do have a dry season each year. These flowers, too, last only a few days.

Epicrianthes haniffii (Carr) Garay & Kittredge (1985)

SYNONYMS
Bulbophyllum haniffii Carr (1932)

This plant grows in Thailand, Myanmar, Malaya, and Laos at 800 to 1000 m altitude. It has a creeping, branching, pendent habit, and the very small pseudobulbs are carried on the thick rhizomes about 1 to 2 cm apart. The leaves are 4 cm long, and the flower is less than 3 cm across with the sepals all quite similar, 0.5 to 0.7 cm long. The petals are minute and have two groups of slender, hirsute palae that can be 0.5 cm long. The labellum is about 0.3 cm long and carries many tiny globular protrusions along either side. This species, too, is best grown on slabs in moderate temperatures and light. A dry period stimulates flowering. This flower is absolutely fascinating with the globules on the labellum and the wonderful mobile appendages to the petals. The flowering season may be short, but the unusual flowers make it all worthwhile.

Epicrianthes javanica Blume (1825)

SYNONYMS
Bulbophyllum epicrianthes Hooker fil. (1890), *B. epicrianthes* var. *sumatranum*
  (J. J. Smith) J. J. Vermeulen (1982)
Bulbophyllum javanicum J. J. Smith (1918), *B. javanicum* var. *sumatranum*
  J. J. Smith (1920), *Phyllorchis javanica* (Blume) Kuntze (1891)

This species, too, is pendent, with about 1 to 2 cm between pseudobulbs, leaves approximately 4 cm long, and short inflorescences bearing a single interesting flower. All sepals are similar, less than 1 cm long, yellow with red-brown suffusion at the base. The petals are minute, with about a dozen fleshy, mobile appendages that are white with dark spots. The labellum is almost 1 cm long with a papillose surface and base. This species grows in Myanmar, Sumatra, Borneo, Java, and Indonesia on trees without moss at low elevations. It can be grown on tree slabs without padding, in somewhat shaded areas that are warm and have a seasonal dry period.

Epicrianthes undecifila (J. J. Smith) Garay & Kittredge (1985)

SYNONYM
Bulbophyllum undecifilum J. J. Smith (1927)

This pendent species has small pseudobulbs only 1 or 2 cm apart and ovate leaves about 5 cm long and 2 cm wide. The single-flowered inflorescence is 1 cm long. The petals and sepals are white or yellow with reddish spots, and the petals have many filiform, elliptic, green appendages. These plants grow in shaded areas on moss-covered tree trunks from 600 to 1700 m elevation in Java and Borneo. The specific name is of Latin derivation—*undecim* means "eleven" and *filum* means "thread"—and refers to the many appendages on the petals. This species can be grown on small pieces of cork, tree fern, or osmunda with spaghnum padding, in shady areas at intermediate temperatures and with copious moisture.

Ferruminaria Garay, Hamer & Siegerist (1994)

In this genus the plants are epiphytes with slender rhizomes, and the pseudobulbs are close together and have a single leaf. The inflorescences are fasciculate and have but one flower each. The dorsal sepal is free, and the lateral sepals are spreading and laterally adnate to the column foot. The petals are small, and the labellum is fleshy and firmly fused to the column foot. The column is short with a distinct foot which is confluent with the base of the labellum. There are four pollinia in two pairs, without caudicles or viscidia. The generic name means "to cement, bind or join" and refers to the fusion of the labellum to the column foot. Type: *Bulbophyllum brastagiense* Carr (1933)

Ferruminaria brastagiensis (Carr) Garay, Hamer & Siegerist (1994)

SYNONYM
Bulbophyllum brastagiense Carr (1933)

Cedric E. Carr found this species in the woods behind the Brastagi Hotel in Malaya and named it for the hotel. The rhizomes are covered with dry sheaths, and the pseudobulbs can be 1.7 cm tall, grooved, and 1.5 cm apart. The leaf can be as large as 6 cm long and 1 cm wide. There are six or more inflorescences that arise from the base of the ovoid pseudobulbs, and each one is about 4 cm long and has one flower. The dorsal sepal is 1 cm long and has ciliate margins, the lateral sepals are narrow, 1 cm long, with ciliate margins, and the petals are less than 0.5 cm long. The sepals are yellow green with red markings, and the petals are pale green with black dots. The labellum is about 0.7 cm long and 0.3 cm wide. The plants are found at approximately 1600 m above sea level and need intermediate conditions in which to grow.

Ferruminaria melinantha (Schlechter) Garay, Hamer & Siegerist (1994)

BASIONYM
Bulbophyllum melinanthum Schlechter (1905)

This species is similar to *Ferruminaria brastagiensis*, but the small flowers are yellow to orange. The plants grow on trees in Papua New Guinea at elevations of 50 to 100 m above sea level. Cultivation requires warm temperatures and high humidity.

Hapalochilus (Schlechter) Senghas (1978)

The column is arcuate, without a foot, and basally tumid. The labellum is fused to the column and thus does not move. All three sepals are free from one another (possibly the lateral sepals may be connate), and almost all species are native to New Guinea. Type: *Bulbophyllum nitidum* Schlechter (1912)

Hapalochilus aristilabris (J. J. Smith) Garay & Kittredge (1985)
SYNONYM
Bulbophyllum aristilabre J. J. Smith (1912)

The pseudobulbs are close together and 1.5 cm tall, and the leaf is about 11 cm long. The large solitary flower is held on a scape almost 6 cm tall, the sepals are about 5 cm long and 3 cm wide, the petals are minute, and the labellum is more than 4 cm long and about 0.3 cm wide. The flower is white with dark red-violet markings. This species grows as an epiphyte in riverine forests in New Guinea at about 300 m above sea level. It can be cultivated in pots with media that retains some moisture, in warm conditions, with slight shade and good air movement.

Hapalochilus bandischii Garay, Hamer & Siegerist (1995)

This species resembles *Hapalochilus coloratus* in the shape of the flowers and the general appearance, but the petals are quite different as they are fili-form, 1 cm long, and have rounded, broad bases. This species grows in Papua New Guinea near Lake Kutubu at 950 m elevation. The type specimen was collected by Wolfgang Bandisch, after whom the species was named.

Hapalochilus capillipes (J. J. Smith) Garay & Kittredge (1985)
SYNONYM
Bulbophyllum capillipes J. J. Smith (1908)

The small pseudobulbs are close together and have one leaf about 5 cm long. The 2-cm long flower is reddish brown with an orange labellum and is held well above the leaves. The sepals are all about 1 cm long, the petals are minute, and the verrucose labellum is held parallel to the ground and is widened at the middle. The species grows in New Guinea at about 500 m above sea level and can be cultivated in light shade at warm temperatures in containers filled with a medium that drains well.

Hapalochilus coloratus (J. J. Smith) Garay & Kittredge (1985)
SYNONYM
Bulbophyllum coloratum J. J. Smith (1911)

The pseudobulbs are close together, 5 cm tall, and have one leaf that is 18 cm long. The single flower has sepals slightly more than 1 cm long, white with purple markings, and the labellum is thickened, bright orange with dark maroon spots, and is about 1 cm long. This species grows as an epiphyte on moss-covered tree limbs in New Guinea's coastal areas. Plants can be main-tained in small pots with a mix of moisture-retentive material and warm, moist, shady conditions. The striking contrast of colors makes this a most desirable plant to grow.

Hapalochilus cruciatus (J. J. Smith) Garay & Kittredge (1985)

SYNONYM
Bulbophyllum cruciatum J. J. Smith (1911)

This species grows in New Guinea on the trunks and branches of large trees in low-altitude rainforests. The pseudobulbs are about 1 cm apart on the rhizomes and are 1.5 cm tall. The leaves are 10 cm tall and apiculate. The inflorescences are exceedingly short, less than 1 cm long, and have only one small white-and-purple flower that opens only during the day. Unfortunately, the flower lasts only two or three days and since it is carried almost at ground level, it takes a keen eye to catch it open. This species requires a moist environment and does best mounted on slabs of cork. Good air circulation and moderate shade are helpful.

Hapalochilus formosus (Schlechter) Garay & Kittredge (1985)

SYNONYM
Bulbophyllum formosum Schlechter (1912)

The pseudobulbs of this very graceful species are 4 cm tall with leaves approximately 13 cm long. The scape is 12 cm tall, erect, with one large, beautiful flower. The sepals are more than 6 cm long, only 0.5 cm wide, and white with wine-colored stripes. The labellum is about the same length, yellow at the base with wine-colored papillae, and shading to white on the long, acuminate apex. This species grows as an epiphyte on trees in forests of New Guinea at 800 m altitude. It is easily cultivated in small pots with a well-drained mix such as those containing a good proportion of bark or tree fern chunks, in warm to intermediate temperatures with regular watering but not continuously damp conditions. It has a striking flower with thin and elegant sepals that are quite colorful.

Hapalochilus immobilis (Schlechter) Garay, Hamer & Siegerist (1995)

SYNONYM
Bulbophyllum immobile Schlechter (1913)

This species is very similar to *Hapalochilus cruciatus* and was originally thought to be synonymous with it, but new collections have shown the flowers to be quite a bit smaller and the petals to have small differences. It grows in much the same areas and can be cultivated in the same manner.

Hapalochilus lohokii (Vermeulen & Lamb) Garay, Hamer & Siegerist (1994)

SYNONYM
Bulbophyllum lohokii Vermeulen & Lamb (1994)

This species is the westernmost member of this genus as yet recorded. The 2-cm tall pseudobulbs are about 1 cm apart on the rhizome, and the leaf can be as tall as 6 cm. The inflorescence rises nearly to the top of the leaves and bears one well-displayed flower. All the sepals are slightly more than 1 cm long, the petals are about half that size, and the labellum is immobile, about 1 cm long with thick, papillose margins. The flower is pale yellow with dark maroon markings, and the labellum is yellow. The species has been found in Malaysia on small branches in the understory of forests from 1700 to 2000 m above sea level.

Hapalochilus longilabris (Schlechter) Garay & Kittredge (1985)

SYNONYMS
Bulbophyllum efogi name used in gardening
Bulbophyllum longilabre Schlechter (1912)

This species was named, of course, for the very much elongated labellum which can reach 3.5 cm long. The sepals are also elongated, being as much as 3 cm long, but the petals are only 0.2 cm long. The petals are yellow with dark red veins and shading, but the labellum is white, making a great contrast. This species has been awarded as *Bulbophyllum efogi* 'Fox Den' CBM/AOS in New York in August 1977.

Hapalochilus neoebudicus Garay, Hamer & Siegerist (1995)

The authors felt this new species from Tanna Island, Vanuatu, is closest to *Hapalochilus stenophyton* Garay & Kittredge (1985) but differs in flowers that are approximately twice as large and have a linear petal with a rounded apex that is 0.3 cm long and 0.1 cm wide. The type specimen was grown in the collection of the Missouri Botanical Garden in St. Louis, and the specific name is derived from the Latin *ebudicus*. This orchid is from Vanuatu (formerly known as New Hebrides).

Hapalochilus nitidus (Schlechter) Garay & Kittredge (1985)

SYNONYM
Bulbophyllum nitidum Schlechter (1912)

The pseudobulbs of this species are 2 cm tall and have one 11-cm long leaf. The scape is about 9 cm long and has one flower which has long, gracefully curved white with red-striped sepals 4.5 cm long, minute petals, and a labellum as long as the sepals that is white with dark red spots. The species grows as an epiphyte in the forests of New Guinea at approximately 1200 m altitude. It is an extremely attractive species and can be cultivated in pots or baskets, or on slabs but must be kept warm and in the shade, and be given considerable moisture daily. PLATE 61

Hapalochilus stabilis (J. J. Smith) Garay & Kittredge (1985)

SYNONYM
Bulbophyllum stabile J. J. Smith (1911)

The pseudobulbs of this species are clustered together and are usually less than 1 cm tall with leaves that are about 4 cm long. The inflorescence is about 6 cm tall and bears only one flower that is 2.5 cm long. The dorsal sepal is roughly 1 cm long and concave, and the lateral sepals are widely reflexed, about the same length. The labellum is slightly shorter, swollen, and does not move. The flower is rose purple and lasts only three days. This species is endemic to New Guinea and can be found in low-altitude rain forests growing on twigs. It is essential to supply adequate moisture, shade, and air movement to assure proper growth throughout most of the year, then a short dry period to initiate flowering.

Hapalochilus stenophyllum (Schlechter) Garay & Kittredge (1985)

SYNONYM
Bulbophyllum stenophyllum Schlechter (1912)

This small plant has crowded pseudobulbs that are 1 to 2 cm tall with one thin 7-cm long leaf. The inflorescence is about 4 cm long and carries one 1-cm white-and-purple flower which has a bright yellow-and-white labellum with purple spots. The flowers are diurnal and last only a few days. The plants can be cultivated in pots or baskets and need warm temperatures and abundant moisture. This species is native to New Guinea.

Hapalochilus striatus Garay & Kittredge (1985)

SYNONYM
Bulbophyllum pulchrum Schlechter (1912), not *B. pulchrum* J. J. Smith (1912)
    which is *Cirrhopetalum pulchrum* N. E. Brown (1886)

This species is about 18 cm tall with pseudobulbs that are 3 cm tall and are close together. The leaves can be 15 cm long. The scape is about 10 cm long and bears one flower. The sepals are lanceolate and more than 4 cm long, and the petals are minute. The labellum is about 4 cm long, lanceolate, with the apex acuminate and papillose. The flower is pale cream with dark red suffusions and stripes. This species grows as an epiphyte in forests of New Guinea at about 800 m altitude. It is a strikingly beautiful orchid and can be cultivated on tree fern or wood mounts or in pots or baskets with bark and fiber mixes in warm, lightly shaded, moist conditions.

Hapalochilus trachyglottis (Schlechter) Garay & Kittredge (1986)

BASIONYM
Bulbophyllum trachyglottis Schlechter (1905)

The dark red sepals of this beautiful flower open widely and have pure white borders. The labellum is also dark red with the edges fading to white. The species comes from the Solomon Islands and Fiji.

Ione Lindley (1853)

In this interesting genus the rostellum is shaped like a horseshoe with diverging points, each of which accepts pollinia independently through stipes or glands. *Ione* has at times been considered conspecific with the genus *Sunipia*. The plants are found from the Himalayas to Myanmar and the northern areas of Thailand at rather high altitudes. They require cool to intermediate temperatures, frequent watering, moderate shade, and good air circulation. Lectotype: *Sunipia bicolor* Lindley (1883)

Ione angustipetala (Seidenfaden) Seidenfaden (1995)
BASIONYM
Sunipia angustipetala Seidenfaden (1980)

This species is endemic to Chiengmai (Thailand). It has pseudobulbs about 1 cm tall and 2 to 2.5 cm apart on the rhizomes. The leaves are 8 cm long and 1 cm wide, and the inflorescence has three to four flowers. The sepals and petals are spreading, each more than 1 cm long, and the petals have inrolled edges. Intermediate temperatures and a bit of shade are needed for successful cultivation.

Ione rimannii (Reichenbach fil.) Seidenfaden (1995)
SYNONYMS
Acrochaene rimannii Reichenbach fil. (1882), *Monomeria rimannii* (Reichenbach fil.) Schlechter (1915), *Sunipia rimannii* (Reichenbach fil.) Seidenfaden (1980)
Ione salweenensis (Phillimore & W. W. Smith) Schlechter (1915), *Sunipia salweenensis* (Phillimore & W. W. Smith) Hunt (1971)

This species occurs in northern Thailand, and when Heinrich Gustav Reichenbach described *Acrochaene rimannii* in the *Gardener's Chronicle* (June 1882), he made these comments:

Mr. Rimann, who is travelling for Mr. F. Sander in tropical Asia, has just sent a very curious Orchid which has flowers of the finest lilac-purple, nearly equal to those of *Dendrobium kingianum*, with a most remarkable lip of the darkest purple, having each lateral lobe semicircular and denticulate. The middle lobe is fleshy and triangular. Sepals oblong lanceolate, the lateral ones connate, bidentate at the top. The petals are short, oblong, denticulate, and make an admirable contrast from purple and blackish purple, flowers being of clearest white.

Of all known Orchids, only *Acrochaene punctata* Lindley comes near it. I have, however, not been able to find the content of any anther. Had it not been necessary to do so at once, I would not have named and described the plant now. I like much to give it, at all events, a specific name in honour of its discoverer, and hope he will find many more curiosities and grand novelties.

Protection from direct sunlight and intermediate temperatures are needed for growing this small orchid.

Mastigion Garay, Hamer & Siegerist (1994)

The distinguishing features of this genus are a large space on the column between the dorsal sepal and the lateral sepals (that is, an exposed column foot), petals with cilia or palae, and but a single flower per inflorescence. The lateral sepals twist and form a union of their outer margins into a long whip-like tail. The generic name is derived from the Greek *mastix*, which means "whip," in reference to the shape of these lateral sepals. Type: *Cirrhopetalum appendiculatum* Rolfe (1901)

Mastigion appendiculatum (Rolfe) Garay, Hamer & Siegerist (1994)

SYNONYMS
Bulbophyllum appendiculatum (Rolfe) J. J. Smith (1912), *Cirrhopetalum appendiculatum* Rolfe (1901)

This species is occasionally thought to be the same as *Mastigion putidum*, but there are several important differences. *Mastigion appendiculatum* has clavate cilia, petals that are narrowly triangular-lanceolate, and a roundly obtuse labellum. *Mastigion putidum* has irregular lamellate palae, petals that are linear-oblong, and a labellum that is acute to subacuminate. Warm to intermediate conditions are suitable, as are a potting medium that has good drainage and light shade.

Mastigion fascinator (Rolfe) Garay, Hamer & Siegerist (1994)

SYNONYMS
Bulbophyllum fascinator (Rolfe) Rolfe (1908), *Cirrhopetalum fascinator* Rolfe (1908)
Cirrhopetalum appendiculatum var. *fascinator* of gardens

The pseudobulbs of this species are about 2 cm tall and close together, with a leaf that is 5 cm long. The scape is 10 cm tall and has only one flower which is light greenish white with red markings. The dorsal sepal is 3 cm long and fimbriate, and the lateral sepals are 18 cm long, caudate, and connate for the majority of their length but with the tips free. The petals are 2 cm long, linear-oblong, decurved, with long paleolate or clavate ornaments. The labellum is triangular and purple, and has two pubescent keels. This plant grows throughout the lowlands of Malaya and Laos. It can be cultivated in pots or baskets and requires warm, moist conditions and shade.

Mastigion ornatissimum (Reichenbach fil.) Garay, Hamer & Siegerist (1994)

SYNONYMS
Bulbophyllum ornatissimum (Reichenbach fil.) J. J. Smith (1912), *Cirrhopetalum ornatissimum* Reichenbach fil. (1882), *Phyllorchis ornatissimum* (Reichenbach fil.) Kuntze (1891)

The pseudobulbs are about 2 cm tall and 3 cm apart on the rhizomes, and the leaf is about 8 cm long. The scape is approximately 10 cm tall, and the flower 14 cm long. The 2-cm tall dorsal sepal has threadlike palae on its edges. The lateral sepals form tails about 12 cm long with the tips twisted. The petals are falcate and are distinguished by having broad palae clustered at the apices. The flowers are yellowish green with dark purple marking, and the labellum and the palae are bright red purple. This species grows in the eastern Himalayas, Assam (India), Sikkim, Myanmar, and the Philippines. It can be cultivated at intermediate temperatures in partial shade and in baskets or pots with a good mix and frequent watering. PLATE 62

Mastigion proboscidium (Gagnepain) Garay, Hamer & Siegerist (1994)

SYNONYMS
Bulbophyllum proboscidium (Gagnepain) Seidenfaden & Smitinand (1961), *Cirrhopetalum proboscidium* Gagnepain (1931)

This species is native to Laos and Thailand. The pseudobulbs are about 3 cm apart on the rhizome and have leaves 6 to 7 cm long. The inflorescence is 5 cm long and carries very interesting flowers with rounded 1-cm long dorsal sepals, petals the same length but narrowly triangular, and lateral sepals at least 2.5 cm long that have rounded basal areas as wide as 1 cm and long, curved, inrolled apices. The exposed column foot is very evident. This species can be grown in protected intermediate conditions in pots or baskets with good drainage.

Mastigion putidum (Teijsmann & Binnendijk) Garay, Hamer & Siegerist (1994)

SYNONYMS
Bulbophyllum putidum (Teijsmann & Binnendijk) J. J. Smith (1912), *Cirrhopetalum putidum* Teijsmann & Binnendijk (1862)

The lateral sepals gradually taper into a long twisted tail, the petals are linear-oblong with long-ciliate margins, and the labellum is triangular and has three glabrous keels. This species, too, can be grown in pots or baskets at intermediate temperatures with some shade and moist conditions.

Monomeria Lindley (1888)

This genus is similar in some respects to the genus *Sunipia*. It is characterized by the two pollinia attached to the distinct stipe and by the lateral sepals that are twice as long as the dorsal sepal and attached at the apex of the long column foot. The petals are decurrent along the column foot. The genus is native to the area from the Himalayas to Thailand and Vietnam. Type: *Monomeria barbata* Lindley (1830)

Monomeria barbata Lindley (1830)

SYNONYMS
Epicrianthes barbata (Lindley) Reichenbach fil. (1861)
Monomeria crabo Parish & Reichenbach fil. (1874)

This species has pseudobulbs more than 5 cm tall and leaves 30 cm long and 5 cm wide. The erect inflorescence can be 30 cm tall with about 10 to 15 flowers. These yellow flowers are about 2.5 cm long, the petals are covered with red dots, and the labellum is purple. The species grows at high altitudes in Nepal, Assam (India), Myanmar, and Thailand and requires cool conditions with moderate shade for maximum results.

Monomeria dichroma (Rolfe) Schlechter (1914)

SYNONYMS
Bulbophyllum dichromum Rolfe (1907), *Ione dichroma* (Rolfe) Gagnepain
  (1934), *Sunipia dichroma* (Rolfe) Ban & Huyen (1983)
Bulbophyllum jacquetii Gagnepain (1930)

This species has pseudobulbs more than 5 cm tall and solitary leaves that are 30 cm long and 5 cm wide. The inflorescence is erect, to 30 cm tall, and often with 15 flowers. These yellow flowers are about 5 cm long, with red-dotted petals and a purple labellum. The plants grow in Laos and Vietnam and do well when grown at intermediate temperatures. They can be potted or slabbed and must be shielded from direct sunlight.

Monomeria longipes (Reichenbach fil.) Garay, Hamer & Siegerist (1994)

SYNONYMS
Bulbophyllum longipes Reichenbach fil. (1861), *Henosis longipes* (Reichenbach
  fil.) Hooker fil. (1890)

The genus *Henosis* was established by Joseph Hooker for this species, however, the flower he examined had a stipe that had become detached from the pollinia and so the flower was pictured as having a stipe sticking out from the anther which was not correct. A year later he gave credit to his artist, Miss

Smith, for pointing this error out to him. The branching floral scapes are approximately 20 cm tall which means they stand well above the 9-cm long leaves and 3-cm high pseudobulbs. The plants grow from 1200 to 1500 m above sea level in Moulmein, Myanmar, and need intermediate to cool temperatures and some sun protection.

Monosepalum Schlechter (1913)

In this genus the lateral sepals are united with the dorsal sepal to form a tube which is split in the front. The column foot is elongated, and the labellum is movable. The genus is native to the montane forests of New Guinea. Type: *Bulbophyllum muricatum* Schlechter (1913)

Monosepalum muricatum (J. J. Smith) Schlechter (1913)
SYNONYM
Bulbophyllum muricatum J. J. Smith (1911)

This small terrestrial has pseudobulbs that are 2 cm tall and several centimeters apart on the rhizomes with one 4- to 6-cm long leaf. The erect inflorescence is very tall, sometimes 50 cm, and has one attractive pendulous flower. The dorsal sepal is closely adherent to the lateral sepals which are free from one another, and all are about 8 cm long with their apices caudate. The petals are triangular, only 0.5 cm in size, and have three long glabrous appendages: the upper two are echinulate, 1 cm long, with round apices that look like balls, while the lower appendage is about the same length but flattened and only partially echinulate. The labellum is ligulate, less than 0.5 cm long, and hirsute. The flowers are light green or yellow, mottled with purple or brown on the outside. This plant is endemic to New Guinea and grows in grasslands from 2000 to more than 3000 m above sea level, thus making it a candidate for cool to intermediate growing conditions. Pots of fertile loam and shade from direct sun would be appropriate with, of course, ample moisture to ensure good growth.

Osyricera Blume (1825)

In this genus the column is without a foot, and the inflorescence is racemose with a more or less fusiform rachis. Type: *Osyricera crassifolia* Blume (1825)

Osyricera crassifolia Blume (1825)
SYNONYMS
Bulbophyllum crassifolium (Blume) J. J. Smith (1905)
Bulbophyllum osyricera Schlechter (1911)

The pseudobulbs are minute, less than 0.5 cm tall, and about 1 cm apart on the rhizomes, and the leaves can be as large as 11 cm long and 2 cm wide. The inflorescence is more than 20 cm long, and the rachis is deflexed and has more than 20 flowers. The narrow dorsal sepal is 0.6 cm long and held at right angles to the rachis, while the lateral sepals are slightly broader and are parallel to the labellum. The petals are triangular, half the length of the sepals. The labellum is swollen, ligulate, papillose, and less than 0.5 cm long. The flowers are pink with red markings, and the labellum is orange. It is found in Java and Sumatra from 300 to 1000 m above sea level and can be cultivated in small pots or baskets or on moss covered slabs in warm, moist, somewhat shaded conditions.

Osyricera erosipetala (C. Schweinfurth) Garay, Hamer & Siegerist (1994)

SYNONYM
Bulbophyllum erosipetalum C. Schweinfurth (1951)

This small epiphyte has pseudobulbs less than 0.5 cm tall and leaves to 14 cm long. The inflorescence can be 13 cm long, erect, with many tiny flowers. The lateral sepals are connate, and the petals have an erose, dentate margin. The species grows in the Philippines and can be cultivated in warm, moist conditions with light shade and either in pots or baskets or on slabs with a pad of moss over the roots.

Osyricera spadiciflora (Tixier) Garay, Hamer & Siegerist (1994)

SYNONYM
Bulbophyllum spadiciflorum Tixier (1966)

This species was described from a specimen that came from Vietnam and is quite similar to *Osyricera crassifolia* but is larger with leaves that are sometimes 25 cm tall and an inflorescence as tall as the leaves before it bends downward with its flowers. The labellum is quite distinctive with a papillose surface and numerous filiform projections. Culture is the same as for *O. crassifolia*, that is, warm, shaded, and moist.

Pedilochilus Schlechter (1905)

These species are all small plants, most of which grow at high altitudes in the alpine regions (the mist belt) of Papua New Guinea, although one species has been reported from Sulawesi, and one from Vanuatu. The single flowers are a good size for such small plants and since they are held well above the leaves they are easily seen. The petals are twisted a bit at the midvein to form an S. The labellum has a thick callus between the auricles, the margins of the labellum are thickened, and the midveins are keeled. The plants require cool growing conditions and thick moss in which to sink their roots. Type: *Pedilochilus papuanum* Schlechter (1905)

Pedilochilus majus J. J. Smith (1916)

The pseudobulbs of this species are about 2.5 cm long and are pressed closely against the rhizome with narrow leaves that can be 20 cm long. Several single-flowered, 18-cm long inflorescences arise from the same spot on the rhizome. The ovary is 1.5 cm long and recurved. The dorsal sepal is acute, ciliate, 2 cm long and 0.5 cm wide, and the lateral sepals are ciliate, 2.5 cm long and 1 cm wide, with revolute margins. Petals are less than 1 cm long, and the labellum is 2 cm long and 0.5 cm wide. The flowers are yellow-green with brown markings. This species is found between 2800 and 3400 m above sea level. It requires cool, wet conditions for successful cultivation.

Pedilochilus obovatum J. J. Smith (1929)

SYNONYM
Pedilochilus oreadum van Royen (1979)

The pseudobulbs are 0.5 cm tall, rather close together on the rhizome, and the leaves are 3 cm long and 0.7 cm wide. The single flower is held on an inflorescence that can be 4 cm long; it is yellow and slightly less than 1 cm overall. The species grows in very wet, moss-covered areas of Papua New Guinea at altitudes of 3500 to 4000 m above sea level. It can be cultivated in cool temperatures with copious watering and light shade.

Porpax Lindley (1845)

The flattened pseudobulbs are between 1 and 2 cm wide, each with two leaves. There are one to three minute flowers which appear from the apex of the pseudobulbs, and their sepals are united to some degree. The plants usually grow in moss on tree trunks or on rocks. Type: *Porpax reticulata* Lindley (1845)

Porpax fibuliformis (King & Pantling) King & Pantling (1898)

SYNONYM
Eria fibuliformis King & Pantling (1895)

This species has pseudobulbs about 1 cm in diameter that are clustered together on the rhizomes. The two leaves are more than 3 cm long with ciliate edges. There are two tiny, dull red, hirsute flowers that appear between the base of the leaves. The sepals are united to form a sac, and the labellum is three-lobed with a carunculate apex. The species grows in India at 300 to 500 m above sea level and can be cultivated in shady, warm, damp conditions either on small padded mounts or in small pots or baskets with a moss cover on the roots.

Porpax jerdoniana (Wight) Rolfe (1908)

SYNONYMS

Cryptochilus wightii Reichenbach fil. (1892)

Eria jerdoniana (Wight) Reichenbach fil. (1859), *Lichenora jerdoniana* Wight (1851), *Pinalia jerdoniana* (Wight) Kuntze (1891)

Eria lichenora Lindley (1859), *Porpax lichenora* (Lindley) Cooke (1907)

This species is quite similar to the previous one, but the leaves are slightly smaller and there may be three dull brownish orange, tomentose flowers that appear between the leaves. The sepals are only basally united. The species grows in the hills of southern India at about 300 m elevation and can be cultivated in warm, shaded, moist locations on slabs that are padded with moss or in baskets or pots.

Porpax meirax (Parish & Reichenbach fil.) King & Pantling (1898)

SYNONYMS

Cryptochilus meirax Parish & Reichenbach fil. (1874), *Eria meirax* (Parish & Reichenbach fil.) N. E. Brown (1880)

This species has flattened, crowded pseudobulbs less than 1 cm in diameter, and two leaves about 2.5 cm long which appear after the solitary flowers. The brown sepals are united into a tube whose apices are free and recurved. The apex of the dorsal sepal is also recurved. The species grows in India, Myanmar, Thailand, and the Malay Peninsula at 500 to 800 m elevation. It can be raised in warm conditions with copious moisture in the summer and intermediate, much drier conditions during the winter months. A bit of protection from direct sun and good air movement are also needed.

Porpax reticulata Lindley (1845)

SYNONYMS

Aggeianthus marchantioides Wight (1852)

Cryptochilus reticulatus (Lindley) Reichenbach fil. (1862), *Eria reticulata* (Lindley) Bentham (1883), *Pinalia reticulata* (Lindley) Kuntze (1891)

Porpax papillosa Blatter & McCann (1931)

The pseudobulbs of this species are 2 cm across, and the 5-cm long leaves appear after the flowers. The single flowers are tubular and arise from the undeveloped pseudobulbs. The species grows in the southern hills of India and in Laos. It can be cultivated in pots or baskets or on slabs with warm, lightly shaded and very wet conditions in summer and a cooler and drier environment in winter.

Rhytionanthos Garay, Hamer & Siegerist (1994)

The lateral sepals are fully united dorsally and involutely connate by the two lateral margins thus creating a horn- or saclike structure. The column foot is not exposed or naked. The etymology is from the Greek *rhytion*, which means "small drinking horn," and *anthos* or "flower," referring to the shape of the lateral sepals. Type: *Cirrhopetalum cornutum* Lindley (1838)

Rhytionanthos aemulum (W. W. Smith) Garay, Hamer & Siegerist (1994)
SYNONYMS
Bulbophyllum forrestii Seidenfaden (1979)
Cirrhopetalum aemulum W. W. Smith (1921)

The pseudobulbs are about 3 cm tall and less than 3 cm apart on the rhizomes with one leaf that can be 20 cm long. The inflorescence is more than 8 cm tall with an umbel of 3-cm long flowers. The edges of the dorsal sepal are entire, the petals are ciliate, and the whole flower is yellow to yellow-orange. The species is closely related to *Rhytionanthos cornutum* and is found mostly in Yunnan (China), but has also been found in Myanmar, India, and Thailand at about 2000 m above sea level. It can best be grown in pots with a good mix, intermediate temperatures, moderate humidity, and slight shade.
PLATE 63

Rhytionanthos bootanense (Parish & Reichenbach fil.) Garay, Hamer & Siegerist (1994)
SYNONYM
Bulbophyllum bootanense Parish & Reichenbach fil. (1874)

This species has pseudobulbs that are 1.5 cm tall and about 2 cm apart on the rhizome, and leaves that are more than 6 cm tall. The inflorescence is quite short and has several flowers that are slightly more than 1 cm long. The flowers are orange with red spots, and the lateral sepals fold over to partially enclose the labellum, giving it the shape of a small boot. The species is native to India and Thailand and can be maintained at intermediate temperatures in small pots with the usual well-draining mix and moderate shade.

Rhytionanthos cornutum (Lindley) Garay, Hamer & Siegerist (1994)
SYNONYMS
Bulbophyllum cornutum (Lindley) Reichenbach fil. (1861), not *B. cornutum* (Blume) Reichenbach fil. (1861) of the section *Sestochilos*, and not *B. cornutum* Ridley (1886) which is *B. forbesii* Schlechter (1913), *Cirrhopetalum cornutum* Lindley (1838)
Bulbophyllum helenae (Kuntze) J. J. Smith (1912), *Phyllorchis helenae* Kuntze (1891)

This species is very similar to *Rhytionanthos aemulum* except that the dorsal sepal is erose, not entire. It is native to the western Himalayas, Nepal, Sikkim, Myanmar, and Thailand and grows as an epiphyte or lithophyte at 1800 to

2000 m above sea level. It can be cultivated in small pots with some shade, moderate humidity, and intermediate temperatures. It should be noted that this species is very frequently sold under its synonym *Bulbophyllum helenae*.

Rhytionanthos mirum (J. J. Smith) Garay, Hamer & Siegerist (1994)

SYNONYMS
Bulbophyllum mirum J. J. Smith (1906), *Cirrhopetalum mirum* (J. J. Smith) Schlechter (1913)

This species has pseudobulbs about 2 cm tall, almost 2 cm apart on the rhizomes, with leaves about 7 cm tall. The inflorescence is short and has only two flowers that are white with red dots. The dorsal sepal is a little over 1 cm long, the lateral sepals may be 3.5 cm long and form a long tube, while the minute petals are semicircular and have about 20 very mobile linear palae at the edges. These palae are purple with white apices and project from under the dorsal sepal; they appear quite attractive to pollinators, especially in the early morning. The species has been found in Indonesia, peninsular Malaysia, Sumatra, Bali, and Java at 1200 to 1500 m above sea level. It, too, can be grown in pots at intermediate temperatures with light shade, and moderate amounts of moisture.

Rhytionanthos plumatum (Ames) Garay, Hamer & Siegerist (1994)

SYNONYMS
Bulbophyllum jacobsonii J. J. Smith (1935)
Bulbophyllum plumatum Ames (1915)

This species grows in the Philippines and Sumatra. The pseudobulbs are 3 to 4 cm apart on the rhizome, the leaf is 10 cm long, and the inflorescence can be equally as long. The flower is most unusual with the dorsal sepal almost round and less than 1 cm long and with the lateral sepals more than 9 cm long and joined, as is typical of this genus. The most remarkable parts of the flower are the petals which, although only about 0.1 cm long, have a wonderful 0.2-cm long thick fringe on the apices, giving the flowers an otherworldly appearance. This species should do well in intermediate to warm temperatures in pots or baskets with the usual well-draining potting mix and with shading from direct sunlight.

Rhytionanthos spathulatum (Rolfe ex Cooper) Garay, Hamer & Siegerist (1994)

SYNONYMS
Bulbophyllum spathulatum Rolfe ex Cooper (1929), *Cirrhopetalum spathulatum* (Rolfe ex Cooper) Seidenfaden (1970)

The pseudobulbs are about 5 cm apart on the rhizome and have leaves approximately 8 cm long. The flowers are borne on a 2-cm long spike, and there are four or more in the umbel. The dorsal sepal is about 0.6 cm long, and the lateral sepals are 1.2 cm long, curved inwards and joined along both margins, and densely papillose. The petals are linear-oblong and approximately 0.4 cm long, and the stelidia are short. The species occurs in Sikkim, Myanmar, Thailand, and Vietnam at about 1000 m elevation. This interesting plant with unusual flowers can be grown in lightly shaded areas either in pots or on mounts. Considering the sprawling growth habit, the plants probably would be easiest to contain on mounts of some sort. Intermediate conditions are suitable for good growth and flowering.

Saccoglossum Schlechter (1913)

In this genus all three sepals are free from one another, and the labellum is saccate and movably attached to the column. The column is declined and extends over the labellum. There are presently only a few species, all from Papua New Guinea where they inhabit the mist forests above 1000 m elevation.

Saccoglossum papuanum Schlechter (1913)

The small pseudobulbs are appressed to the rhizomes and are 1.5 cm tall and about 2 to 3 cm apart. The single leaf is cordate, 5 cm long and 3.5 cm wide. The inflorescence has one rather small flower that is noticed for the saccate labellum and for the clinandrium which has long thick fringelike segments. The flowers are pale yellow with brown petals, and the labellum is white with red streaks on the interior. In 1913 Rudolf Schlechter described another species, *Saccoglossum maculatum*, which is much the same but the flowers are white with the dorsal sepal and petals dotted red. Both species can be cultivated in pots but mounting on slabs would give them a more natural appearance. They require constantly humid conditions so a moss pad under and perhaps over the roots and good humidity and light shade are essential to successful cultivation. Other members of this genus are *S. lanceolatum* L. O. Williams (1941) and *S. verrucosum* L. O. Williams (1938).

Sunipia Lindley (1833)

The pollinia are attached to the short subquadrate-truncate to emarginate rostellum through a Y-shaped stipe and a single gland. The four pollinia of this genus are held in pairs, each pair with its own stipe. Lectotype: *Sunipia scariosa* Lindley (1888)

Sunipia andersonii (King & Pantling) Hunt (1971)
SYNONYMS
Ione andersonii King & Pantling (1898), *I. andersonii* var. *flavescens* (Rolfe)
   Tang & Wang (1951)

Ione bifurcatoflorens Fukuyama (1939), *Sunipia bifurcatoflorens* (Fukuyama)
  Hunt (1971)
Ione flavescens Rolfe (1914)
Ione purpurata Braid (1924), *Sunipia purpurata* (Braid) Hunt (1971)
Ione sasaki Hayata (1912), *Sunipia sasaki* (Hayata) Hunt (1971)

This species has leaves 3 cm long and only one or two flowers on each very short inflorescence. The flowers are slightly less than 1 cm across with recurved sepals, petals with a broad base and ciliate edges, and a labellum with rounded hypochile and caudate epichile, both of which are roughly the same length. The flowers are pale yellow and the labellum purple. The species has been collected in Vietnam, Bhutan, India, southern China, Taiwan, Myanmar, and Thailand at about 900 to 1800 m above sea level. It is best grown in pots or baskets with any good mix and a pad of moss or some other moisture-retentive material under the roots. Intermediate temperatures and slight shade with good air circulation and sufficient moisture are indicated.

Sunipia angustipetala Seidenfaden (1980)

This species has pseudobulbs about 1 cm tall and 2.5 cm apart on the rhizome, and a leaf 7 to 8 cm long. The inflorescence is 4 cm long with three to four flowers. The sepals are pale with darker spots, 1.5 cm long and 0.3 cm wide at the base. The petals are 1.4 cm long, linear, spreading, and are also only 0.3 cm broad at the base; they have ciliate edges near the base, apical edges rolled inward, and are erose. The plants grow in the hills around Chiengmai (Thailand) and do best when cultivated in light shade at intermediate to cool temperatures with considerable moisture.

Sunipia annamensis (Ridley) Hunt (1971)

SYNONYM
Ione annamensis Ridley (1921)

The leaves of this species are about 13 cm tall, and the scape is erect, more than 20 cm tall, with 4 to 10 flowers. The lateral sepals are adnate only when young, the petals are small with erose edges, and the labellum has thick, upturned sides and a triangular, obtuse tip. The species is found in Chiengmai (Thailand) and Annam (Vietnam) at 1800 to 2300 m above sea level. This species, too, can be grown in intermediate to cool temperatures and needs ample water and shade.

Sunipia bicolor Lindley (1833)

SYNONYMS
Bulbophyllum bicolor (Lindley) Hooker fil. (1890), not *B. bicolor* Lindley
  (1830) of *Bulbophyllum* section *Umbellatae*, *Ione bicolor* (Lindley) Lindley
  (1853)

Dipodium khasianum Griffith (1851), *Ione khasiana* (Griffith) Lindley (1853)

This orchid is widespread throughout Nepal, Sikkim, India, Bhutan, Myanmar, Yunnan (China), and Thailand at 1800 to 2100 m and even as high as 2700 m on occasion. The flowers face in all directions on the inflorescence. The scape is thin, nodding, and about the same length as the leaves. The lateral sepals are partially connate, and the side lobes of the labellum have two small auricles at the base, then broaden and have fimbriate edges near the apex. This species must be grown in cool to intermediate conditions with protection from direct sunlight.

Sunipia candida (Lindley) Hunt (1971)

SYNONYMS
Bulbophyllum candidum (Lindley) Hooker fil. (1892), *Ione candida* Lindley
   (1853)

In this species the flowers face in many directions atop the thin scape. The small pseudobulbs are about 4 cm apart on the rhizomes, and the leaf is about 5 cm tall. The lateral sepals are less than 1 cm long, are not joined, and are pale yellow. The petals and the base of the labellum are serrate. The species grows in Khasia (India) at 2100 m altitude. It should be cultivated in cool to intermediate conditions with light shade and ample moisture.

Sunipia cirrhata (Lindley) Hunt (1971)

SYNONYMS
Bulbophyllum cirrhatum (Lindley) Hooker fil. (1888), *Ione cirrhata* Lindley
   (1853)

This orchid grows in the Himalayas at about 2000 m elevation and when John Lindley described it in 1853 as *Ione cirrhata* he said,

> [A]nd the lip is not serrated, but is marked by two elevated white lines, resembling the columnar cirri of a catasetum. Flowers dirty white, with purple streaks and a deep violet lip. My account is almost wholly taken from Mr. Cathcart's figure in Dr. Hooker's possession.

Intermediate to cool temperatures and light shade are needed to successfully grow this species.

Sunipia grandiflora (Rolfe) Hunt (1971)

SYNONYM
Ione grandiflora Rolfe (1908)

In this small species the pseudobulb is about 2 cm tall with a 5-cm leaf and the inflorescence only 2 cm tall. The single flower is white with purple veins and labellum, about 3 cm tall; the petals are reflexed, 1.3 cm long and 0.5 cm wide, with slightly erose edges; and the labellum is 1.2 cm long and 0.9 cm wide, broadly ovate, also with erose edges. The species grows in Myanmar and Thailand at 1100 m above sea level and can be cultivated in small pots or baskets with good air circulation, light shade, and regular misting to keep the humidity high. PLATE 64

Sunipia intermedia (King & Pantling) Hunt (1971)

SYNONYM

Ione intermedia King & Pantling (1897)

These flowers face in all directions on the short inflorescence. The sepals are twice as long as the spreading, somewhat twisted petals. The labellum has an epichile that is longer than the narrow hypochile. The species has been found in the Sikkim Himalayas at 1800 m and can be grown as the others of this genus.

Sunipia racemosa (J. E. Smith) Tang & Wang (1951)

SYNONYMS

Ione racemosa (J. E. Smith) Seidenfaden (1969), *Stelis racemosa* J. E. Smith (1819)

Ione scariosa (Lindley) King & Pantling (1898), *I. scariosa* var. *magnibracteata* Kerr (1933), *Sunipia scariosa* Reichenbach fil. (1875), *S. scariosa* Lindley (1833)

Ione siamensis Rolfe (1908)

Ornithidium bracteatum Wallich (1890)

The flowers of this species are very small and are nearly hidden by the long bracts, there is no column foot, and the petals are as broad as they are long. The species grows in Nepal, Sikkim, India, Myanmar, Thailand, Laos, and China from 1000 to 2500 m elevation. It can be cultivated in light shade at intermediate temperatures.

Sunipia thailandica (Seidenfaden & Smitinand) Hunt (1971)

SYNONYM

Ione thailandica Seidenfaden & Smitinand (1965)

The pseudobulbs are about 1.5 cm tall, closely spaced on the rhizome, and the leaves are about 4 cm long. The thin, nodding inflorescence arises from the base of the pseudobulb and can be 15 cm long with 15 to 35 flowers. The lateral sepals are mostly connate, the petals are almost square, and the labellum is less than 0.5 cm long, shaped like a tongue, tumid, finely papillose, with basal side lobes that are thin and triangular. The sepals are light purple, the petals are paler purple, and the midlobe of the labellum is bright green. This species grows in northeastern Thailand at 1200 m above sea level and needs intermediate conditions with a bit of shade from direct sunlight.

Synarmosepalum Garay, Hamer & Siegerist (1994)

In this genus the sepals are fused together and the petals are much smaller than the sepals. The labellum moves on the column foot and is fleshy. There are four pollinia that are in unequal pairs and have neither calicoes nor viscidia. The plants have pendent rhizomes with the pseudobulbs rather close together with but one leaf. The inflorescence is much shorter than the leaves, and the flowers are held in a raceme of a few to many dark purple flowers. The genus name is derived from the Greek *synarmos*, which means "joined together," and the Greek *sepals* in reference to the three fused sepals. Type: *Synarmosepalum kittredgei* Garay, Hamer & Siegerist (1994)

Synarmosepalum heldiorum (J. J. Vermeulen) Garay, Hamer & Siegerist (1994)

SYNONYM
Bulbophyllum heldiorum J. J. Vermeulen (1991)

The pseudobulbs of this plant are less than 1 cm apart and less than 1 cm tall. The leaves are thick, obovate, sometimes as large as 7 cm long and 2 cm wide. Unfortunately, the inflorescence is only about 2 cm long and nestles under the leaves. The few flowers are very deep purple and cupped, almost forming a globe. The rhizome does not hang down but creeps down trunks of trees on Mt. Kinabalu in Borneo at altitudes of 2000 m above sea level. The species could best be cultivated on relatively narrow but long pieces of cork in intermediate, shady, moist conditions.

Synarmosepalum kittredgei Garay, Hamer & Siegerist (1994)

This species is similar in habit and color to the aforementioned *Synarmosepalum heldiorum*, but the two are readily separable because of the shape of the petals and labellum. In this species the petals are linear with a rounded apex, 0.4 cm long and 0.1 cm wide, and the labellum is 0.4 cm long, fleshy, with two keels, and very papillose near the apex. *Synarmosepalum kittredgei* grows in the Philippines at 1200 m elevation and can be cultivated the same as the others in the genus.

Tapeinoglossum Schlechter (1913)

The plants are repent, and the flowers are ringent, bilabiate, with fully united lateral sepals which form a cup under the labellum. There are two or three species which grow in Papua New Guinea and Irian Jaya between 400 and 800 m altitude. Type not designated.

Tapeinoglossum centrosemiflorum (J. J. Smith) Schlechter (1913)

SYNONYM
Bulbophyllum centrosemiflorum J. J. Smith (1912)

The pseudobulbs are slightly longer than 1 cm and are about 2 cm apart on the pendent rhizome. The dangling leaves are about 7 cm long and less than 1 cm wide. The short inflorescence holds the single flower away from the plant, thus displaying its beauty very effectively. The dorsal sepal is erect, almost 2 cm long and 1 cm wide. The lateral sepals are almost 1 cm long and are slightly less than 1 cm wide. The flowers are white with striking red veining. This species grows as an epiphyte at 600 to 800 m above sea level on tree trunks in the forests of New Guinea and can be cultivated in pots or baskets that allow it to hang over the sides or, if possible, on mounts. Temperature should be warm and moisture ample with protection from direct sunlight.

Tapeinoglossum nannodes (Schlechter) Schlechter (1912)
SYNONYM
Bulbophyllum nannodes Schlechter (1905)

This species is very much smaller in vegetative parts than *Tapeinoglossum centrosemiflorum*, but the flowers are similar in size. They are yellow with brownish markings, and the labellum has violet hairs. Culture would require warm, moist, and shaded areas with the opportunity for the plants to hang unhindered either from pots or slabs.

Trias Lindley (1830)

The name of this genus is derived from the Greek *treis*, which means "three," referring to the three sepals which are broadly ovate, triangular, and very nearly identical. Type: *Trias oblonga* Lindley (1830)

Trias crassifolia (Thwaites ex Trimen) Satish (1989)
SYNONYM
Bulbophyllum crassifolium Thwaites ex Trimen (1885)

The pseudobulbs are less than 1 cm in diameter, very close together, and have a thick leaf about 2 cm long. The flowers are less than 1 cm across, greenish yellow with red spots, and are held on an inflorescence that is approximately 3 cm long. This species grows as an epiphyte on the trunks of trees in the damp forests of Sri Lanka and can be cultivated on a slab or in a small pot in warm temperatures and somewhat shaded and moist areas.

Trias disciflora (Rolfe) Rolfe (1896)
SYNONYM
Bulbophyllum disciflorum Rolfe (1895)

The leaves are more than 10 cm long, sepals about 2.5 cm long, and petals 1 cm. The sepals are yellow green with many dark red-brown spots, especially on the lateral sepals, and the labellum has raised purple spots which make it appear almost solid purple. This species grows in Thailand, Laos, and Vietnam. It can be grown on a slab or in a small pot under warm, lightly shaded conditions with ample moisture.

Trias intermedia Seidenfaden & Smitinand (1961)

This tiny species is endemic to Thailand and has 1.5- to 2-cm round carunculate pseudobulbs that hold a leaf that is 1 cm long, 1.4 cm wide, thick, and slightly retuse. The inflorescence is very short and carries a single flower that is less than 1 cm in size, greenish white with purple veins. The operculum has terete prolongations that form a Y shape. This, too, is best grown on tiny slabs in intermediate to warm temperatures and needs light shade and considerable humidity.

Trias nasuta (Reichenbach fil.) Stapf (1928)
SYNONYMS
Bulbophyllum nasutum Reichenbach fil. (1871)
Trias vitrina Rolfe (1895)

The pseudobulbs of this species are 4 cm tall and crowded together, and the leaves are less than 10 cm long. The flowers are on very short inflorescences with sepals about 1.5 cm long and petals less than 1 cm long. The sepals are yellow green, the petals are purple at their apex, and the labellum has a dark red-purple base with a yellow apex. The species grows in Myanmar, Thailand, and Vietnam and needs warm to intermediate temperatures with light shade.

Trias oblonga Lindley (1830)
SYNONYMS
Bulbophyllum moulmiense Reichenbach fil. (1861)
Bulbophyllum oblongum (Lindley) Reichenbach fil. (1861)
Trias ovata Lindley (1830)

The angular pseudobulbs are close together, 2 cm high, and have one 3-cm long leaf. The inflorescence arises from the base of the pseudobulb and can be 2.5 cm tall with one 2.5-cm wide yellow-green flower. The species grows in Myanmar and Thailand at moderate elevations and requires intermediate to warm temperatures, high humidity, light shade, and a tiny piece of wood or coconut husk on which to grow.

Trias picta (Parish & Reichenbach fil.) Parish ex Hemsley (1882)
SYNONYM
Bulbophyllum pictum Parish & Reichenbach fil. (1874)

The pseudobulbs are ovoid, about 1 cm tall and a little wider, close together, with one leaf that is 6.5 cm long. The short inflorescence holds one 2-cm wide flower that is white with many red-purple spots and a labellum that is densely spotted with dark purple. This species grows in Myanmar and Thailand and can be cultivated in dappled shade at intermediate temperatures, preferably on slabs. PLATE 65

Trias rosea (Ridley) Seidenfaden (1976)

SYNONYMS
Bulbophyllum roseum Ridley (1896)
Trias rolfei Stapf (1928)

The pseudobulbs of this species are less than 1.5 cm tall, approximately, and the leaves are usually less than 7 cm long. The flowers are sessile, greenish white, spotted with pale purple dots, and the labellum is dark purple. Small pieces of coconut husk in moist, intermediate to warm temperatures and some shade are ideal for cultivation.

Trias stocksii Bentham ex Hooker fil. (1890)

The pseudobulbs of this small species are 1.5 cm tall, globose, about 2 cm apart on the rhizomes. The leaf is about 4.5 cm long, and the scape is approximately 1 cm long with a single flower. The flowers are slightly more than 1.5 cm in diameter, yellow orange with red spots. The species grows in India and possibly in Nepal and can be cultivated in small pots or on slabs in intermediate temperatures with good humidity and some shade.

Vesicisepalum (J. J. Smith) Garay, Hamer & Siegerist (1994)

The name of this genus is derived from the Latin *vesicula*, which means "small bladder" and *sepalum*, or "sepal," referring to the manner in which the connate sepals form a bladderlike inflated bag. The plants are pendent on a fractiflex rhizome that is covered with filiform roots. The pseudobulbs are alternate in two rows, basally attached to the rhizome, and have a single leaf. The inflorescences arise from the node of the rhizome, are short, and have one flower. Type: *Bulbophyllum folliculiferum* J. J. Smith (1914)

Vesicisepalum folliculiferum (J. J. Smith) Garay, Hamer & Siegerist (1994)

SYNONYM
Bulbophyllum folliculiferum J. J. Smith (1914)

The pseudobulbs are as tall as 2 cm, the leaves are linear-lanceolate and can be 20 cm long and almost 2 cm wide. The inflorescence has a single flower with the sepals connate at their base, 1.3 cm long, and the dorsal sepal slightly less than 1 cm long. The labellum is mobile, curved, and less than 0.5 cm long. The species grows in New Guinea and can be cultivated in warm to intermediate areas in light shade. It must be given an opportunity to grow in a pendent manner by mounting on slabs or planting in pots than can be angled to allow the plants to hang over the sides.

CHAPTER 9

Hybrids

When an orchid grower decides that two different species of orchids would contribute desirable traits to a proposed plant and transfers the pollen of one to the stigma of the other, the resulting plant is a hybrid. When this hybrid blooms it can be given a name and registered with the Royal Horticultural Society in England, thus officially naming the cross. Anyone else, of course, can make the same hybrid with any plants of the same species, but the hybrid name will be the one that has already been registered.

The earliest registration of a hybrid within the *Bulbophyllum* alliance was made by the Sanders in 1936 when they registered a cross of what they called *Cirrhopetalum longissimum* with *C. ornatissimum* and named it *C.* Louis Sander. The currently preferred genera for these species are *Bulbophyllum longissimum* and *Mastigion ornatissimum* and the resulting hybrid is *Mastiphyllum* Louis Sander (PLATE 66). This beautiful hybrid has the long and graceful sepals of the parents carrying over to the progeny and resulting in a very pleasing array of flowers. An added bonus is that the hybrid is easier to grow than either of the parents, an example of what is commonly referred to as hybrid vigor. In November 1977, a plant of *Mastiphyllum* Louis Sander was exhibited by Ralph W. Hodges in Baltimore, Maryland, with the clonal name 'E. & R.' and was awarded a CCM/AOS of 83 points. It had 80 flowers and 19 buds on 16 inflorescences, and the natural spread was 11 cm vertically. And in November 1984 the clone 'Crownpoint' was awarded an AM/AOS of 80 points with 10 flowers and four buds on seven inflorescences. This plant was owned by Bob and Pat Martin of West Signal Mountain, Tennessee, and had a natural spread of an amazing 30 cm vertically.

That same year Stewart Orchids registered *Bulbophyllum* Fascination (*B. fascinator* × *B. longissimum*). Since *B. fascinator* has been transferred to the genus *Mastigion*, the proper hybrid name is now *Mastiphyllum* Fascination. This, too, has a flower with beautiful, very long lateral sepals.

One year later, 1937, Sanders registered *Bulbophyllum* David Sander (*B. lobbii* × *B. virescens*). This must have been an interesting hybrid because

B. virescens has a whorl of very large flowers with dorsal sepals 10 cm long and lateral sepals 12 cm long, while *B. lobbii* is single flowered and less than half that size. Unfortunately, this hybrid does not seem to be in cultivation at this time.

There seemed to be a lull of almost 30 years until 1966 when the Eric Young Foundation registered *Bulbophyllum* Jersey (*B. lobbii* × *B. echinolabium*). Since *B. echinolabium* is a huge flower with a wonderful dark red papillose labellum that has a very long tubular apex (PLATE 67), this cross should be very interesting but it, too, is not to be found in collections today.

In 1969 J. Chambers through A. Low's Nursery registered *Bulbophyllum* Elizabeth Ann (*B. longissimum* × *B. rothschildianum*; PLATE 68). Both parents contribute the extraordinary sepals that are so elegant that this hybrid is still very much in demand today, both as a beautiful plant to grow, having received at least six American Orchid Society awards, and also as a good hybrid parent. Perhaps the best-known clone of this hybrid is 'Buckleberry' which received both an FCC/AOS of 92 points and a CCM/AOS of 91 points in October 1989 in Dallas, Texas. This spectacular plant was owned by Mr. & Mrs. Fred Timm of Richardson, Texas. When awarded, it had 37 flowers and 40 buds on 13 inflorescences and the vertical spread of the flowers was 28.4 cm, a truly impressive size. A different plant of this same grex was awarded a CCM/AOS of 98 points in Philadelphia, Pennsylvania, in December 1993. It had the astonishing number of 293 flowers and 16 buds on 45 inflorescences with a vertical spread of 20 cm. It was owned by Nancy and Joe Volpe of Tabernacle, New Jersey, and was grown in a 25-cm wooden basket with spaghnum moss and osmunda.

Also in 1969 a very different hybrid, *Cirrhopetalum* Daisy Chain (*C. makoy-anum* × *C. amesianum*) was registered by Stewart Orchids. This hybrid forms a very attractive whorl of flowers that are much shorter than the *Bulbophyllum rothschildianum* type hybrids but are very nice in their own right. A colorful clone, 'Woodbridge', received a JC/AOS (Judge's Commendation) for "distinctive charm of a primary hybrid." It was owned by William Hammond of Birmingham, Alabama, and the award was made in Atlanta, Georgia, in 1981. Fortunately, this hybrid is still available to collectors, and since it is very easy to grow it is an excellent plant to add to a collection.

Cirrhopetalum Vindobona was registered by W. Voth in 1975 as a cross of *C. ornatissimum* and *C. rothschildianum*, which we now call *Mastigion ornatissi-mum* and *Bulbophyllum rothschildianum*, and the correct hybrid name is *Masti-phyllum* Vindobona. This should be a magnificent hybrid with long, graceful lateral sepals but does not seem to be grown at present.

In 1977 *Cirrhopetalum* Kalimpong was registered by G. Pradhan (PLATE 69). It is now called *Mastiphyllum* Kalimpong because the parents are *Bulbo-phyllum guttulatum* and *Mastigion ornatissimum*. It is a very desirable hybrid as it grows easily in baskets (or pots if you prefer) and quickly establishes itself. It is a faithful bloomer and has many medium-sized yellow-and-red flowers, all of which make it a valuable plant to have.

There was another lapse in registrations of these plants until 1985 when W. Upton registered *Cirrhophyllum* Alpha (*C. umbellatum* × *Bulbophyllum baileyi*). This should be a very interesting and quite variable hybrid because of the great difference in the flowers of the parents. *Cirrhopetalum umbellatum* has a beautiful whorl of flowers with long lateral sepals and *Bulbophyllum baileyi* is a nonresupinate single flower with wide, spreading laterals sepals.

One hybrid that is still very much in evidence is *Mastiphyllum* Fred Fuchs which was registered in 1987 by T Orchids for F. J. Fuchs Jr. It is a cross of *Bulbophyllum macranthum* and *Mastigion putidum* and is a vigorous grower that rewards the owner with many engaging medium-sized flowers. This orchid, when happy, will fill a cedar or redwood basket very quickly and drape itself over the sides. When in bloom the entire plant is covered with colorful flowers.

Suphachadiwong Nursery produced *Bulbophyllum* Emly Siegerist (*B.* Elizabeth Ann × *B. lasiochilum*) in 1989. It has lateral sepals that, although much shorter than those of *B.* Elizabeth Ann, are much longer than the sepals of *B. lasiochilum*. The lateral sepals also have the slightly extended appearance of *B. lasiochilum*. This hybrid is easy to grow in intermediate temperatures with ample humidity.

J & R (Orchid Art) registered *Bulbophyllum* Lovely Elizabeth (*B.* Elizabeth Ann × *B. rothschildianum*) in 1994. The cross, which lives up to its hybrid name, "lovely," was made by Lucien Tempera of Copaigue, New York, and named for his wife, Elizabeth. This hybrid is easily grown in intermediate to warm conditions and rewards the grower with many very long and colorful flowers.

That same year *Bulbophyllum* Warren's Wizardry (*B. lobbii* × *B. digoelense*) was registered by Mrs. Ralph Levy for Dr. Richard Warren who made the hybrid (PLATE 70). It has the appearance of a very graceful *B. lobbii* and is quite attractive. In 1994 Mrs. Levy also registered *Mastiphyllum* Bengalese Nights (*M.* Kalimpong × *Bulbophyllum dayanum*), which has a dark red, dusky flower with much the same shape as *Mastiphyllum* Kalimpong and does indeed have an oriental flavor. Another cross made by Mrs. Levy and registered in 1994 is *M.* Pulled Taffy (*M.* Louis Sander × *Bulbophyllum rothschildianum*). It has exceptionally long, thin, and graceful lateral sepals. The last three hybrids can all be grown in intermediate conditions with good air movement and considerable moisture. The latter hybrid does best in a basket which gives the lengthy lateral sepals an opportunity to show off unhindered.

In 1995 Suphachadiwong Nursery produced *Mastiphyllum* Santa Claus (*Bulbophyllum* Elizabeth Ann × *Mastigion fascinator*) which has a pretty single flower per inflorescence with long, pale lateral sepals that are spotted with red, while the rest of the flower is predominately a dark vibrant red. The nursery also made the hybrid *Triasphyllum* Emly's Delight (*Bulbophyllum* Emly Siegerist × *Trias disciflora*; PLATE 71). The trias seems to be the dominant parent, and the resultant flower is yellow with dark red spots and has full, beautifully spreading lateral sepals with long pointed apices. The plant is small and easily grown and flowered. Other hybrids registered by this nursery are *Bulbophyllum* Pale Face (*B.* Elizabeth Ann × *B. macranthum*); the magnificent *B.* Thai Spider (*B. medusa* × *B. gracillimum*), which has a proudly displayed mass of long, thin lateral sepals that is well worth adding to any group of orchids; and *Cirrhopetalum* Emly's Angel (*C. campanulatum* × *C. auratum*), which has a whorl of widely spreading pale flowers with yellow dorsal sepals that is held well above the leaves. All these hybrids are attention-getters and highly recommended to the grower. Another Suphachadiwong registration of 1995 was *C.* Sunshine Queen (*C. mastersianum* × *C. coralliferum*) which looks like a very nice, full *C. coralliferum* and is displayed a good distance above the leaves. *Cirrhopetalum* Sunshine Queen comes in two color varieties, yellow and a brilliant orange. The nursery also registered *Cirrhophyllum* Lion King (*Bulbophyllum medusae* × *Cirrhopetalum mastersianum*), which has the long, graceful lateral sepals that one would expect from this cross (PLATE 72).

The whimsically named *Cirrhophyllum* Freudian Slip (*Bulbophyllum eublepharum* × *Cirrhopetalum lepidum*) was registered by J. Hermans in 1995. This should be a most unusual cross because the *B. eublepharum* parent is a large plant with a very long raceme of many lax white and pink flowers, while the *C. lepidum* parent, now correctly known as *C. flabelloveneris*, is a small plant with many flowers per inflorescence.

Another plant registered in 1995 was *Mastiphyllum* Mandarin (*M. fascinator* × *Bulbophyllum psittacoglossum*) by K. Dreithaler. This unlikely twosome pairs the exceptionally long and conjoined lateral sepals and heavily ornamented dorsal sepal and petals of *Mastiphyllum fascinator* with the very widely spreading and relatively short lateral sepals of *Bulbophyllum psittacoglossum*.

In 1996 the emerging interest in bulbophyllums and their allies was very evident in the number of hybrid registrations of those genera. Suphachadiwong Nurseries in Thailand again registered six hybrids, Mrs. Ralph Levy registered five, including *Bulbophyllum* Nannu Nannu (*B. trigonosepalum* × *B. nabawanense*; PLATE 73); B. Thoms registered four; W. R. Williams contributed *B.* Wilmar Galaxy Star (*B. dearei* × *B. lobbii*); and M. Uchida produced *Mastipetalum* Thonputi (*Mastigion putidum* × *Cirrhopetalum umbellatum*). Among the introductions from Suphachadiwong Nurseries is *Bulbophyllum* Peppermint Miss (*B. lobbii* × *B. capillipes*), a beautiful white version of *B. lobbii* that has red stripes on the sepals and petals, while the anther cap and column are suffused with yellow. *Cirrhophyllum* Sunny Boy (*Cirrhopetalum mastersianum* ×

Bulbophyllum rothschildianum) has brilliant orange-yellow lateral sepals that seem to be only one flower part and bright red petals which make a very pretty picture. *Mastiphyllum* Dancing Angels (*Bulbophyllum* Lovely Elizabeth × *Mastigion fascinator*) looks very much like a slightly shorter version of *Bulbophyllum* Elizabeth Ann, one of the grandparents, but with darker coloration and only two flowers per inflorescence. *Mastipetalum* Banana Split (*Mastigion fascinator* × *Cirrhopetalum mastersianum*) looks just as you would expect: long, partially joined lateral sepals of a tasty banana color, yellow dorsal sepal, and reddish petals. It usually bears three or more flowers per inflorescence, and they are held nicely above the leaves.

Suphachadiwong also recorded two unusual trias crosses in 1996 which they named after their sons, Meechai and Prasong. *Triaspetalum* Meechai (*Trias disciflora* × *Cirrhopetalum* Elizabeth Ann) has the usual trias shape but with elongated and apically upturned lateral sepals. It is very pale yellow with dark red dots forming stripes on all floral parts. *Triasphyllum* Prasong (*Bulbophyllum lobbii* × *Trias vitrina*; PLATE 74) has retained more of the trias shape but is very pale off-white with light reddish dots. Both are small plants with beautiful and unusual flowers and would add interest to any group of miniature orchids.

B. Thoms (Richella) registered *Bulbophyllum* Memoria Richard Mizuta (*B. lobbii* × *B. affine*), *B.* Stella Mizuta (*B. lobbii* × *B. macranthum*), *Mastiphyllum* Cindy Dukes (*Bulbophyllum rothschildianum* × *Mastigion putidum*), and *Mastiphyllum* Doris Dukes (*Mastigion fascinator* × *Bulbophyllum rothschildianum*) in 1996. *Cirrhophyllum* Hilde (*Bulbophyllum mirum* × *Cirrhopetalum picturatum*) was registered that year by K. Dreithaler but *B. mirum* is now *Rhytionanthos mirum*, so the hybrid cross is *Rhytiopetalum* Hilde. Dreithaler also made the hybrid *Mastipetalum* Rebecca (*Cirrhopetalum picturatum* × *Mastigion ornatissimum*). And Mrs. Ralph Levy named *Bulbophyllum* Crab Claw (*B. rothschildianum* × *B. dayanum*; PLATE 75) and *Mastiphyllum* Magnifico (*M.* Louis Sander × *Bulbophyllum phalaenopsis*; PLATE 76) as well as a hybrid she called Short Changed (*Mastiphyllum* Louis Sander × *Cirrhopetalum andersonii*; PLATE 77). Since the latter is the first multigeneric cross of *Bulbophyllum*, *Cirrhopetalum*, and *Mastigion*, the new hybrid name *Joara* is proposed for it.

In 1997 *Cirrhopetalum* Sandi Ting (*C. sikkimense* × *C. makoyanum*) was registered, as was *Mastiphyllum* Cheryl Kurazaki (*Bulbophyllum lasiochilum* × *Mastigion fascinator*), *Mastiphyllum* Fantasia (*M.* Fascination × *Mastigion fascinator*), and *M.* Wayne Oyama (*Bulbophyllum lasiochilum* × *Mastigion putidum*). H. Christiansen made *Mastiphyllum* Han's Delight (*Mastigion putidum* × *Bulbophyllum cruentum*), and *Mastiphyllum* Wilmar Sunrise (*M.* Fascination × *Bulbophyllum rothschildianum*) was registered by W. R. Williams. Also entered into the record books by B. Thoms (Richella) was the hybrid *Mastiphyllum* Jim Krull (*Bulbophyllum lobbii* × *Mastigion ornatissimum*).

In 1998 the hybrid *Mastiphyllum* Gary Haggen (*Bulbophyllum* Elizabeth Ann × *Mastiphyllum* Louis Sander) was registered and also *Bulbophyllum* Stars and Stripes (*B. bicolor* × *B. lobbii*).

All these hybrids have interesting and unusual flowers and are highly recommended for ease of growing. The often used phrase "hybrid vigor" is not just an empty expression but has valid meaning. For a beginning orchid grower there is no better way to start a collection than with a few hybrids.

Conversion Chart

Centimeters / Inches		Centimeters / Inches	
0.1	$\frac{1}{32}$ in.	1	$\frac{3}{8}$ in.
0.2	$\frac{1}{16}$ in.	2	$\frac{3}{4}$ in.
0.3	$\frac{1}{8}$ in.	3	$1\frac{1}{4}$ in.
0.4	$\frac{5}{32}$ in.	4	$1\frac{5}{8}$ in.
0.5	$\frac{3}{16}$ in.	5	2 in.
0.6	$\frac{1}{4}$ in.	6	$2\frac{3}{8}$ in.
0.7	$\frac{9}{32}$ in.	7	$2\frac{3}{4}$ in.
0.8	$\frac{5}{16}$ in.	8	$3\frac{1}{4}$ in.
0.9	$\frac{11}{32}$ in.	9	$3\frac{5}{8}$ in.
1.0	$\frac{3}{8}$ in.	10	4 in.

Meters / Feet	
100	330 ft.
200	660 ft.
300	990 ft.
400	1320 ft.
500	1650 ft.
600	1980 ft.
700	2310 ft.
800	2640 ft.
900	2970 ft.
1000	3330 ft.

Glossary

Acuminate. Narrowing to a sharp point with angle less than 45 degrees
Acute. Apical angle between 45 and 90 degrees, sharp point not extended
Adherent. Dissimilar parts touching but not joined
Adnate. Unlike parts joined
Aggregate. Close together, clustered
Alate. Having a straight wing
Anterior. The front side
Anther. Cap containing the pollen
Apical. Near the tip
Apiculate. Acute tip
Appressed. Closely against, angle of divergence less than 15 degrees
Approximate. Close together but not joined
Aristate. With a long, narrow bristlelike projection
Articulate. Jointed
Auricles. Earlike appendages
Axil. Angle between upper surface of leaf and stem where they join
Basal. At the base of a plant part
Bicuspidate. Having two prongs
Bidentate. Having two teeth
Bilateral. Two vertical planes
Bilobed. Having two lobes
Bract. Modified, reduced leaflike organ below an inflorescence or pseudo-bulb
Caespitose. Matted, tufted
Capitate. Having dense clusters or heads
Carinate. Shaped like the keel of a boat
Carnose. Fleshy
Caruncle. Small, lumpy outgrowth
Caudate. With a tail
Caudicle. The long, narrow part that connects pollen masses to the stigma

Caulescent. Having an obvious leafy stem

Channeled. Grooved longitudinally

Cilia. Minute but conspicuous hairs

Ciliate. Fringed with minute but conspicuous hairs

Cirrus. From the Latin *cirrus*, meaning "tendril, fringe"

Clavate. Club shaped

Cleistogamous. Self-fertilizing

Clinandrium. The cavity at the apex of the column which contains the anthers

Coherent. Similar parts superficially joined but not fused

Column. Structure formed by fusion of stamens and pistils

Compressed. Flattened laterally

Concolor. All one color

Conduplicate. One half folds over the other

Confluent. The merging of one or more parts

Conjoined. United

Connate. Having similar parts joined

Connivent. Parts coming together but not fused

Conspecific. The same species

Contiguous. Parts touching but not fused

Cordate. Heart shaped

Coriaceous. Leathery

Cornute. Horn shaped

Cucullate. Hood shaped, cowl shaped

Cuneate. Wedge shaped

Deciduous. Leaves are shed after a growing period

Declined. Bent down or forward

Decumbent. Refers to stems that lie close to the ground

Decurrent. Extending downwards

Decurved. Curved downward

Deflexed. Bent down abruptly

Dentate. With margins that have sharp teeth

Denticulate. Finely dentate

DIffuse. Spreading widely

Discoid. Disc shaped

Distal. Toward the apex, farthest away from point of attachment

Distichous. With two ranks of flowers or leaves in opposite rows

Divergent. Spreading widely with angle less than 15 degrees

Dorsal sepal. In nonresupinate orchids, the uppermost sepal

Echinulate. Covered with small, pointed spines

Elliptical. Flattened circle more than twice as long as broad

Emarginate. Having a shallow notch at the tip

Endemic. Native to a certain geographical area
Entire. Smooth
Epichile. Terminal portion of the articulated orchid labellum
Epiphyte. Plant living upon another plant but not parasitic on it
Erect. Upright, vertical
Erose. Having a jagged margin
Falcate. Sickle shaped
Fasciculate. Bundled
Fenestrate. With windowlike areas
Filiform. Threadlike
Fimbriate. Having margins fringed with long, coarse hairs
Flaccid. Flabby
Flavescent. Yellowish
Fractiflex. Zigzag
Fugacious. Short lived
Fusiform. Thickest in the middle and tapering toward each end like a spindle
Glabrous. Not hairy
Globose. Rounded, spherical
Gynostemium. The column of an orchid flower
Hirsute. Covered with stiff hairs
Hort. Abbreviation for *hortorum*, meaning "of the gardens, not described"
Hypochile. Lower portion of the labellum
Imbricate. Overlapping
Incurved. Curved inward or upward
Inflorescence. Arrangement of flowers on a floral axis
Involute. Having the margins inrolled
Keeled. Having a ridgelike structure
Kirros. From the Greek word for yellow
Labellum. The modified petal of an orchid flower, lip
Lamellate. Made of thin plates
Lanceolate. Lance shaped, tapering at both ends
Lectotype. Specimen serves as nomenclatural type when holotype is missing or not designated by the original author
Ligulate. Tongue shaped
Linear. Sides almost parallel, 10 times longer than broad
Lip. Orchid labellum
Lithophyte. A plant that grows on rocks
Lobe. Portion of a leaf or flower that is curved or rounded with an undivided central area
Maculate. Spotted
Mentum. Extension of base of column, chin

Moniliform. Like a string of beads

Mucro. Having a sharp terminal point

Muricate. With many sharp points

Navicular. Boat shaped

Oblong. Longer than broad with parallel sides, width plus or minus one-third the length

Obovate. Basal half narrower than the apical half

Obtuse. Rounded apex, sides forming an angle of more than 90 degrees

Obverse. The front side, opposite to reverse

Operculum. Anther cap

Oval. Elliptical, with the width more than half the length

Ovate. Egg shaped, widest basally

Palae. Somewhat rounded, flat, movable projections attached by a thin thread

Panicle. Inflorescence indeterminate, main axis branching with flowers on secondary branches

Papillose. Having small, nipplelike protuberances

Patent. Spreading, horizontal

Pedicel. Stalk of an individual flower in an inflorescence

Peduncle. Stalk of inflorescence or solitary flower

Pendent. Nodding, hanging down

Petiole. Stem of a leaf

Pollen. The male part of the flower

Pollinium. Mass of pollen grains that form a unit

Porrect. Extended or stretched horizontally

Proteranthous. Inflorescence arises from base of the leaves before development of new pseudobulbs

Pseudobulb. The stem of sympodial orchids

Pseudoumbellate. All pedicels seem to arise from base of pedicel, but in fact they do not

Proximal. Nearest the point of origin, basal

Pubescent. Covered with short trichomes

Quadrate. Four sided, square

Raceme. Unbranched inflorescence with individual flowers on pedicels along main axis

Rachis. The major axis of an inflorescence

Recurved. Bent down or back

Reflexed. Abruptly recurved

Repent. Creeping along the ground and rooting at the joints

Resupinate. With the dorsal sepal uppermost, pedicellate ovary twisted 180 degrees

Retuse. Having a shallow notch in the apex

Revolute. Rolled downward or back

Rhizome. The stem parallel to the earth

Rhombic. Somewhat diamond shaped

Ringent. Gaping open

Rostellum. Sterile modified stigmatic lobe

Rugose. Wrinkled

Saccate. Shaped like a pouch

Samara. A fruit with winglike growths that aid in wind dispersion

Scabrous. Having short, stiff hairs making surface rough

Scandent. Climbing

Scape. A flower stalk, rachis

Semilunate. Shaped like a half moon

Sepal. In orchids the three outermost parts of the flower

Sequentially. One at a time, in sequence

Serrate. With saw-toothed margins

Sessile. Without a stalk

Setaceous. Bristly

Setae. Bristly hairs

Spathulate. Spoon shaped

Species. A group of things classified according to attributes they have in common

Spike. An indeterminate, unbranched inflorescence with sessile flowers, not a synonym for raceme

Stalk. The main supporting axis, stem

Stamen. The part that holds the anther

Stelidia. Projection on either side of the column

Stigmatic surface. The female part of the flower

Stipe. A supporting stalk, as with pollinia

Subacuminate. Almost acuminate

Subquadrate. Not quite square

Subtend. Immediately below

Subulate. Awl shaped, narrow, pointed, and somewhat flat

Sympodial. Growing on creeping rhizomes

Synsepal. A sepal formed by some degree of fusion of the sepals

Terete. With the cross section circular

Tomentose. With matted, woolly hairs

Trichome. Glandular hair

Trimerous. Having three sepals and three petals

Truncate. The abrupt ending of a base or apex, similar to being cut off, squared

Tumid. Inflated, swollen

Type. Usually the herbarium specimen upon which the published description of a new species is based

Umbel. All pedicels arise from apex of peduncle

Undulate. Margin wavy in the vertical plane

Unifoliate. Having one leaf

Verrucose. Warty

Viscidium. Sticky area of column

Zygomorphic. Bilateral symmetry; having identical halves when divided by a single plane through the axis of the flower

Bibliography

Abraham, A., and P. Vatsala. 1981. *Introduction to Orchids.* Trivandrum, India: St. Joseph's Press.

Ames, O. 1914. *Philippine Journal of Science.* 9(1): 2.

———. 1932. "New or Noteworthy Philippine Orchids." *Philippine Journal of Science.* 47(2).

Ames, O., and D. Correll. 1952. *Orchids of Guatemala. Fieldiana* 26.

Averyanov, L. V. 1988. *Vietnam Orchids.* St. Petersburg, Russia: Komarov Botanic Institute.

Ball, J. S. 1978. *Southern African Epiphytic Orchids.* Johannesburg, South Africa: Conservation Press.

Banerji, M. L. 1982. *Orchids of Nepal.* Dehra Dun, India: Bishen Singh Mahendra Pal Singh.

Bedford, R. B. 1969. *A Guide to Native Australian Orchids.* Sydney: Angus & Robertson.

Cady, L., and E. R. Rotherham. 1970. *Australian Native Orchids.* Sydney: A. H. & A. W. Reed.

Chan, C. L., A. Lamb, P. S. Shim, and J. J. Wood. 1994. *Orchids of Borneo.* Vol. 1. England: Royal Botanic Gardens, Kew.

Comber, J. B. 1990. *Orchids of Java.* England: Royal Botanic Gardens, Kew.

Cribb, P. 1984. *Flora of Tropical East Africa. Orchidaceae.* England: Royal Botanic Gardens, Kew.

Darwin, C. 1898. *On the Fertilization of Orchids by Insects.* New York: D. Appleton & Company.

de la Bâthie, H. P. 1939–1941. *Flore of Madagascar, Orchidacées.* Tananarive.

Dockrill, A. W. 1969. *Australian Indigenous Orchids.* Sydney: The Society for Growing Australian Plants.

Dressler, R. L. 1981. *The Orchids.* Cambridge, Massachusetts: Harvard University Press.

Foldats, E. 1969–1970. *Flora de Venezuela.* Caracas: Instituto Botanico.

Gamble, G. S. 1984. *Orchidaceae of the Presidency of Madras.* Rpt. India: Secretary of State for India. England: Royal Botanic Gardens, Kew.

Garay, L. A. 1999. "Orchid Species Currently in Cultivation." *Harvard Papers in Botany* 4(1): 301–309.

Garay, L. A., F. Hamer, and E. S. Siegerist. 1990. "A Note on *Bulbophyllum fletcherianum* and Its Alias." American Orchid Society *Bulletin.* 59(8): 810–812.

————. 1992a. "Beitraege zu kultivierten *Bulbophyllum*-Arten." *Die Orchidee* 43(6): 262–268.

————. 1992b. "Bemerkungen zu *Bulbophyllum* Sektion *Hyalosema.*" *Die Orchidee* 43(6).

————. 1992c. "Observations on 'New Guinea Field Note Extracts Part II *Bulbophyllum*' by N. H. S. Howcroft." *Papua New Guinea Orchid Society News* 21–22 (November–December).

————. 1994. "The Genus *Cirrhopetalum* and the Genera of the *Bulbophyllum* Alliance." *Nordic Journal of Botany* 14(6): 609–646.

————. 1995. "Inquilina Orchidacea." *Lindleyana* 10(3): 174–182.

————. 1996. "Inquilina Orchidacea II." *Lindleyana* 11(4): 224–235.

Garay, L. A., and W. Kittredge. 1985. "Notes from the Ames Orchid Herbarium." *Botanical Museum Leaflets* 30(3).

Garay, L. A., K. Senghas, and K. Lemcke. 1996. "*Bulbophyllum woelfliae.*" *Journal für den Orchideenfrend* 3(1).

Garay, L. A., and H. R. Sweet. 1974. *Orchids of the Southern Ryukyu Islands.* Cambridge, Massachusetts: Harvard University Press.

Grant, B. 1895. *The Orchids of Burma.* Rpt. Dehra Dun, India: Bishen Singh Mahendra Pal Singh.

Hamer, F. 1974. *Las Orquídeas de El Salvador.* 2 vols. San Salvador: Minister of Education.

Hamer, F., and L. A. Garay. 1995. "*Bulbophyllum* Section *Bulbophyllaria* in the Neotropics." *Boletin, IBUG* 3: 1–3, 5–26.

Holttum, R. E. 1964. *Flora of Malaya*, vol. 1. *Orchids of Malaya.* 3rd ed. Singapore: Government Printing Office.

Hooker, J. D. 1890. *Flora of British India*, vols. 5 & 6. Rpt. 1978. India: Secretary of State for India.

Hu, S. Y. 1972. "The Orchidaceae of China." *Quarterly Journal Taiwan Museum.* Taiwan: Taiwan Museum.

————. 1977. *The Genera of Orchidaceae in Hong Kong.* Hong Kong: Chinese University Press.

Jayaweera, D. M. A. 1981. *Orchidaceae, Flora of Ceylon.* New Delhi, India: Amerind Publishing Company.

Kamemoto, H., and R. Sagarik. 1975. *Beautiful Thai Orchid Species.* Bangkok: Orchid Society of Thailand.

Lewis, B., and P. Cribb. 1989. *Orchids of Vanuatu*. England: Royal Botanic Gardens, Kew.

Lin, T. 1975. *Native Orchids of Taiwan*. Vol. 1. Taiwan.

Lindley, J. 1830. *Genera and Species of Orchidaceous Plants*. Rpt. 1983. India: Secretary of State, India.

Little, J., and C. E. Jones. 1980. *Dictionary of Botany*. New York: Van Nostrand Reinhold.

McVaugh, R. 1985. *Flora Novo-Galiciana*. Vol. 16, *Orchidaceae*. Ann Arbor, Michigan: University of Michigan.

O'Byrne, P. 1994. *Lowland Orchids of Papua New Guinea*. Singapore: SNP Publishers.

Pabst, G. F. J., and F. Dungs. 1975–1977. *Orchidaceae Brasilienses*. 2 vols. Germany: Brucke-Verlag Kurt Schmersow.

Perrier, H. 1981. *Flora of Madagascar*. Translation. Lodi, California: S. D. Beckman.

Piers, F. 1968. *Orchids of East Africa*. 2nd ed. Germany: Cramer.

Pradhan, U. C. 1979. *Indian Orchids: Guide to Identification and Culture*. Kalimpong.

Rolfe, R. A. 1898. Orchidaceae. *Flora of Tropical Africa*. Rpt. 1984. England: Royal Botanic Gardens, Kew.

Santapau, H., and Z. Kapadia. 1966. *The Orchids of Bombay*. Calcutta, India: Government of India.

Schlechter, R. 1982. *The Orchidaceae of German New Guinea*. Translated by R. S. Rogers, H. J. Katz, and J. T. Simmons. Melbourne, Australia: Australian Orchid Foundation.

Seidenfaden, G. 1969. "Notes on *Ione*." *Dansk Botanisk Arkiv*. 137–143

———. 1970. Contributions to Orchid Flora of Thailand II. Copenhagen: Botanisk Museum.

———. 1972. *An Enumeration of Laotian Orchids*. Paris.

———. 1974. "Notes on *Cirrhopetalum* Lindl." *Dansk Botanisk Arkiv* 29: 1–260.

———. 1975. "Orchid Genera in Thailand." *Dansk Botanisk Arkiv*. 70: 12–21, 83–89, 104–105, 225–226

———. 1977. Contributions to Orchid Flora of Thailand VIII. Copenhagen: Botanisk Museum.

Seidenfaden G., and T. Smitinand. 1958–1965. *The Orchids of Thailand*. Bangkok: The Siam Society.

Seidenfaden, G., and J. J. Wood. 1992. *The Orchids of Peninsular Malaysia and Singapore*. Fredensborg: Olsen & Olsen.

Siegerist, E. S. 1991. "*Bulbophyllum macranthoides* Rediscovered." *Papua New Guinea News* 9: 5–6.

———. 1997. "Novelties in the *Bulbophyllum* Alliance." *Orchids* 6: 573–581.

Teo, C. K. H. 1985. *Native Orchids of Peninsular Malaysia.* Singapore: Times Books International.

Thouars, A. 1822. *Histoire Particulière des Plantes Orchidées Recueillies sur les Trois Îles Australes d'Afrique.* Rpt. 1979. New York: E. M. Coleman.

Tootill, E., and S. Blackmore. 1984. *Dictionary of Botany.* Aylesbury, England: Penguin Books.

Vermeulen, J. J. 1987. *Orchid Monographs.* Vol. 2, *A Taxonomic Revision of the Continental African Bulbophyllinae.* Leiden, Holland: Rijksherbarium.

————. 1991. *Orchids of Borneo.* Vol. 2, *Bulbophyllum.* England: Royal Botanic Gardens, Kew.

————. 1993. *Orchid Monographs* Vol. 7. Leiden, Holland: Rijksherbarium.

Williams, L. O. 1951. *The Orchidaceae of Mexico.* Rpt. 1986. India: Escuela Agricola Panamericana.

Williams, L. O., and P. H. Allen. 1980. *Orchids of Panama.* Rpt. St. Louis, Missouri: Missouri Botanical Garden.

Williamson, G. 1977. *The Orchids of South Central Africa.* New York: David McKay Company.

Index